Chris,

Warmest Regards

Simon

Restraint of Trade and Business Secrets:

Law and Practice

Second Edition

Simon Mehigan

Barrister

David Griffiths

Partner, Clifford Chance

© Longman Group UK Ltd 1991

Published by
Longman Law, Tax and Finance
Longman Group UK Ltd
21–27 Lamb's Conduit Street
London WC1N 3NJ

Associated Offices
Australia, Hong Kong, Malaysia, Singapore, USA

British Library Cataloguing in Publication Data

Mehigan, Simon
    Restraint of trade and business secrets:
    law and practice.—(Longman commercial
    series)
    1. Restraint of trade—England
    I. Title   II. Griffiths, David
    344.203'723   KD 2212

ISBN 0-85121-669-2

Printed in Great Britain by Mackays of Chatham Ltd, Chatham

Contents

Foreword to Second Edition

This book is a practical guide to the drafting and litigation problems associated with the law of restraint of trade and business secrets. It is not an academic study and therefore deals with the law as it is rather than as it should be, although criticism is offered where thought appropriate.

The book is written for the commercial practitioner and accordingly it does not cover such matters as personal confidences or government secrets.

We are primarily concerned with an examination of the common law. Mention is made of United Kingdom and EEC statutory and quasi-statutory regulations where necessary, but these topics are not covered in detail.

Whereas few of the cases lay down principles, it is valuable to have an easy form of access to decided cases because they do indicate the way the court is likely to react to factual situations. This is particularly important in the field of restraint of trade where the result of so many cases depends on whether the court will grant an interlocutory injunction. For this reason we have included as Appendix I a table giving brief descriptions of recently decided cases.

The need for a second edition has been demonstrated by the corpus of new case law which has come into existence since July 1986 when the first edition was completed.

We would like to thank Lord Griffiths, John Osborne, Julian Christopher, Robert O'Sullivan, Martin Evans and Sebastian Payne for their assistance and their helpful comments and guidance, but we, of course, accept all responsibility for all views and mistakes. The law is stated as at 1 June 1991.

Simon Mehigan   David Griffiths
5, Paper Buildings   Clifford Chance
Temple

Table of Cases

Table of Statutes

Table of Statutory Instruments

Table of EC Legislation

To Amanda and Henrietta

Chapter 1

Introduction

1 The restraint of trade doctrine

The essence of the restraint of trade doctrine is still contained in the famous speech of Lord MacNaghten in *Nordenfelt v Maxim Nordenfelt Guns and Ammunition Co* [1894] AC 535:

> The public have an interest in every person's carrying on his trade freely: so has the individual. All interference with individual liberty of action in trading, and all restraints of trade of themselves, if there is nothing more, are contrary to public policy . . . .

A more recent re-statement is given in the judgment of Lord Morris of Borth-y-gest in *Esso Petroleum Co Ltd v Harper's Garage (Stourport) Ltd* [1968] AC 269:

> In general, the law recognises that there is freedom to enter into any contract that can lawfully be made. The law lends its weight to uphold and enforce contracts freely entered into. The law does not allow a man to derogate from his grant. If someone has sold the goodwill of his business, some restraint to enable the purchaser to have that which he has bought may be recognised as reasonable. Some restraints to ensure the protection of confidential information may be similarly regarded. The law recognises that if business contracts are fairly made by parties who are on equal terms such parties should know their business best. If there has been no irregularity, the law does not mend or amend contracts merely for the relief of those for whom things have not turned out well. But when all this is fully recognised yet the law, in some circumstances, reserves a right to say that a contract is in restraint of trade and that to be enforceable it must pass a test of reasonableness. In the competition between varying possible principles applicable, that which makes certain covenants and in restraint of trade unenforceable will in some circumstances be strong enough to prevail. Public policy will give it priority.

The restraint of trade doctrine is, therefore, an aspect of public policy and before relying on older authorities it must be remembered that the perception of what constitutes public policy may change.

2 Purpose of restraint of trade clauses

The usual purpose of most restraint of trade clauses is to limit competition. But public policy leans against the achievement of such an aim. In *Morris (Herbert) Ltd v Saxelby* [1916] 1 AC 688, Lord Atkinson said '. . . no person has an abstract right to be protected against competition *per se* in his trade or business'. The most important words there are '*per se*': for a person can legitimately prevent competition indirectly if the restraint is reasonable and is attached to a proper interest which merits protection. Usually the restraint must protect either business goodwill or business secrets.

Accordingly the law insists that a former employee cannot be prevented from turning to his own account his professional skill and knowledge even though it may have been acquired whilst in employment and at the employer's expense. On the other hand, where circumstances are such that the employee has been put in a position of acquiring special intimate knowledge of the clients of his employer or the means of influence over them there exists subject matter which is entitled to the court's protection. Otherwise, as Evershed J said in *Routh v Jones* [1947] 1 All ER 179 '. . . the master would be exposed to unfair competition on the part of his former servant—competition flowing not so much from the personal skill of the assistant as from the intimacies and knowledge of the master's business acquired by the servant from the circumstances of his employment'.

Part I

Restraint of Trade Doctrine

Chapter 2

The Issues

There are four issues which must be considered in any case in which it is thought a restraint of trade problem exists. These are, in logical order of application:

(a) Does a restraint of trade exist in this case/does the restraint of trade doctrine apply to this class of case?
(b) Is there an interest meriting protection?
(c) Is the restraint reasonable as between the parties?
(d) Is the restraint reasonable in the public interest?

Each question is now examined in turn.

1 Does a restraint of trade exist in this case/does the restraint of trade doctrine apply to this class of case?

It is necessary before undertaking an analysis of whether a restraint in a particular case is reasonable to decide whether in the first place the doctrine has any part to play. If it does not, then quite clearly questions of reasonableness are irrelevant. First, in many cases the doctrine will, on a common sense view, be irrelevant and no court will permit a defendant to raise it. For example, if there is a simple contract for the sale of a chattel it would be impractical to say that the restraint of trade doctrine applied. On the other hand the doctrine clearly applies to contractual terms by which the covenantee, an employer or a purchaser of a business, seeks to forbid the covenantor (the employee or seller) from carrying on his trade or restricts the way in which he may carry it on *after* the purchase and sale of labour or the business, has been completed.

In recent years there have been several judicial attempts to define the scope of the doctrine.

1.1 Modern judicial views on the ambit of the doctrine

In *Petrofina (Great Britain) Ltd v Martin* [1966] Ch 146 two members of the Court of Appeal attempted to define what amounts to a restraint of trade. Lord Denning MR said:

Every member of the community is entitled to carry on any trade or business he chooses and in such manner as he thinks most desirable in his own interests, so long as he does nothing unlawful: with the consequence that any contract which interferes with the free exercise of his trade or business, by restricting him in the work he may do for others, or the arrangements which he may make with others, is a contract in restraint of trade. It is invalid unless it is reasonable as between the parties and not injurious to the public interest.

Diplock LJ said 'A contract in restraint of trade is one in which a party (the covenantor) agrees with any other party (the covenantee) to restrict his liberty in the future to carry on trade with other persons not parties to the contract in such manner as he chooses'.

As Lord Morris said in the *Esso* case these are helpful expositions provided that they are not used too literally. Two years after *Petrofina* the House of Lords laid down guidelines as to what did and what did not, fall within the doctrine in *Esso Petroleum Co Ltd v Harper's Garage (Stourport) Ltd* [1968] AC 269.

The appellants, suppliers of petrol to garage owners, entered into two agreements with the respondents in relation to two garages, M and C. The agreements were on the appellants' standard forms. In respect of garage M the appellants agreed to sell and the respondents agreed to buy from the appellants for a period of four years and five months their total requirements of petrol for resale. The respondents agreed, *inter alia*, to keep the garage open at all reasonable hours and if they sold the garage, to ensure that the buyer entered into a similar agreement with the appellants. In respect of garage C the agreement was identical except that the period was 21 years. In addition, garage C was subject to a mortgage whereby the appellants advanced, under a loan agreement, £7,000 to the respondents who covenanted to repay it by instalments over a period of 21 years. In the mortgage deed the respondents further covenanted that they would purchase all their requirements from the appellants exclusively. Each agreement also contained a resale price mainten-ance clause. Subsequently, because low priced petrol came onto the market the appellants wrote to all of their dealers, including the respondents saying that they would not insist on the implementation of the resale price maintenance clause. In answer to this the respondents who were in favour of this clause and its enforcement said that they now deemed that the sale agreements were null and void and they began to sell another brand of petrol at both garages. They also announced their intention of redeeming the mortgage. The appellants considered the mortgage could not be redeemed without their consent unless in accordance with the covenant for repayment over a period of 21 years. The appellants sought injunctions restraining the respondents from buying or selling petrol other than that supplied by them at the two garages during the subsistence of the agreements and in respect of garage C during the period of the mortgage.

It was argued on behalf of the appellants that there were two distinct categories of restraint. Firstly, there were contracts restraining a person from carrying on some trade or business; these were clearly subject to the doctrine. Secondly, there were restrictive covenants affecting land and so imposing a burden on the land rather than on any person. It was argued that such covenants are often contained in conveyances, leases and mortgages, and that they had never been subject to the doctrine of restraint of trade and consequently the test of reasonableness. The present case fell into the second category and not the first as far as garage C was concerned. It was argued on behalf of the respondents that the doctrine applied to a covenant which was imposed for the benefit of the trade of the covenantee and which either forbids the covenantor to carry on his trade or restricts the way in which he may carry it on. Further, when a covenant is taken for the benefit of property, the doctrine does not apply, but when it is taken to protect both property and a business, or solely a business, the doctrine applies and therefore the question of reasonableness arises.

A variety of tests were proposed. The first was stated by Lord Reid who said:

> Restraint of trade appears to me to imply that a man contracts to give up some freedom which otherwise he would have had. A person buying or leasing land had no previous right to be there at all, let alone to trade there, and when he takes possession of that land subject to a negative restrictive covenant he gives up no right or freedom which he previously had.

As the respondents were already in possession when they entered into the solus agreements, he concluded that the agreements were within the doctrine of restraint of trade. Lord Reid's view that the restraint of trade doctrine only applies if the convenantor has given up a freedom which he previously possessed was supported by Lords Morris and Hodson. An attempt was made in *Lobb (Alec) (Garages) Ltd v Total Oil (Great Britain) Ltd* [1985] 1 All ER 303, to take advantage of this view. The oil company granted a lease-back with a tie to the individual shareholders of a company; the company itself having granted the lease. It was argued that the doctrine could not apply as the shareholders had given up nothing, only the company had. However this was described by the Court of Appeal as a device and the doctrine was applied. See also *Amoco Australia Pty Ltd v Rocca Bros Motor Engineering Co Pty Ltd* [1975] AC 561, *Sadler v Imperial Life Assurance Co of Canada Ltd* [1988] IRLR 388 and the discussion at pp 163–6 below.

The second test is also contained in Lord Reid's judgment. He concluded that not only had the respondents agreed negatively not to sell other petrol but that they had agreed positively to keep their garage open for the sale of the appellant's petrol at all reasonable hours throughout the period of the tie. It had been argued that this merely regulated the respondent's trading and tended towards the promotion rather than the restraint of his trade. To this Lord Reid said that to regulate a person's existing trade may be a greater restraint than prohibiting him from engaging in a new trade. He seemed to imply in this that even if the covenantor had *not* previously enjoyed a certain freedom then the restraint of trade doctrine might still apply if he is, as a result of the restraint, under a *positive* duty to do something which restricts his current freedom.

The third test appears first in Lord Pearce's judgment but is most clearly stated by Lord Wilberforce:

> No exhaustive test can be stated—probably no precise non-exhaustive test. But the development of the law does seem to show that judges have been able to dispense from the necessity of justification under a public

policy test of reasonableness such contracts or provisions of contracts as, under contemporary conditions, may be found to have passed into the accepted and normal currency of commercial or contractual or conveyancing relations. That such contracts have done so may be taken to show with at least strong *prima facie* force that, moulded under the pressures of negotiation, competition and public opinion, they have assumed a form which satisfies the test of public policy as understood by the courts at the time, or, regarding the matter from the point of view of the trade, that the trade in question has assumed such a form that for its health or expansion it requires a degree of regulation. Absolute exemption from restriction or regulation is never obtained: circumstances, social or economic, may have altered, since they obtained acceptance, in such a way as to call for a fresh examination; there may be some exorbitance or special feature in the individual contract which takes it out of the accepted category: but the court however must be persuaded of this before it calls upon the relevant party to justify a contract of this kind.

He expanded this view by referring to a number of authorities, which could only be truly explained by saying that certain contracts have become part of 'the accepted machinery of a type of transaction which is generally found acceptable and necessary; so that instead of being regarded as restrictive they are accepted as part of the structure of a trading society'. Thus sole agency contracts had become part of the accepted pattern or structure of trade. They therefore encouraged or strengthened the trade rather than limited it. Applying these notions to the particular contracts in question he decided that the solus system was both too recent and too variable for it to have become part of the 'accepted machinery'. Part of Lord Wilberforce's test is extremely difficult for the practitioner to apply. It would have been tempting for an adviser to have thought in 1968 that a solus agreement involving the exclusive purchase of petrol was of sufficiently established commercial importance to fall within that class of cases to which Lord Wilberforce said the restraint of trade doctrine would not apply. Indeed, it was found as a fact in the case that out of 36,000 petrol stations in the United Kingdom nearly 35,000 were subject to solus agreements. Of the 35,000 over 6,600 were solus agreements with Esso. Moreover, the provisos and developments which Lord Wilberforce admitted might make an accepted commercial agreement subject to the doctrine in any event make this test difficult to apply. This test was considered in *Schroeder (A) Music Publishing Co Ltd v Macaulay* [1974] 1 WLR 1308 where Lord Reid, by way of answer to the argument that a standard form of publishing agreement which had stood the test of time was the very same agreement about which the defendant was then complaining, said that this test could only be satisfied when the contracts were 'made freely by parties bargaining on equal terms' or 'moulded under the pressures of negotiation, competition and public opinion'. These requirements were not satisfied in *Schroeder* because the contract was imposed on the plaintiff by a defendant who had greater bargaining power which he used oppressively.

A fourth test proposed in *Esso Petroleum Co Ltd v Harper's Garage (Stourport) Ltd* [1968] AC 269 was the second test stated by Lord Wilberforce.

In concluding his judgment, Lord Wilberforce examined the claim that the designation of the transaction as a mortgage in itself protected the entire contents of the mortgage deed from the scrutiny of the restraint of trade doctrine. He said, referring to the contents of a mortgage deed: 'If their purpose and nature is found not to be ancillary to the lending of money upon security, as, for example, to make the lending more profitable or safer, but some quite independent purpose, they may and should be independently scrutinised' (ie subject to the restraint of trade doctrine). What Lord Wilberforce was saying was that one examines the content and not the form of a restraint and if there appears 'some quite independent purpose' behind the restraint, ie a purpose outside the essence of the agreement, then the doctrine applies. This test appeared to have the support of Lords Morris and Pearce.

There may be some merit in the argument put forward on behalf of the respondents in the *Esso* case that all contracts are subject to the doctrine but that most contracts are quite clearly reasonable. All contracts could be described quite properly as being in restraint of trade, but this was not a term of abuse, and only those contracts which were in unreasonable restraint of trade would be struck down by the courts. This is an attractive argument which seems to provide an easy answer to the problem by disregarding it entirely. It is supported by Lord Hodson in *Esso* and in *Pharmaceutical Society of Great Britain v Dickson* [1970] AC 403. The difficulty with the argument is that it may provide a rogues' charter. But in practice we think it is a reasonable approach because of the powers which the court has to deal with unmeritorious points.

An important aspect of the *Esso* case is that it illustrates that the restraint of trade doctrine is not simply applicable to those restraints which continue after the end of the contract period. Indeed, there is earlier authority for the application of the doctrine during the period of contract though as these cases are very much in the minority, they are sometimes forgotten. In *McEllistrim v The Ballymacelligott Co-op Agricultural & Dairy Society* [1919] AC 548 a co-operative society had changed its rules so as to prevent any member from selling milk other than to the society. If a member did so there was a heavy penalty. Moreover there could be no termination of membership without the society's permission. The House of Lords applied the restraint of trade doctrine. In *English Hop Growers Ltd v Dering* [1928] 2 KB 174 the Court of Appeal had to consider an agreement under which the defendant contracted to sell his crop to the plaintiffs for a period of five years. The Court of Appeal applied the restraint of trade doctrine and found that the agreement was reasonable.

In *Foley v Classique Coaches Ltd* [1934] 2 KB 1 the restraint of trade doctrine was applied to an agreement whereby a purchaser of land agreed to take from the seller all the petrol required for the purchaser's business carried out on that land. See also *Servais Bouchard v Prince's Hall Restaurant Ltd* (1904) 20 TLR 574.

In *R v General Medical Council, ex parte Colman* [1990] 1 All ER 489 the Court of Appeal on one view appear to have refused to apply the restraint of trade doctrine when asked to do so by a doctor who complained that the General Medical Council (GMC) had refused to allow him to advertise. It was found that the decision of the GMC to prevent advertising in the press was a lawful exercise of the statutory powers conferred on it by s 35 of The Medical Act 1983, and that if a statutory power was exercised *intra vires*, reasonably and in accordance with the purpose of the Act conferring the power, (even though it restricted the plaintiff's freedom to trade or practice his profession) the court could not review the exercise of the power on the basis that it caused a restraint of trade, since the exercise of the power in accordance with the policy and the purpose of the Act could not be contrary to public policy and any review by the court would be unconstitutional. An alternative view might be that as the court considered whether the GMC had exercised its power in accordance with the Act it was in fact embarking on an exercise which involved making a finding of reasonableness (or the lack of it) in a fashion analogous to an application of the restraint of trade doctrine.

1.2 Extension of the principles

In recent years there has been an extension of the principles behind the restraint of trade doctrine so as to embrace:

(a) restraints in contracts which do not fit neatly into what was hitherto regarded as amounting to a restraint of trade;

(b) situations where the contract in question was not between the plaintiff and defendant and to which the plaintiff was not privy although he was affected by the working of the contract; and

(c) situations when no contract existed at all but the plaintiff could claim that a set of rules or certain conduct affected him prejudicially.

See *Schroeder (A) Music Publishing Co Ltd v Macaulay* [1974] 1 WLR 1308; *Eastham v Newcastle Football Club Ltd* [1964] Ch 413, *Nagle v Feilden* [1966] 2 QB 633 and *McInnes v Onslow Fae* [1978] 3 All ER 211.

These cases are referred to as 'restraint of trade' cases and indeed that phrase was used in them. They can rightly be described as such because in each case the plaintiff's freedom and ability to earn a living was affected. It was that which gave him *locus standi*. The *Schroeder* case concerned an agreement between a young songwriter and a music publisher. There came a stage when the songwriter no longer wanted to be bound by the agreement so he sought a declaration that it was contrary to public policy and therefore unenforceable. The case reached the House of Lords and at every hearing the plaintiff succeeded. Lord Reid identified why the agreement was in restraint of trade. He said that the agreement was on its face unduly restrictive having regard to:

(a) its likely duration;

(b) the publishers' right to assign copyright in songs which they had acquired in full under the agreement, so that it could not be argued that they would be unlikely to act oppressively and so damage their goodwill;

(c) the fact that the publishers were not bound to publish or promote the songwriter's work if they chose not to do so, so that he might earn nothing, and his talents be sterilised, contrary to the public interest; and

(d) the absence of any provision entitling the songwriter to terminate the agreement.

Lord Reid went on to point out that this case was not of the type which would usually have been described as in restraint of trade; there was for example no provision which prevented the plaintiff from working once the contract had run its course. He said:

> Any contract by which a person engages to give his exclusive services to another for a period necessarily involves extensive restriction during that period of the common law right to exercise any lawful activity he chooses in such manner as he thinks best. Normally, the doctrine of restraint of trade has no application to such restrictions: they require no justification.

However he went on in an important passage to say that if contractual restrictions appear to be unnecessary or to be reasonably capable of enforcement in an oppressive manner then they must be justified before they can be enforced. By 'justified' he meant 'proved to be reasonable'. Therefore, there seem to be two bases on which a contractual term can be attacked even though it does not attempt to restrain a party after the contractual period had ended. These are:

(a) Is the restriction necessary?
(b) Is the restriction reasonably capable of enforcement in an oppressive manner? (There appears to be some foundation for this approach in Lord Pearce's judgment in *Esso*.)

Note that it does not have to be shown that there has actually been oppressive enforcement simply that such is 'reasonably capable'. What is clear is that the word oppressive does not necessarily mean that the defendant has been induced to enter the restriction by fraud, misrepresentation, deceit or forced to enter it by duress. The question of oppression or unconscionable conduct was further considered in *Lobb (Alec) (Garages) Ltd v Total Oil (Great Britian) Ltd* [1985] 1 All ER 303. There it was pointed out by Dillon LJ that inequality of bargaining power was not sufficient on its own to enable a court to strike down a contract. It was also necessary to show unconscionable conduct etc. Moreover, as was pointed out in *Multiservice Bookbinding Ltd v Marden* [1979] Ch 84 unreasonableness is not sufficient to amount to unconscionable conduct. This is the traditional view. It is generally accepted that in order to succeed on a plea of unreasonableness it is not necessary for the covenantor to show that the covenantee had acted oppressively. *Schroeder* however does appear to equate unreasonableness with oppression but it is suggested that it was not laying down any principle to that effect: it so happened that on the facts in that case unreasonableness and oppression both existed.

The *Schroeder* case was applied in *Davis (Clifford) Management Ltd v WEA Records Ltd* [1975] 1 WLR 61, in which Lord Denning MR pointed out that the agreement was not in restraint of trade in the traditional sense because:

> It does not preclude a man from exercising his trade at all. But it is an agreement which is 'restrictive of trade' in this sense, that it requires a man

to give his services and wares to one person only for a long term of years to the exclusion of all others.

See further *Lloyds Bank Ltd v Bundy* [1975] QB 326.

A further example of the wide application of the restraint of trade doctrine is found in *Eastham v Newcastle Football Club Ltd* [1963] 3 All ER 139. In that case, the plaintiff was a professional footballer registered with a league club, Newcastle United. He had asked to be transferred, but his club had given him notice of retention and refused to release him. He refused to sign again with his club and sought, *inter alia*, declarations that the rules of the Football Association relating to the retention and transfer of football players, including the plaintiff, and the regulations of the Football League relating to retention and transfer were not binding on him, because they operated in unreasonable restraint of trade. He also claimed a declaration that the refusal of the directors of Newcastle United to release him from its retention list or alternatively to put him on its transfer list was unreasonable. Wilberforce J held, among other things, firstly, that the retention provisions, which operated after the end of the employee's employment, substantially interfered with his right to seek employment and therefore operated in restraint of trade; secondly, that the transfer system and the retention system, when combined, were in restraint of trade and that, since the defendants had not discharged the onus of showing that the restraints were no more than was reasonable to protect their interests, they were in unjustifiable restraint of trade and *ultra vires*; thirdly, that the court could examine a contract between employers only and declare it void on grounds on which such a contract would be declared void if it had been a contract between an employer and employee, and that it was open to an employee to bring an action for a declaration that such a contract was in restraint of trade, inasmuch as it threatened his liberty of action in seeking employment, which was a matter of public interest; and, fourthly, that it was a case in which the court could and should grant the plaintiff the declarations sought. See also Chapter 19 below for discussion of other similar cases.

In *Balston Ltd v Headline Fillers Ltd* [1987] FSR 330 it appears that an express confidential information clause which sought to protect secrets other than 'business secrets' (in the narrow sense that that phrase is used in *Faccenda Chicken v Fowler*, see pp 78–9 below) was subjected by Scott J to the restraint of trade doctrine (see also Harman J in *Systems Reliability Holdings plc v Smith* [1990] IRL R 377). This is consistent with the principles enunciated by Lord Morris in *Esso* (see p 1 above) although it is unusual to find a specific reference to the doctrine in this context. The usual approach of the courts is to examine whether any confidential information exists, whether it is protected by an express or implied term and, subject to arguments as to the balance of convenience, grant or refuse the injunction sought.

1.3 Conclusion

One can conclude that:

(1) The following classes of case are usually subject to the doctrine:

(a) employment contracts regarding the period after the contract has ended;

(b) contracts analogous to (a) such as some agency agreements and partnership agreements;

(c) business sales contracts which preclude the vendor from competing with his former business;

(d) solus agreements; and

(e) any situation, not necessarily involving a contract, in which it appears a party has acted unreasonably, unfairly or oppressively so as to restrict another party, usually the plaintiff in the action, in the exercise of his trade, profession or employment.

(2) The following classes of cases are usually not subject to the doctrine:

(a) those which include a restraint which does not involve the convenantor in giving up a freedom which he would otherwise have enjoyed unless the restraint creates a positive duty to do something which restricts his freedom during the period of its operation;

(b) those which, under contemporary conditions, may be found to have passed into the accepted and normal currency of commercial or contractual or conveyancing relations; and

(c) those in which the purpose and nature of the restraint is coterminous with the purpose of the contract.

2 An interest meriting protection

In order to succeed the party arguing for the validity of the restraint of trade must first persuade the tribunal that the facts demonstrate the existence of a legitimate interest meriting protection. The nature of the interest meriting protection will differ according to the type of restraint under consideration. In employment contracts the interests are usually business secrets, trade connections or goodwill. In solus agreements efficiency of distribution, and in cases concerning sporting organisations the proper promotion of the sport, have been held to be interests meriting protection.

'Goodwill' is made up of two components: trade connections and reputation. The latter is only really relevant when considering business sales, however the former is important in all types of situation.

The application of these principles is well illustrated in *Stenhouse Australia Ltd v Phillips* [1974] AC 391. Lord Wilberforce examined the interests which an insurance-broking business might have in preventing an employee canvassing its clients once he had left. He said that in the business of insurance and insurance broking, a successful enterprise depends upon a number of factors which vary according to the nature of the customer, or client, with whom business is done. The more varied or diversified the business of the client, and the larger the amount of insurance to be placed, the more likely it is that he will look around the market for himself in order to obtain the best terms. With a less diversified business, the likelihood grows that, while he is satisfied with the service he gets, he will keep his business, at least for a period, with the same insurer, and place it through the same broker. The advice and guidance, based on collation of information, by the broker, will be more valuable in such a case, to both broker and customer. In either case, in order to obtain and to retain business it is necessary to cultivate and accumulate knowledge of the client's requirements and of his record, so as to be able to offer him attractive terms. To develop this may be a fairly long-term affair: even if it has been developed there is always the risk that the client may decide to go elsewhere if better prospects offer. It is clear from this, he said, that the connection between an insurer or insurance broker and his client is not nearly so firm as, for example, that between a solicitor and his client. On the other hand its comparative fragility makes the risk of solicitation of clients by a former employee the more serious. A client is not easily detached from a solicitor who has been handling his affairs over a period of years, but a comparatively mild solicitation may deprive an insurance broker of valuable business which otherwise might safely be reckoned on for a period. He concluded that the facts demonstrated the existence of a protectable interest.

Regarding business secrets, a problem which arises in practice is the necessity in employment cases to make a distinction between what is a business secret and what is simply the general skill of the employee. That distinction is dealt with in Chapter 3 at p 18. However the courts have consistently recognised the interest that the employer or any other covenantee has in protecting business secrets. For example, in *Littlewoods Organisation Ltd v Harris* [1978] 1 All ER 1026 Megaw LJ said:

> . . . it is appropriate that a covenant, restricting an employee from full freedom of taking other employment when he leaves his existing employment, should be included in the contract of employment where there is a real danger that the employee will in the course of that employment have access to and gain information about matters which could fairly be regarded as trade secrets; and that applies even though the information may be carried in his head and even though (perhaps, particularly though) it may be extremely difficult for the employee himself, being an honest and scrupulous man, to realise that what he is passing on to his new employers is matter which ought to be treated as confidential to his old employers.

Once the party seeking to enforce the restraint has established that there is an interest meriting protection the next question is whether the restraint is reasonable between the parties.

3 Reasonableness between the parties

The question whether a particular restraint is reasonable in the interests of both parties generally divides into three parts:

(a) Is the scope of the activities which the clause restrains reasonable?
(b) Is the geographical extent of the restraint reasonable?
(c) Is the duration of the restraint reasonable?

In all three parts 'reasonable' means providing no more than relevant and necessary protection for the legitimate interest of the covenantee. Before relying on any case as a precedent for what is reasonable between the parties the important observations made in the case of *Esso Petroleum Co Ltd v Harper's Garage (Stourport) Ltd* [1968] AC 269 must be noted. Lord Reid said that where a party, who is in no way at a disadvantage in bargaining, chooses to take a calculated risk, then he could see no reason why the court should say that he had acted against his own interests. Lord Hodson said that in the case of agreements between commercial companies for regulating their trade relations the parties are usually the best judges of what is reasonable. In such a case, as Lord Haldane said in *North Western Salt Co Ltd v Electrolytic Alkali Co Ltd* [1914] AC 461, the law 'still looks carefully to the interests of the public, but it regards the parties as the best judges of what is reasonable as between themselves'.

3.1 Scope: activities restrained

In order to demonstrate that a particular provision is reasonable between the parties it is necessary to demonstrate that the scope of those activities is reasonably referable to a legitimate interest, although it is not necessary to have absolute consistency between the restraint and the relevant interest. In *M & S Drapers v Reynolds* [1957] 1 WLR 9 Morris LJ said 'I do not consider that a restriction . . . would necessarily be held to be unreasonable merely because it could be shown possibly to extend to one or two cases beyond the range of contemplated protection'. It is submitted that this is sensible: if the party seeking to enforce the restraint were required to match the restraint exactly to the interest very few restraints, if any at all, would be found to be reasonable.

3.2 Geographical extent

Important factors to be considered when examining a geographical area are not simply the distance involved (usually a radial measurement from a given place) but the character of the area, the ease of travel/communication and the character of the business in question. It is generally true to say that if the area is predominantly rural then the geographical extent of the restriction can sometimes be greater than if an urban area is under consideration. For example, in *Routh v Jones* [1947] 1 All ER 179 Evershed J paid especial regard to the rural nature of an area in deciding that a restriction which extended to ten miles from a certain place was not unreasonable.

3.3 Time restrictions

If there is no mention of a time restriction in a covenant then the courts will normally infer that it is intended that the restriction should last forever. No general rules can be laid down as to the reasonableness of a time period because these obviously depend on the facts of each case, however as Lord Shaw said in the *Morris (Herbert)* case 'as the time of the restriction lengthens and the space of its operation extends, the weight of the onus on the covenantee grows'. It is important to remember that a classic type of restraint of trade clause frequently mentions two quite separate time periods. The first and obvious one is the period to which the covenant relates once the contract is at an end. The second occurs in those clauses which seek to circumscribe contact with those who were, for a given period, clients of the covenantee. An example of such a clause is one which says the employee is not to canvass or solicit during a period of five years from the date of the determination of this agreement for whatever reason any person, company or firm who were customers of the employer with whom he dealt during the last three years of his employment. There is no reason why both periods should not be scrutinised.

4 Reasonableness in the public interest

It has been common in the past to underestimate the importance of public policy or the public interest in the restraint of trade doctrine. See *A-G of the Commonwealth of Australia v Adelaide Steamship Co* [1913] AC 781. Although it is usually true that if the interests of the covenantee and the covenantor are satisfied then so is the public interest, it is important to realise that in some cases the courts have chosen to examine the restraint primarily from the point of view of the public interest rather than from that of the parties.

In the *Esso* case Lord Reid said 'as the whole doctrine of restraint of trade is based on public policy its application ought to depend less on legal niceties or theoretical possibilities than on the practical effect of a restraint in hampering that freedom which it is the policy of the law to protect'. Lord Reid went on to say that the reason that the court will not enforce a restraint which goes further than affording protection to the legitimate interests of a party is because too wide a restraint is against the public interest.

What is public policy? Although, as Lord MacMillan said in *Vancouver Malt & Sake Brewing Co Ltd v Vancouver Breweries Ltd* [1934] AC 181, it is important to realise that 'public policy is not a constant' it appears to have some easily recognisable and immutable general characteristics. For example, the two competing public interests in employment cases are:

(a) a person should be held to his promise; and

(b) every person should be free to exercise his skill and experience to the best advantage of himself and of those who may want to employ him (see Lord Atkinson in *Morris (Herbert) v Saxelby* [1916] 1 AC 688).

In business sales cases the conflicting public interests are that a man is not at liberty to deprive himself or the community of his labour and expertise unreasonably and yet he must have a freedom to sell his business for the best price; which may be only obtainable if he precludes himself from entering into competition with the purchaser (see James VC in *Leather Cloth Co v Lorsont* (1869) LR 9 Eq 354).

However, judicial opinion has varied in its view of what is the dominant ingredient of public policy. For example, in *English Hop Growers Ltd v Derring* [1928] 2 KB 174 Scrutton LJ said 'I have always for myself regarded it as in the public interest that parties who, being in an equal position of bargaining, make contracts, should be compelled to perform them, and not to escape from their liabilities by saying that they had agreed to something which was unreasonable'. However, it should be noted that Scrutton LJ's words were said in a case involving a contract between commercial parties and it now seems that the insistence that public policy is primarily concerned with holding people to their agreements is now out of favour. Likewise, it is submitted that no modern court would say as Sir George Jessell MR did in *Printing and Numerical Registering Co v Sampson* (1875) LR 19 Eq 462:

> ... if there is one thing which more than another public policy requires it is that men of full age and competent understanding shall have the utmost liberty of contracting, and that their contracts when entered into freely and voluntarily shall be held sacred and shall be enforced by courts of justice. Therefore, you have this paramount public policy to consider—that you are not lightly to interfere with this freedom of contract.

If one sets that quotation against the context of modern cases such as *Schroeder (A) Music Publishing Co v Macaulay* [1974] 1 WLR 1308 one is left in no doubt that the courts nowadays, whilst paying tribute to the sanctity of contract, will vigorously refuse to uphold contracts which in their view are oppressive or unreasonable. Indeed, it is submitted that the reasoning in *Schroeder's* case was based on public policy and Lord Diplock explained what was meant by public policy. He said that the public policy which the court was implementing was not some 19th century economic theory about the benefit to the general public of freedom of trade, but the protection of those whose bargaining power is weak against being forced by those whose bargaining power is stronger to enter into bargains that are unconscionable. It is submitted that this is not a complete modern definition of what amounts to public policy but is one facet of that definition.

Important cases in which public policy has been the paramount or only reason for striking down a provision as an unreasonable restraint of trade include *Morris (Herbert) v Saxelby* and *Leng (Sir WC) & Co Ltd v Andrews* [1909] 1 Ch 763. Moreover, in *Strange (SW) Ltd v Mann* [1965] 1 WLR 629 Stamp J said that an employee's skill and knowledge 'is in no sense the employer's property and it is contrary to public policy to restrain its use in any degree'. In the *Esso* case both Lords Hodson and Pearce specifically rested their judgments in striking down a solus agreement which extended to 21 years on the basis of public policy.

Finally, it can be said that the public interest and public policy have played an especially important part as a vehicle for providing a reason for giving redress in those cases in which the parties are not contractually bound. For example, Slade J in *Greig v Insole* [1978] 3 All ER 449 charmingly described the public interest in that case as the 'public pleasure' in watching cricket played by talented cricketers, and described the Football Association and the Football League in *Eastham v Newcastle Football Club Ltd* [1964] Ch 413 as being 'custodians of the public interest'.

Chapter 3

Restraint of Trade

1 The form of the agreement

The form of a restraint is irrelevant. Only its contents are important. It may be a direct or an indirect restraint or it may be contained in an agreement outside the primary contract between the parties.

1.1 Direct and indirect restraints

Most cases quite obviously involve a direct restraint on the covenantor from doing a certain thing or things. However, some cases do involve indirect restraints. In *Wyatt v Kreglinger and Fernau* [1933] 1 KB 793 the restraint was contained in a letter dealing with the plaintiff's retirement rather than in his contract of employment and it effectively said that the defendants would pay him a pension if he refrained from working in the wool trade. This restraint was held by the court to be an indirect one and on the facts of the case it was found to be unreasoanble and therefore the plaintiff was not entitled to his pension.

A further example of an indirect restraint is found in the case of *Mineral Water Bottle Exchange and Trade Protection Society v Booth* (1887) 36 Ch D 465 where a trade association had a rule that no member should employ an employee who had left the service of another member without the consent in writing of his late employer until a period of two years had elapsed from the time of the end of his employment. This was quite clearly not an agreement between the employer and the employee but had the effect of being an indirect restraint on any employee who wanted to work for another member of the trade association within the two year period. The rule was struck down as being an unreasonable restraint of trade when the Society attempted to prevent the defendants from employing an employee who had recently left another member of the association.

A recent example of an indirect restraint is found in the case of *Kores Manufacturing Co Ltd v Kolok Manufacturing Co Ltd* [1957] 3 All ER 158. In that case the plaintiffs and the defendants were two companies who manufactured similar goods. They entered into an agreement by correspondence, each company writing in substantially the same terms to the other that they would not, without the written consent of the other, at any time, employ any person who during the past five years had been an employee of the other. The covenant was held to be an unreasonable restraint of trade. See also *Bull v Pitney-Bowes Ltd* [1967] 1 WLR 273.

In *Sadler v Imperial Life Assurance Co of Canada Ltd* [1988] IRLR 388 the question of whether an indirect restraint of trade existed was considered. The defendants, a life assurance company employed the plaintiff as an insurance agent. He was in fact an employee rather than an independent agent and had worked for the defendants for 17 years. He then resigned from his employment in accordance with the terms of his employment contract and brought an action against his former employers relating to commission payments. The plaintiff was remunerated by a commission calculated by reference to the premium paid by the insured persons introduced by him. The purchaser of a life assurance contract does not make one payment at the beginning of the contract but pays a premium in instalments over a number of years. This fact was reflected in the commission structure that the defendants agreed to pay the plaintiff. Commission was payable to the plaintiff on premiums paid during the first ten years of any policy. The commission was paid on a reducing basis so a substantial amount of commission was paid in respect of the premium paid in the first policy year and a lower commission in subsequent years up to the tenth year. Accordingly, the total commission payable to the plaintiff in respect of a policy effected through his introduction would take ten years to accrue. It was recognised by the defendants that when the employment of an agent came to an end it was likely that there would be in existence a number of policies which would have been effected during the period of the plaintiff's employment in respect of which commission would normally be paid in future years if the employment had continued. The employment contract between the parties dealt with this eventuality by the continuance of such payments to the employee after he had ceased to be employed 'provided that the agent's entitlement to such commission will immediately cease if the agent enters into a contract of service or for services directly or indirectly with any limited company, mutual society, partnership or brokerage operation involved in the selling of insurance or would be in breach of any part of clause 9A hereof were this contract still subsisting'. Clause 9A of the contract incorporated a restraint on competing activities during employment. It effectively prevented him from working for another insurance company during that period.

In his statement of claim the plaintiff admitted that since termination of the contract he had by reason of continuing to work within the insurance industry acted in such a way that, if the contract were still subsisting, he would have been in breach of clause 9A. It was in the light of that breach that the defendants had refused to pay the plaintiff any post-determination commission.

It was argued on behalf of the plaintiff that:

   (a) the proviso quoted above constituted an unlawful restraint of trade;
   (b) the proviso was severable and might be struck out of the contract without affecting the remainder;
   (c) the plaintiff's entitlement to post-determination commission accordingly continued notwithstanding his admitted breach of clause 9A.

The defendants argued that:

(a) The proviso quoted above came within the first test enunciated by Lord Reid in the *Esso* case (see p 7 above) ie that it did not deprive the plaintiff of any freedom which he would otherwise have had; accordingly that it did not operate as a restraint of trade and therefore that it was effective on the admitted facts to terminate the plaintiff's entitlement to commission.

(b) That if the effect of the proviso were to impose a restraint of trade then the consequence was that not only the proviso but also the whole of the paragraph to which the proviso related and which contained the stipulation that post-termination commission would be paid was void. Therefore, the plaintiff would have no entitlement to post-termination commission at all.

It was agreed by the parties that if the proviso on its true construction operated as a restraint of trade it could not be justified on the ground of reasonableness. The judge found that the substance of the post-termination commission clause was that in the event of termination following a prescribed period of service, commission would be paid to the plaintiff in respect of premiums actually paid under the relevant policies issued during his appointment but that it was subject to the proviso that the agent's entitlement to such commission would cease if he entered into competing activities. The judge concluded that there was thus a direct financial inducement for the agent not to enter into such activities but to restrict his post-termination employment to non-competing activities. The effect of the proviso was that if the plaintiff were to recover post-termination commission he would be required to give up some freedom which he would otherwise have had, namely the freedom to take employment in whichever field he wished. He therefore found that the facts of the case were indistinguishable from those of *Wyatt* and *Bull*.

1.2 Proximity of the restraint to the main contract

A covenant in restraint of trade is usually contained in a contract. For example, an employee will have a written contract of employment in which clauses will provide for the restraint of trade and for the protection of business secrets. However, it is not necessary for the restraint of trade clause to be part of the main contract so long as it is possible to argue that it is referable to it or is in some other way of contractual force. In *Commercial Plastics Ltd v Vincent* [1965] 1 QB 623 the contract of employment was concluded on 20 December 1959 and yet the restraint of trade clause was contained in a letter of 27 November 1959. It was accepted by the Court of Appeal that the letter had to be construed as part of the written contract. In *Stenhouse Australia Ltd v Phillips* [1974] AC 391 the restraint of trade clause was part of an agreement made between the parties after employment had ceased as it had been in *Wyatt's* case. In the *Esso* case, the restraint in a supply and purchase contract was reinforced in a mortgage deed. The court refused to accede to the appellant's argument that the fact that the restraint was contained in a mortgage deed excluded the application of the restraint of trade doctrine. Lord Morris said that a consideration of the facts and documents led him to the view that the solus agreement, the loan agreement and the mortgage could be linked together as an instance of one transaction and that the intention was that in providing that the mortgage should be irredeemable for the period of the tie it should become a support for the solus agreement.

2 The time at which reasonableness is considered

It is generally accepted that the relevant time at which reasonableness is to be considered is the time of entering the contract. Therefore a court will ask the question was the restraint reasonable when it was entered by the parties? The matter was discussed extensively in *Commercial Plastics Ltd v Vincent* [1965] 1 QB 623. Pearson LJ said when construing the restraint 'although the time for ascertaining the competitors is the time of termination of a contract of employment, the time for ascertaining the reasonableness of a restrictive covenant or provision is the time of the making of the contract'. This highlights one of the problems of the approach that the time at which reasonableness should be considered is the time of contract. Many restraints, as in *Commercial Plastics*, refer to the fact that a party may not solicit or compete with the other party in relation to those who were customers at the date of the determination of the contract. One therefore has the dichotomy of examining what is reasonable at one time (ie the start of the contract), whilst also examining the ultimate purpose of the restraint at another (ie the end of the contractual period). However, there is no doubt that the majority of authorities do favour an examination of reasonableness at the time of contracting. The practical effect of this is illustrated by the case of *Strange (SW) Ltd v Mann* [1965] 1 WLR 629 where at the time of entering the contract the business was exclusively a credit-betting business and it was accepted by all parties that the validity of the covenant fell to be tested without regard to the fact that subsequently betting shops became legal and that a betting shop had been set up by the plaintiff. Stamp J therefore considered the reasonableness of the restraint purely in the context of a credit-betting business. Indeed, it was this fact which principally led him to describe the restraint as unreasonable.

An important consequence of this approach is that generally the courts have refused to accept that supervening events (ie events subsequent to the time of contract) can render an initially reasonable covenant unenforceable. It seems that the reason for this is that to hold otherwise would be to give rise to an unacceptable degree of uncertainty. In *Gledhow Autoparts Ltd v Delaney* [1965] 1 WLR 1366 Diplock LJ said 'It is natural . . . to tend to look at what in fact happened under the agreement; but the question of the validity of a covenant in restraint of trade has to be determined at the date at which the agreement was entered into and has to be determined in the light of what may happen under the agreement, although what may happen may be and always is different in some respects from what did happen. A covenant of this kind is invalid *ab initio* or valid *ab initio*. There cannot be a moment from which it passes from the class of invalid into that of valid covenants'. Moreover, in *Schroeder* Lord Reid said that a consequence of examining validity at the time when the contract was signed made it unnecessary to deal with the reasons why the respondent (originally the plaintiff) now wished to be freed from it. This must mean that cross-examination about these reasons is irrelevant.

Although one looks at reasonableness at the time the agreement is entered into, it is only practical also to take into account the legitimate expectations of the parties at that time regarding the future, and what is reasonably foreseeable. See *Putsman v Taylor* [1927] 1 KB 741 and *Lyne-Pirkis v Jones* [1969] 1 WLR 1293 per Edmund Davies LJ. However it may be that expansion of the business goes beyond the reasonable expectation of the parties; in which case it may be necessary for the covenantor to renegotiate the ambit of the restraint. In order to attempt to provide for this possibility there should be a contractual provision which permits renegotiation and see *R S Components Ltd v Irwin* [1974] 1 All ER 41.

In *Shell UK v Lostock Garage Ltd* [1976] 1 WLR 1187 Lord Denning MR explained what he thought was meant by the proposition that reasonableness is to be considered at the time when the contract is made:

> If the terms impose a restraint which is unreasonable in the sense that it may work unfairly in circumstances which may reasonably be anticipated, the courts will refuse to enforce the restraint: but it will not hold it to be unenforceable simply because it might work unfairly in certain exceptional circumstances outside the reasonable expectation of the parties at the time of making the agreement.

He found that the circumstances which had arisen were not foreseeable at the time of the contract but he still decided to take into account supervening events: this made the contract unenforceable and unreasonable. He specifically disagreed with Diplock LJ's judgment in *Gledhow* quoted above and he particularly said that there was no such thing in this area of law as a contract which was void or invalid *ab initio* because an unreasonable restraint was only unenforceable if a party attempted to enforce it. He said that there were two situations in which the court would not enforce a clause:

(a) if at the time of making the contract it is seen that it may in the future operate unfairly or unreasonably; or

(b) if after the time of making the contract it is found to operate unreasonably or unfairly even if those circumstances were not envisaged beforehand.

Therefore it was possible to have supervening unenforceability. It seems that Kerr J at first instance had come to the same conclusion as Lord Denning via a public policy route. However, Lord Denning was in the minority in the Court of Appeal for both Ormrod LJ and Birdge LJ disagreed with him. Furthermore as authority for his departure from Diplock LJ's judgment, Lord Denning relied on dicta of their Lordships in *Esso Petroleum Co Ltd v Harper's Garage (Stourport) Ltd* [1968] AC 269 which are of doubtful support. However, whilst Lord Denning's view does not represent the law on this topic, it is submitted that his lack of faith in the traditional approach because the question of reasonableness is bound to be viewed with hindsight, is a valid criticism. It is rare for counsel to be stopped from corss-examining on what actually did happen during the currency of an agreement, or addressing the court on this, even if such events were not reasonably foreseeable. Moreover in the area of business secrets there may be a different approach. If what was a secret at the time that the contract was entered into subsequently becomes public knowledge then it would be unrealistic if the court were simply to examine the question of reasonableness at the time when the contract was entered. On the other hand, it could be said that this type of objection does not relate to reasonableness but is concerned with breach.

3 Construction

The problem of construction only arises if ambiguity exists. Throughout the cases it is possible to discern two distinct approaches to construction. The first, which is currently out of favour, although it made a brief reappearance in *Commercial Plastics Ltd v Vincent*, is the literal approach. The second, which has recently been heavily supported in *Littlewoods Organisation Ltd v Harris* [1978] 1 All ER 1026, holds that the object and intent of the whole contract should be found and that the specific restraint should be construed in its light. The problem with a literal approach is that it has frequently been used to persuade a court that wholly unlikely consequences might arise and that the court should, in the light of those consequences conclude that the restraint is unreasonable. On the whole, the champions of the literal approach have been the party attempting to strike down a particular clause whilst the object and intent approach tends to favour parties who are attempting to uphold the restraint. In our view, particularly because of the extravagant results that have arisen in some cases by applying the literal rule, there can be no doubt that in the modern context the object and intent rule is much fairer. The object and intent rule really has its basis in the reaction of the courts against the *reductio ad absurdum* type of argument put forward by counsel on behalf of defendants. In *Rannie v Irvine* (1844) 7 Man & G 969 Tindal CJ said 'if the contract is reasonable at the time it is entered into, we are not bound to look out for improbable and extravangant contingencies in order to make it void'. In *Nevanas (SV) & Co Ltd v Walker & Foreman* [1914] 1 Ch 413 Sargant J said 'The covenant has not been held bad because it might work unreasonably in certain exceptional circumstances not within its main and principal purpose and meaning'.

Other cases which have consistently championed the object and intent approach are *Mills v Dunham* [1891] 1 Ch 576, *Moenich v Fenestre* (1892) 61 LJ Ch 737, *Underwood (E) & Son Ltd v Barker* [1899] 1 Ch 300, *Haynes v Doman* [1899] 2 Ch 13, and *Caribonum Co Ltd v Le Couch* (1913) 109 LT 385 in which Eve J used the object and intent approach in order to construe a business secrets clause.

More recent cases such as *Home Counties Dairies Ltd v Skilton* [1970] 1 WLR 526 and *Plowman (GW) & Sons Ltd v Ash* [1964] 1 WLR 568 show the sense of the approach. In *Plowman's* case it was argued that on its true construction the restrictive covenant was too wide as it applied to goods of all kinds and would prevent canvassing by the employee in articles of trade of any kind. Harman LJ agreed that no specification existed but in applying the object and intent test he said:

... one must regard the contract as a whole, and this is a contract where a sales representative in South Lincolnshire serving a firm which, as appears from the very clause in question ... is a corn and agricultural merchant and animal feeding stuffs manufacturer. In my opinion it is no wider than that: the articles in which he may not canvass are the very articles in respect of which his employer employed him.

See also *White (Marion) Ltd v Francis* [1972] 1 WLR 1423.

In *Littlewoods Organisation Ltd v Harris* Lord Denning MR said that by construing a restriction according to the object and intent rule the courts refuse to hold a covenant bad merely because of unskilful drafting and will cut it down so as to reveal its essential reasonableness. However he said that the courts will only do so if the covenant is 'intrinsicaly just and reasonable'. Therefore it would seem on this approach that the court first has to decide whether the covenant is intrinsically just and reasonable before it applies the object and intent test. In practice this may be a very difficult exercise to undertake because in order to decide what is intrinsically just and reasonable the court will surely have to apply some rule of construction. However Lord Denning MR also put forward an alternative test. This applies when the words are so wide that on a strict construction they cover improbable and unlikely events. In such cases the court should not apply the strict construction so far as to make the whole clause void or invalid or unenforceable. All that should be done is that, if that improbable and unlikely event ever takes place, the courts should decline to enforce the clause. He then construed the words in a restrictive covenant which prevented the defendant from working for Great Universal Stores (GUS) or any of its subsidiaries. The clause read:

In the event of the determination of this Agreement for any reason whatsoever [Harris] shall not at any time within 12 months after such determination: (i) enter into a Contract of Service or other Agreement of a like nature with GUS Ltd or any company subsidiary thereto or be directly or indirectly engaged concerned or interested in the trading or business of the said GUS Ltd or any such company aforesaid ...

Did the inclusion of 'subsidiary' invalidate the restrictive covenant as it was accepted that many subsidiaries did not deal in the mail order business (one was a restaurant in Alice Springs). He concluded that it was proper to look at the GUS group as a single entity. Therefore it was fair for the provision to cover subsidiaries as well. As the group was under one unified control it was possible for an employee to be moved around within the group or at least have 'his information and knowledge' so transferred making it important that Littlewoods should have protection regarding the whole GUS group. If they did not and Harris had been free to work for a GUS company which was not in the mail order business he could still have passed Littlewoods' business secrets back to the mail order companies because of the structure of the GUS group.

The next point which posed a problem in this case was that the clause was unlimited in geographical area and the business of Littlewoods was solely within the UK whereas the businesses of the GUS group were worldwide. Lord Denning decided that if the clause was limited by its perceived object it applied only to such part of the GUS group as operated within the UK. It was therefore reasonable on this basis. The final point was that the only business of Littlewoods which could reasonably require protection was their mail order business and not their retail chain store business. However, the clause did not make this clear. Lord Denning said that it should be limited to the mail order business only because Harris' contract was at all relevant times with the mail order part of Littlewoods' business. The problem with this reasoning is that it comes very close to construing a clause to the extent that the plaintiffs seek to enforce it rather than as it stands. This approach was specifically rejected in *Gledhow* by Sellers LJ and it is submitted that he was right to do so.

Megaw LJ agreed with Denning MR but Browne LJ dissented: he said that the majority were effectively remaking the contract which was something which the court was not entitled to do. It is submitted that there is a great deal to be said for Browne LJ's view. On the majority view the defendant was actually left free to work for a subsidiary of GUS which was not involved in the mail order business in the United Kingdom even though that would have been in clear breach of the restriction. The approach of the majority seems to have been that even if there was such a breach the courts would refuse to acknowledge that it existed. It is submitted that the views of Browne LJ in *Littlewoods* case are to be preferred and that the approach of the majority is an extreme example of the object and intent approach which should not be followed.

In his judgment Lord Denning MR was highly critical of the decision in *Commercial Plastics Ltd v Vincent* because the agreement there was just and made in good faith. In that case the Court of Appeal was very much attracted by a *reductio* argument put forward on behalf of the defendant. However they decided the case on another basis and Pearson LJ said

'it may be said in answer to the possibility of such a *reductio ad absurdum*, though no doubt, it has to be taken into account, is far from conclusive, because it may involve unlikely hypotheses, which would be outside the reasonable expectations of the parties at the time of the making of the contract of employment'.

This is correct though we doubt if a *reductio* has to be taken into account and prefer the approach of non-fanciful construction which has been recently reaffirmed in *Home Counties Dairies v Skilton* (see p 63). This seems to chart a safe course between the extremes of *Littlewoods* on the one hand, and *Commercial Plastics* on the other. It is submitted that a number of cases which in the past applied the literal rule would now be decided in the opposite way.

The literal approach to construction has been most consistently and in our view, most erroneously applied in a line of cases concerning general medical practitioners. In *Routh v Jones* [1947] 1 All ER 758 the Court of Appeal held that a restraint on a medical assistant to a partnership which prevented him from practising 'in any department of medicine, surgery or midwifery (or accepting) any professional appointment' was unreasonable because it covered, *inter alia*, practice as a consultant or medical officer of health. There were other good reasons for not enforcing the covenant—length of time and its geographical scope, instead of resorting to an unconvincing analysis of the contrast between the legitimate interest of the plaintiffs and the width of the restraint as construed on a literal basis.

Routh v Jones was followed by Romer J in *Jenkins v Reid* [1948] 1 All ER 471 in which a restraint on a medical assistant to an ordinary country general medical practice was struck down because, as it prevented practice as 'a physician, surgeon or apothecary', the plaintiff would be unable to practice as a consultant in the geographical area covered by the restraint. Once again there were other reasons for not enforcing the covenant which did not involve taking an unrealistic and literal approach to the activities restrained. A similar approach was taken in *Lyne-Pirkis v Jones* [1969] 1 WLR 1293 and in *Peyton v Mindham* [1972] 1 WLR 8.

We are pleased to state that since the appearance of the first edition of this book the Court of Appeal has at last seen sense in its approach to construction in cases involving general medical practitioners: see *Clarke v Newland* [1991] 1 All ER 397. The case is important because the Court of Appeal considered in some detail the way in which a restraint of trade clause should be construed. The parties were partners in a general medical practice in central London. The plaintiff was the senior partner and the defendant the junior partner. Clause 15 of the partnership agreement stated: 'in the event of a partnership being [so determined] the salaried partner undertakes not to practice within the practice area . . . .', the practice area being defined. At first instance the judge, in refusing the injunction, decided that he was bound by the decision in *Lyne-Pirkis v Jones* and the plaintiff appealed. The case for the plaintiff was argued on four bases:

   (a) The verb 'practice' in the relevant clause had to be construed in the context of the agreement as a whole and in the proper factural matrix. In particular the attention of the court was drawn to clause 1 of the agreement which referred to the practice carried on by the parties as a 'practice of general medical practitioners'.

   (b) The agreement had to be given a purposive construction.

   (c) If so construed the word 'practice' plainly meant practice as a general medical practitioner. It was not a question of implying a term but giving the proper construction to the relevant word.

   (d) The decision in *Lyne-Pirkis v Jones* and the early decision of the Court of Appeal in *Routh v Jones* were clearly distinguishable. In both those cases the express words used and the relevant clause could be compared with other express words used elsewhere.

On behalf of the defendant it was argued that some limitation had to be placed on the word 'practice' and the natural and proper limitation was to imply the words 'as medical practitioners'. There was no warrant for implying the more restrictive limitation 'as general medical practitioners'. Both the plaintiff and defendant were free to practice either as doctors in a hospital or as medical consultants. In approaching this case the court first stated that there were many cases where a court has to construe a standard clause in, for example, a charter party, and there may be some earlier decisions on the same clause or on a clause which is in terms which are indistinguishable. In some of these cases the earlier decision would be a binding authority and it would have to be followed. In other cases in this category the earlier case, though not formally binding, was often followed in order to provide certainty and consistency in an area where commercial relations may depend on an accepted construction. In the present case however the court was not concerned with a standard clause and therefore it decided its approach should be different. The court was satisfied that the right approach was to try to reach a conclusion on a proper construction of the relevant clause before turning to any other cases where similar clauses had been used. Having reviewed the authorities which dealt with the construction of restraint of trade clauses, the court applied the following rules:

(a) The question of construction should be approached in the first instance without regard to the question of legality or illegality.
(b) The clause should be construed with reference to the object sought to be obtained.
(c) In restraint of trade cases the object is the protection of one of the partners against rivalry in trade.
(d) That the clause should be construed in context in the light of the factural matrix at the time when the agreement was made.

Applying those rules to the facts of this case the Court of Appeal decided that the word 'Practice' in the partnership agreement clearly meant practice as a general medical practitioner and did not mean anything wider. *Lyne-Pirkis v Jones* was distinguished on the basis that in that case there was an express antithesis between the phrase 'as general medical practitioners' in a recital and 'as a medical practitioner' in the relevant clause. What this case clearly shows is that one has to be very careful in assuming that in restraint of trade cases a phrase ascribed a meaning in one case will also be ascribed the same meaning in another.

In *Business Seating (Renovations) Ltd v Broad* [1989] ICR 729 it was claimed by the defendant that a non-solicitation covenant was void because the business not to be solicited was not defined. Millett J had to deal with the argument that it would be a breach of the covenant if the defendant were during the remainder of the period of restraint, to solicit any business of any kind from any company which happened to have been a customer of the plaintiff company during the relevant period. It was said that if the defendant took employment as a milk roundsman he would not be able to solicit orders for milk from any of the customers who had had their chairs renovated by the plaintiff company. The judge pointed out that another clause in the contract of employment expressly described the prohibited business: it was clearly restricted to repairing or renovation of office furniture and commercial seating. The evidence before the judge also showed that that was the nature of the plaintiff's business. The defendant was employed as a sales representative who sold the service of renovating and repairing office furniture and commercial seating and the judge correctly decided that that must be the business which was referred to by the restraint of trade clause.

4 Phrases and words

In *Rex Stewart etc v Parker* [1988] IRLR 483 the court was asked to consider a non-solicitation clause which related to any person '. . . who to your knowledge is or has been during the period of your employment a customer of the company ...'. It was successfully argued that the phrase 'is or' could only relate to a customer when the soliciting is taking place. Accordingly it would catch persons who may not have been customers of the plaintiff at the time when the defendant left his employment but who had become customers subsequently. This is a clear example of inept drafting. The phrase should simply have said 'was'.

In *Allied Dunbar (Frank Weisinger) Ltd v Frank Weisinger* [1988] IRLR 60 Millett J when discussing a clause which prevented soliciting (but not dealing) appeared to give judicial approval to the defendant's understanding that the clause prevented him approaching a client on a secret or confidential basis and telling him that 'he can still advise him but only if the client makes the approach'.

Finally, there are four general points. The first is that in cases of doubt the courts will construe the restriction *contra proferentes*. Secondly, it seems that the courts construe business sale covenants more liberally than restraints of trade in employment contracts and do so in an effort to make business sale covenants more easily enforceable: *Ronbar Enterprises Ltd v Green* [1954] 1 WLR 815. Thirdly, it is of fundamental importance in a few cases to consider whether the covenant is too vague to be enforced or void for uncertainty. This is a general ground for striking down a covenant. See *Davies v Davies* (1887) 36 Ch D 359 where a covenant which sought to restrain trade 'so far as the law allows' was found to be too uncertain to be enforced. Vagueness was resorted to by the judge in *Jenkins v Reid* in order to explain why a reformulation of a clause was unacceptable and in *Gledhow Autoparts Ltd v Delaney* [1965] 1 WLR 1366 Dankwerts LJ criticised the phrase 'districts in which the traveller had operated' as being too vague especially as instructions given as to where he should work were purely oral. Fourthly, it was pointed out sensibly in *Littlewoods* by both Lord Denning MR and Megaw LJ that a clause made '*inter rusticos*' (ie without legal help on either side) can be properly construed in the light of the way in which both parties thought it would be likely to be interpreted. See also *Normalec Ltd v Britton* [1983] FSR 318.

5 Severance

There are two different uses of the word severance. The first concerns whether the offending covenants can be cut out altogether from the contract—leaving an entire contract behind: see *Lobb (Alec) (Garages) Ltd v Total Oil (Great Britain) Ltd* [1985] 1 Al ER 303 and *Stenhouse Australia Ltd v Phillips* [1974] AC 391. Thus, in some cases where the covenant is all, or substantially all, the consideration, a consequence of a finding of unreasonableness is to strike down the whole contract. However, even if the covenantee would not have entered the agreement without the covenant, the contract may not be invalidated as a whole if there is consideration independent of the covenant: see *Vancouver Malt & Sake Brewing Co Ltd v Vancouver Breweries Ltd* [1934] AC 181 and *Amoco Australia Pty Ltd v Rocca Bros Motor Engineering Co Pty Ltd* [1975] AC 561. The ultimate question for the court is whether the absence of the covenant changes the contract in character from the original. The second approach is to consider whether an objectionable part of a covenant can be severed so as to leave an enforceable obligation. This is the approach most commonly discussed in restraint of trade cases.

Severance of the constituent parts of a restraint, if more than one part exists, can often be critical. The availability of severance frequently has a direct effect on whether at the end of the day the court considers the clause to be reasonable. A party seeking to enforce the clause which has been attacked as being an unreasonable restraint of trade will usually argue in the first place that the restriction as a whole is reasonable and secondly that any part which is unreasonable can be severed thereby leaving only the reasonable part which should be enforced. It is therefore important to know when severance is available. There appear to be two distinct approaches. The first, which is much more liberal, is most frequently found in business sales cases. This strains to make severance available in order to enforce the restraint. The second approach, is much more strict and applies predominantly in employment cases.

In *Attwood v Lamont* [1920] 3 KB 571 it was said by Lord Sterndale MR '. . . a contract can be severed if the severed parts are independent from one another and can be severed without the severance affecting the meaning of the part remaining'. Younger LJ said that severance was only permissible where the covenant is not really a single covenant but is in effect a combination of several distinct covenants. It is submitted that this is the strict and correct approach to severance. Earlier authority for it is found in *Mills v Dunham* [1891] 1 Ch 576. It was recently applied in *Commercial Plastics Ltd v Vincent* [1965] 1 QB 623 where it was said that as the provision was a single one and could not correctly be divisible into two or more parts severance could not take place. However, in *Ronbar Enterprises Ltd v Green* Jenkins LJ, having reviewed some earlier business sale cases in which severance had taken place *viz Goldsoll v Goldman* [1914] 2 Ch 603 and *British Reinforced Concrete Engineering Co Ltd v Schelff* [1921] 2 Ch 563, said that *Attwood v Lamont* could be distinguished because it concerned an employment contract. This distinction has been criticised recently in *Lucas (T) and Co Ltd v Mitchell* [1974] Ch 129. The court struck down an area restraint on dealing by an employee but severed that from a restraint on soliciting and supplying. The court held that there were two relevant questions: is there in reality more than one restraint? If so, is the excision of the unenforceable part capable of being achieved without other addition or modification? It rejected the majority view in *Attwood* that, in employment cases, there existed a third consideration *viz*: it is for the court to decide in its discretion whether or not to treat the two restraints as separate or not. It may have been this subjective judicial approach which led to the strange result in *Attwood*.

However, whichever approach is applied, it is quite clear that whether severance is available is entirely dependent on the facts of the case. A very good example of what cannot be achieved by severance is found in *Baker v Hedgecock* (1888) 39 Ch D 520. In that case there was an agreement by the defendant with his employer, a tailor, not to carry on 'any business whatsoever' for a period of two years within a certain area. The employee set up as a tailor within the relevant area within two years of leaving his employment. It was held that the agreement was void and that effect could not be given to it by rejecting the general restraint which appeared in it and limiting the agreement for the purposes of the action to carrying on the business of a tailor.

For a recent example of a case dealing with severance see *Business Seating (Renovations) Ltd v Broad* [1989] ICR 729 the facts of which are set out at p 98 below. There Millett J having held that the part of a non-solicitation clause which gave protection to the plaintiff was valid but that the part which sought to give protection to an associated company of the plaintiff was invalid had then to decide whether the invalid part could be severed or whether the whole clause was invalid. He concluded that in this case there were two companies each with its own separate and distinct business and each with its own customers although many of the customers were common to both. He said that although there was a single clause there were in effect two separate covenants each taken with the plaintiff but for the protection of the respective business of each company. He decided that there was not only no difficulty gramatically in severing the two covenants but that severance left entirely unaffected the covenant which related to the customers of the plaintiff company itself. Accordingly he severed the invalid part from the valid part and granted an injunction based on the latter. See also *Rex Stewart Jeffries Parker Ginsberg Ltd v Parker* [1988] IRLR 483 in which that part of a clause which related to 'associated companies' was severed.

The question of the availability of severance was crucial in the recent case of *Sadler v Imperial Life Assurance Co of Canada Ltd* [1988] IRLR 388, the facts of which are set out in para 1.1 of this chapter. In that case the judge found that a proviso to a clause dealing with the payment of post-termination commission to an insurance agent was an indirect and unreasonable restraint of trade. The former employee, who was the plaintiff and who sued for the payment to him of commission under the first part of the clause argued that the proviso could be severed and that therefore the obligation of the defendants to pay him such sums remained. The defendants argued that the proviso could not be severed and that as it had been found to be an unreasonable restraint of trade the whole of the clause was void. The judge having reviewed the relevant authorities said that a contract which contains an unenforceable provision nevertheless remains effective after removal of the severance of that provision if the following conditions are satisfied:

(a) The enenforceable provision is capable of being removed without the necessity of adding to or modifying the wording of what remains.
(b) The remaining terms continue to be supported by adequate consideration.
(c) The removal of the unenforceable provision does not so change the character of the contract that it becomes 'not the sort of contract that the parties entered into at all'.

He concluded that all three conditions were satisfied in this case and gave judgment for the plaintiff.

Finally, under the Treaty of Rome, if Art 85(1) applies, then only the relevant clauses are automatically void; the remainder of the contract is severable: see *La Technique Miniere* [1966] ECR 235. Whether, in fact, the whole contract is void is a matter for national law. See *Société de Vente de Ciments et Betons de l'Est SA v Kerpen and Kerpen GmbH* (Case 319/82) [1985] 1 CMLR 511.

6 Assignment

There is no doubt that the benefit of a restrictive covenant can be assigned in accordance with normal contractual rules. It most frequently happens in employment contracts after the first employer has sold his business. *Wessex Dairies Ltd v Smith* [1935] 2 KB 80 is an example of such a case, though there the plaintiffs sued as equitable assignees as that agreement to assign had not been executed. In business sales cases the assignment of the benefit of a restrictive covenant is usual upon a sale of goodwill and will be implied if not excluded: *Townsend v Jarman* [1900] 2 Ch 698. What if there is no express covenant on a business sale and X purchases the business from Y and eventually sells it to Z? Can Y, the original vendor, then solicit or canvass customers of his old business? There is no doubt that there is an implied restraint as between Y and X and between X and Z and it would equally seem that the benefit of the implied covenant between Y and X would pass to Z upon the sale of goodwill. The benefit of the restrictive covenant attaches to the business itself and not to the owner and is therefore assignable. Finally the fact that a covenantor agrees only to sell to another who will accept a restraint is not in itself unreasoanble: *Esso Petroleum Co Ltd v Harper's George (Stourport) Ltd* [1968] AC 269 per Lord Reid.

7 The consequences of a finding of unreasonableness

It can be stated with some degree of certainty that both academic and judicial opinion is divided as how to characterise a contract in unreasonable restraint of trade and the consequences thereof. Treitel describes such contracts as illegal and contrary to public policy and says that restraint of trade clauses are *prima facie* void. Anson agrees they are illegal whilst Cheshire and Fifoot specifically claim they are void—but not, illegal. They say that a restraint is '*prima facie* void' but 'become binding' on proof of reasonableness. Chitty, on the other hand says that an agreement in unreasonable restraint of trade is generally not unlawful if the parties choose to abide by it. It is however unenforceable if the parties choose not to do so. There is judicial support for the word 'void': *Nordenfelt v Maxim Nordenfelt Guns and Ammunition Co* [1894] AC 535; *Haynes v Doman* [1899] 2 Ch 13 per Lindley MR and *Greig v Insole* [1978] 1 WLR 302. Lord Denning MR waivered in his view. In the *Littlewoods* case he described a restraint of trade clause as void, invalid and unenforceable. However, in *Office Overload Ltd v Gunn* [1977] FSR 39 he settled for 'unenforceable' and rejected 'void or invalid'. Indeed the trend of modern authority seems to have chosen 'unenforceable' as the appropriate description. See Lord Wilberforce in *Stenhouse* and Lord Reid in *Esso*: '. . . an agreement in restraint of trade is not generally unlawful if the parties choose to abide by it: it is only unenforceable if a party chooses not to abide by it'.

It is suggested that the words used are important. If a covenant in unreasonable restraint of trade is described as illegal then it will be impossible to recover any money paid under it. If the unreasonableness produces voidness that means that so far as the law is concerned the clause has never existed: it may well then be possible to claim in tort for the restitution of money or goods although no specific action can be brought on the basis of the contractual force of the clause. On the other hand to characterise a bad clause as voidable must mean that it is possible for one party to bring contractual relations to an end and sue for the return of money/goods. Finally, the description unenforceable really means that up until the time of judgment it was valid but thereafter cannot be used as a basis for an action. The consequences, as pointed out in *Schroeder (A) Music Publishing Co v Macaulay* [1974] 1 WLR 1308 in the Court of Appeal, is that all acts taken under the clause prior to judgment remain undisturbed but that future ones will, assuming the successful party chooses to rely on the judgment, be unenforceable.

8 Consideration

In any contract there has to be consideration but the question which has frequently arisen in restraint of trade cases is whether the court is at all concerned as to the adequacy of the particular consideration in the instant case. One view is that the court is not concerned to examine the adequacy of the consideration. Support for this is found in the judgment of Lord Parker in *Morris (Herbert) v Saxelby* [1916] 1 AC 688 where he said 'the court no longer considers the adequacy of the consideration in any particular case'. There is no doubt that in the 19th century the courts did consider the adequacy of consideration in restraint of trade cases, but more recently in *M & S Drapers v Reynolds* [1957] 1 WLR 9 Hodson LJ said '. . . although the position of the employee has to be considered, the court will not inquire into the adequacy of the consideration or weigh the advantages accruing to the covenantor under the contract against the disadvantages imposed on him by the restraint'. However in our view although many judgments pay lip service to Lord Parker's words they do, in fact, go on to examine the adequacy of consideration as relevant to the question of reasonableness. Authority for this view is found in Lord MacNaghten's judgment in the *Nordenfeldt* case where he said 'Of course the quantum of consideration may enter into the question of the reasonableness of the contract'. This was specifically endorsed by Lord Pearce in *Esso* where he explained that what Lord MacNaghten meant was that the adequacy of consideration was a key to oppression and that oppression is a key to reasonableness. In *Davis (Clifford) Management v WEA Records* [1975] 1 WLR 61 Lord Denning MR expressly considered the adequacy of the consideration. He said that the publisher got the copyright in each song written by the defendant for one shilling. He described this as 'grossly inadequate' and said that this was effectively a symptom of the basic unreasonableness of the contract. In *Foley v Classique Coaches Ltd* [1934] 2 KB 1 the *Amoco* case and *Bridge v Deacons* [1984] AC 705 the adequacy of consideration was closely linked to the question of reasonableness. In *Amoco* Lord Cross said the fact that a covenantor had obtained and would continue to enjoy benefits under the agreement which he claimed to be unenforceable was *pro tanto* a reason for holding that the covenant was not in unreasonable restraint of trade. Dillon LJ echoed this point in *Alec Lobb*.

9 Pleading restraint of trade

In the typical case of an action by an employer against a former employee the employer will plead in his statement of claim that by doing a certain thing the employee has breached express or implied terms of his contract. This follows the usual contractual claim for breach. There may also be a claim against third parties for inducing breach of contract and/or tortious conspiracy. However, does the defendant in his defence have to plead specifically the unreasonableness of the restraint? In all cases it is necessary that the defendant specifically pleads that a certain term in a contract is in unreasonable restraint of trade. However, if he fails to do so can he still ask the court to examine the contract in the light of the restraint of trade doctrine because of the existence of the public interest? The answer appears to be in the negative following the judgment of Diplock LJ in *Petrofina (Great Britain) Ltd v Martin* [1966] Ch 146. However the courts have frequently allowed a restraint of trade argument to be adduced at trial even though not pleaded. Judicial intervention is not unknown: see *White (Marion) Ltd v Francis* [1972] 1 WLR 1423. However, in addition to pleading that a provision is in unreasoanble restraint of trade a defendant can also plead repudiation, vagueness and that in any event he has not acted in breach of the clause. Whether breach has occurred is usually a matter of construction.

10 Burden of proof

Dealing first with the question of reasonableness as between the parties it is now accepted that the burden of proof falls on the party seeking to enforce the restraint. Typically this is an employer or the purchaser of a business. Support for this proposition is found in *Mason v Provident Clothing and Supply Co Ltd* [1913] AC 724 in *Morris (Herbert) v Saxelby*, and in *Attwood v Lamont* [1920] 3 KB 571. The earlier cases of *Mills v Dunham* [1891] 1 Ch 576 and *Haynes v Doman* [1899] 2 Ch 13 are now wrong on this point. The only recent murmur of dissent occurred in Lord Reid's judgment in *Pharmaceutical Society of Great Britain v Dickson* [1970] AC 403 in which he expressed a doubt as to whether, in a case where a restraint was part of a professional code of conduct, the burden of proof regarding justification fell on the professional body. However the majority view was otherwise. It is important to note that the burden does not amount to proof of reasonableness itself, for that is a question for the judge, but to prove the facts from which reasonableness can be inferred. But, as Heydon says, judges attach little significance to the point and it really only plays a part if, as in *Dickson's* case, one side refuses to adduce any evidence of reasonableness at all.

Secondly, regarding public policy the burden of proof is on the party raising public policy (see *Morris (Herbert) v Saxelby* and the *A-G of the Common-*

wealth of Australia v Adelaide Steamship Co [1913] AC 781). Even in cases in which a declaration is sought, such as the *Schroeder* case, the burden of proof appears to be on the party arguing that the restraint was reasonable. The whole question of the burden of proof was nicely summed up in the *Esso* case by Lord Hodson where he said:

> It has been authoritatively said that the onus of establishing that an agreement is reasonable as between the parties is upon the person who puts forward the agreement, while the onus of establishing that it is contrary to the public interest, being reasonable between the parties, is on the person so alleging . . . . The reason for the distinction may be obscure, but it will seldom arise since once the agreement is before the court it is open to the scrutiny of the court in all its surrounding circumstances as a question of law.

Lord Pearce said 'When the court sees its way clearly, no question of onus arises'.

Part II

Business Secrets

Chapter 4

Interaction between Business Secrets Clauses and Restraint of Trade Clauses

It has long been recognised by the courts that the protection of business secrets is a legitimate ground for the imposition of restrictions on persons to whom such secrets have been disclosed. Two types of contractual provision are commonly used for the purpose of protecting business secrets. Firstly there are undertakings to maintain the confidentiality of business secrets and not to use them except for limited purposes. However, this type of business secrets clause suffers from the problem of detecting breach. Secondly there are restraints upon the business in which the person receiving the business secrets may engage (ie not to compete in a certain way for a particular time because of the risk of use or disclosure of business secrets). The restraint of trade doctrine is relevant to both types of provision.

The effect of the restraint of trade doctrine on the first type of provision is to place limits on the type of information which may be made subject to the confidentiality provision. Apart from the restraint of trade considerations there would seem to be no reason why a contract under which one person undertakes to keep silent on a particular subject should not be enforceable in accordance with its terms. However where the restraint of trade doctrine applies, for example in contracts of employment, a confidentiality obligation will only be enforced if the information in question can fairly be regarded as a separate part of the employee's stock of knowledge which a man of ordinary honesty and intelligence would recognise to be the property of his employer and not his own to do what he likes with. (See *Printers and Finishers Ltd v Holloway* [1965] 1 WLR 1.) This is, in practice, the same as saying that the obligation of confidentiality will not be enforced where the information concerned does not include a trade secret or its equivalent (see *Faccenda Chicken Ltd v Fowler* [1985] 1 All ER 724).

The effect of the doctrine on provisions of the second type has been the subject of more numerous decisions of the court. The protection of business secrets is one of the two grounds upon which a restraint of trade clause can in general be justified (the other being the protection of customer connections). The term 'business secrets', where used in this book, is intended to cover any confidential information of value used in business. It is not used in the more restricted sense given to the term 'trade secrets' in *Faccenda Chicken v Fowler* [1985] 1 All ER 724 but which has now been effectively viewed as being too narrow by two members of the Court of Appeal in *Lansing Linde Ltd v Kerr* [1991] 1 All ER 418: see p 82 below, we think the approach in *Lansing Linde* is to be preferred. The extent to which covenants in restraint of trade can be justified on the grounds of protection of business secrets is discussed in general terms in Part I and in relation to specific types of contracts in Parts III to VI.

Chapter 5

The Characteristics of Confidentiality

Three elements are normally required for a case of breach of confidence to succeed. Firstly, the information must have the necessary quality of confidence about it. Secondly, it must have been imparted in circumstances importing an obligation of confidence. Thirdly, there must be an unauthorised use of that information to the detriment of the party communicating it. (See *Coco v Clark (AN) (Engineers) Ltd* [1969] RPC 41.)

Whilst theses three elements have been elaborated upon in subsequent cases they are a convenient starting point for consideration of the case law.

1 The necessary quality of confidence

In *Saltman Engineering Co v Campbell Engineering Co Ltd* [1963] 65 RPC 203, Lord Greene MR defined the necessary quality of confidence thus: 'it must not be something which is public property and public knowledge'. As will be seen the courts have not applied this test literally. When determining whether information is public knowledge they have regard to the form in which it is available. If substantial work is required to collate the publicly available information into the material in which protection is sought then this will usually be sufficient to take the material out of the public domain. Lord Greene MR stated in *Saltman* that it is perfectly possible to have a confidential document, be it a formula, a plan, a sketch, or something of that kind, which is the result of work done by the maker on materials which may be available for the use of anybody. He explained that what makes the document confidential is the fact that the creator of the document has used his brain and thus arrived at a result which can only be produced by somebody who goes through the same process. In addition it is clear that the route by which information becomes public knowledge may be crucial to determining whether it thereby loses the necessary quality of confidence. In some cases the courts have upheld a duty of confidence even where the information is demonstrably publicly available. The question of public accessibility is only one of the issues which must be addressed in determining whether information has the necessary quality of confidence. The court will also consider whether the information is of a type which it is willing to protect at all. Both these issues are now considered in detail.

1.1 Inaccessibility

The question of the extent to which the information must be inaccessible to the public has arisen in widely differing situations and although it is difficult to formulate any more specific statement of principle than that of Lord Greene MR in *Saltman*, it is useful to consider some of the cases.

The issue of whether publication in one place meant that the information lost its quality of confidence everywhere at that time arose in *Exchange Telegraph Co Ltd v Central News Ltd* [1897] 2 Ch 48. The plaintiffs gathered information as to the results of horse races from various courses and transmitted that information to subscribers on terms that it should be used only in the newspaper or posted only in the club, newsroom, office or other place to which it was delivered. The defendants also ran a wire service and it was found by the judge that they had been obtaining information from a subscriber to the plaintiff's service for republication by them. It was held that the defendants, who had acquired the information in the knowledge that the supply was a breach by that subscriber of his contract with the plaintiff, could be restrained by injunction from surreptitiously obtaining or copying information collected by the plaintiffs. The judge rejected the defendants' argument that the information was made publicly available at the race meeting and that they were accordingly free to publish it.

The *Exchange Telegraph* case is perhaps an early example of what, following the dicta of Roxburgh J in *Terrapin Ltd v Builders' Supply Co (Hayes) Ltd* [1960] RPC 128, has come to be called the 'springboard' doctrine. In that case he said:

> As I understand it, the essence of this branch of law, whatever the origin of it may be, is that a person who has obtained information in confidence is not allowed to use it as a springboard for activities detrimental to the person who made the confidential communication, and springboard it remains even when all the features have been published or can be ascertained by actual inspection by any members of the public.

In the *Terrapin* case the judge held that because all the details relating to the construction of a particular type of portable building could be ascertained by dismantling and measuring an example of it, the possessor of confidential drawings and other information still had a head start. Any other person would have to prepare plans, construct prototypes and conduct tests. Therefore the possessor of that information had to be placed under a special disability in the field of competition in order to ensure that he did not get an unfair start.

The duration and nature of this disability has been the subject of comment in subsequent cases. The passage quoted above was adopted by Roskill J in *Cranleigh Precision Engineering Ltd v Bryant* [1965] 1 WLR 1293. In *Seager v Copydex Ltd* [1967] 1 WLR 923 it was adopted by Lord Denning MR who added the following point concerning the difficulties which arise where part of the information disclosed to the defendant is only partly within the public domain:

> When the information is mixed, being partly public and partly private, then the recipient must take special care to use only the material which is in the

public domain. He should go to the public source and get it: or, at any rate, not be in a better position than if he had gone to the public source.

This paragraph seems to indicate that it may be possible for a person who has received information in confidence which he could have obtained through other sources to relieve himself of the 'special disability' under which he is otherwise placed by going to those sources. A further possibility which is suggested by Lord Denning's judgment is that in such circumstances it may not be a case for injunction but only for damages. However this does not fit well with the result of the *Terrapin* case where Roxburgh J in fact granted an injunction.

In *Coco v Clark (AN) (Engineers) Ltd* Megarry V-C considered the implications of Lord Denning's judgment in *Seager* but was unable to reach any firm conclusion. He said that 'the essence of the duty seems more likely to be that of not using without paying rather than of not using at all'. However this was a matter which he thought might be resolved at the trial.

The point was briefly touched upon again by Lord Denning in *Potters-Ballotini Ltd v Weston-Baker* [1977] RPC 202 where he said 'although a man must not use such information as a springboard to get a start over others, nevertheless that springboard does not last for ever'.

The Court of Appeal has recently clarified the position. In *Bullivant (Roger) Ltd v Ellis* [1987] ICR 464 they held that it was not right to extend the term of the injunction beyond the period for which the advantage might reasonably be expected to continue. Accordingly an injunction against the defendant fulfilling any contract with any person named on a card index which he had obtained from his former employer was discharged, the court saying it was bound to limit the period to one year at the longest.

In practice the question of the duration of the disability imposed by the springboard doctrine does not frequently arise because most cases concerning confidential information do not come to trial following the grant of an interlocutory injunction and it can therefore be assumed that either the parties settle the action or that interlocutory judgment is treated as final.

It is important that the springboard doctrine be understood in its context. What is being said is that the recipient of confidential information cannot use the information as a shortcut to side-step the work which other members of the public would have to do. Thus if the confidential information was published in full detail then the initial recipient would not have a head start. Members of the public would not need to prepare plans, construct prototypes or conduct tests. The need for the special disability would lapse. For example in *Mustad v Allcock and Dosen* [1963] 3 All ER 416 it was held that because the appellants had published the information which they alleged was confidential in a patent specification they were not entitled to an injunction restraining the respondents from disclosing that information. This case was followed by Cross J in *Franchi v Franchi* [1967] RPC 149 where he held that publication of the information in a Belgian patent application was sufficient to cause the plaintiff's claim to fail. Of course for the obligation of confidence to lapse the information published must be the same as the confidential information. In *Cranleigh Precision Engineering Ltd v Bryant* Roskill J held that the defendant who had, whilst a director of the plaintiff company, been made aware of a patent held by a third party which affected the plaintiff's products, could not justify his failure to disclose the existence of the patent to the plaintiffs and his subsequent acquisition of the patent for himself on the ground that it was public knowledge, for what he had misused was his confidential knowledge of the relationship of the information in the patent to the plaintiff's products. It will frequently happen that information disclosed in confidence is or becomes known to a limited number of people or to a specific section of the public only. It is clearly a question of degree whether the information retains the necessary quality of confidence.

In *Ackroyds (London) Ltd v Islington Plastics Ltd* [1962] RPC 97 a subcontractor used the information supplied by the plaintiff to manufacture and sell goods on its own account to the plaintiff's customers. The plaintiffs obtained an injunction to restrain the defendants notwithstanding that the product in question (a swizzle stick embossed with the name of the ship upon which it was to be used) was available to anyone who happened to take a cruise on that ship. The defendants were presumably outside the class of people who were likely to have access to the information publicly. See also the *Exchange Telegraph* case and *Sun Printers v Westminster Press* [1982] IRLR 292. Megarry V-C, in *Marshall (Thomas) (Exports) v Guinle* [1979] Ch 227 set out a test of four elements which is most helpful for determining whether the information is too widely known to retain the necessary quality of confidence. Firstly, the owner must believe that the release of the information would be advantageous to his rivals or injurious to him. Secondly, the owner must believe the information is not in the public domain. (Megarry V-C said that even if some or all of the owner's rivals have the information as long as the owner believes it is confidential he is entitled to try to protect it.) Thirdly, the owner's belief as to the first and second elements must be reasonable. Fourthly, the information must be judged in the light of the usage and practices of the particular trade or industry concerned. It should be noted that this test was expressly limited by Megarry V-C to secrets in industrial or trade settings.

The interesting question of whether publication by or caused by the confidant affects the existence of the confidence was discussed in *Attorney General v Guardian Newspapers Ltd (No 2)* [1988] 3 All ER 545. Lord Donaldson MR said at p 609 that dissemination of confidential information knowingly in breach of the plaintiff's right cannot undermine the right itself: it can however affect the remedies available to the plaintiff especially regarding the appropriateness of injunctive relief. Lord Goff, at p 664, reserved the question whether some limited obligation (analogous to the springboard doctrine) may continue to rest on a confidant, who, in breach of confidence, destroys the confidential nature of the information entrusted to him. In relation to third parties the matter was most sensibly dealt with by Bingham LJ at p 625.

> A third party coming into possession of confidential information is accordingly liable to be restrained from publishing it if he knows the information to be confidential and the circumstances are such as to impose on him an obligation in good conscience not to publish. No such obligation would in my view ordinarily arise where the third party comes into possession of information which, although once confidential, has ceased to be so otherwise than through the agency of the third party.

1.2 Type of information

Sufficient inaccessibility is not the only requirement of the necessary quality of confidence. In addition the type of information must be considered. This book is concerned primarily with business secrets and so such issues as marital confidences and privacy are not considered even though they may occasionally have commercial value. (See for example *Duchess of Argyll v Duke of Argyll* [1967] Ch 302, *Lennon v News Group Newspapers Ltd* [1978] FSR 573, *Woodward v Hutchins* [1977] 1 WLR 760 and *Stephens v Avery* [1988] 2 WLR 1280.)

It is clear that information need not be complex in order to be the subject of confidentiality. In *Coco v Clark* Megarry V-C said '. . . the mere simplicity of an idea does not prevent it being confidential . . . . Indeed, the simpler an idea, the more likely it is to need protection'. See also *Under Water Welders and Repairers Ltd v Street and Longthorne* [1968] RPC 498.

Conversely, mere volume or complexity of information disclosed will not be sufficient. In *Yates Circuit Foil Co v Electrofoils Ltd* [1976] FSR 345 Whitford J said 'I know of no direct authority which has laid it down that a fetter can be placed upon the disclosure of a body of information of a general character if the body of information is over some particular size'.

However, the *Yates* decision should not be regarded as authority for the proposition that a collection of individually non-confidential items of information cannot be the subject of confidentiality where the confidentiality lies in the fact that they are collected together. A typical example of a confidential collection of information might be a list of customers (see for example *Robb v Green* [1895] 2 QB 315 and *Summers (William) & Co Ltd v Boyce & Kinmond & Co* (1907) 23 TLR 724 and *Bullivant (Roger) v Eillis Ltd* [1987] ICR 464 but *cf Auto Securities Ltd v Standard Telephones and Cables Ltd* [1965] RPC 92). It was suggested by Hirst J in *Fraser v Thames Television Ltd* [1983] 2 All ER 101 that some degree of originality is required for confidential information to be protected. However it is clear from the context that all that he meant was that, where what is claimed to be confidential is an idea based on a well-known theme, it must have something such as a significant twist or slant which is not public knowledge. In that case the making of a television series by the defendants based on a concept communicated in confidence by the plaintiffs was held to be a breach of confidence. (See also *Gilbert v Star Newspapers Co Ltd* (1894) 11 TLR 4 and *Frazer v Edwards* (1905) MacG Cop Cas (1905–10) 10.)

One further restriction on the type of information which may be subject to an obligation of confidentiality has been briefly mentioned above. Information acquired by an employee which becomes part of his general skills and stock of knowledge is not the subject of an obligation of confidentiality although during the term of the employment it may be a breach of the employee's duty of good faith to disclose it to third parties. Information relating to customers, prices, technology and business methods have been held to fall into this category (see the discussion of *Faccenda Chicken v Fowler* [1985] 1 All ER 724 in Chapter 8 and *see Printers & Finishers Ltd v Holloway* [1965] 1 WLR 1, and *Stevenson Jordan & Harrison Ltd v MacDonald & Evans* (1952) 69 RPC 10). The courts will normally refuse to allow claims of confidentiality in respect of the names and addresses of employees so as to prevent offers of other employment being made to them by departing staff (*see Baker v Gibbons* [1972] 1 WLR 693 and *Searle (GD) & Co Ltd v Celltech Ltd* [1982] FSR 92).

In *Ixora Trading Incorporated v Jones* [1990] 1 FSR 251 Mummery J struck out the plaintiffs' writ and statement of claim which, *inter alia*, alleged breaches of express and implied duties of confidence. The plaintiffs were part of a group of companies which operated Bureaux de Change. The defendants had been employed as executives by the plaintiffs. The defendants had both received training in the plaintiffs' business, including familiarisation with the contents of two manuals. The defendants had in the course of their employment visited Paris to assess the feasibility of opening Bureaux de Change in France. As a result they produced a document called an 'Initial Feasibility Study'. Since the termination of the defendants' employment a company in the same group as the plaintiffs had opened a number of Bureaux de Change in Paris. The company set up by the defendants had also opened Bureaux de Change in Paris.

The plaintiffs relied on an express term set out in the letters of appointments written to the defendants as follows:

> You will not disclose any of the company's affairs or any of its subsidiary or associated companies business or trade secrets to a third party either during or after you have ceased to be an employee of the company without the express written consent of the company.

In addition, the defendants gave undertakings to the plaintiff, one of which was as follows:

> Any information which I have access to or knowledge which I acquire arising out of or in the course of my contract of service shall remain confidential and shall not be used by me to obtain any gain, benefit or advantage or profits for myself or for any member of my family or connected person.

The judge pointed out that in the statement of claim the confidential information relied on was described in a general way as a fund of technical knowledge and experience relating to a number of matters; in particular the contents of the manuals and the Initial Feasibility Study. The judge concluded that none of the documents or the contents of them satisfied the requirement of the kind of confidential information which an employer is entitled to prevent an ex-employee from using after the termination of the employer/employee relationship. Moreover he found that a concession made in the pleadings to the effect that the plaintiffs did not allege that the defendants had made use of any of the plaintiffs' trade secrets since leaving their employment was, in the light of the judgment of *Faccenda Chicken Ltd v Fowler* [1986] 1 All ER 617 fatal. That concession may not be now as fatal as the judge thought due to the extension of the meaning of the phrase 'trade secret' found in the Court of Appeal judgments in *Lansing Linde Ltd v Kerr*. The judge went on to find that not only was the information contained in the manuals and the feasibility study not a trade secret but that the information contained in the feasibility study was too obvious and too vague and unspecific to be caught by any alleged fiduciary duty that the defendants were under.

In *Berkeley Administration Inc v McClelland* [1990] FSR 505 the plaintiffs were a company related to Ixora. The fifth and sixth defendants had been employed by a group of companies of which the plaintiffs were a part in senior positions for short periods before being dismissed. After their dismissal the first and sixth defendants drafted a business plan for the purpose of raising finance to set up a Bureau de Change business in competition with the plaintiffs. Shortly afterwards they invited the seventh defendant who was employed by the plaintiffs' group to join them. After the seventh defendant had resigned from the plaintiffs the three refined the business plan and set up the fourth defendant and the fifth defendant companies. The plaintiffs alleged the first, sixth and seventh defendants in preparing their business plan had used five specific items of information derived from financial projections contained in an appendix to a business plan ('the blue book') of the plaintiffs namely:

    (a) the average operating profit per Bureau de Change;
    (b) the average profit of the first year of operation as a percentage of a full years profit;
    (c) the average costs per Bureau;
    (d) the average number and/or transactions per Bureau;
    (e) the average value of each transaction.

The plaintiffs contended that their business plan was confidential, that the items of information relied upon were sufficiently confidential to be protectable after termination of the defendants' employment and that it could be inferred that the defendants had used those items by virtue of alleged similarity between figures appearing in the respective business plans. Wright J accepted that the blue book was described as a confidential memorandum by the plaintiffs and that confidentiality was heavily emphasised in its pages. A limited number of copies were produced, each copy was numbered and a record was kept of the persons to whom the copy was issued. It was plain that the document as whole was intended to be kept confidential by the plaintiffs and that this fact was firmly impressed upon anyone who had anything to do with it. Although the three individual defendants had either signed or had been made aware of undertakings of confidentiality when they entered the employment of the plaintiff, counsel on behalf of the plaintiffs did not rely upon such undertakings before the judge but relied upon general implied principles of law in this area. The judge declined to find that any of the information contained in the blue book bore the stamp of confidentiality within the criteria laid down in *Faccenda Chicken*, ie it could not be described as a trade secret or anything approximating thereto.

This question has also been the subject of a recent decision by the Court of Appeal. In *Johnson and Bloy (Holdings) Ltd v Wolstenholme Rink Plc* [1989] IRLR 499 the Court of Appeal granted an injunction to the plaintiffs to prevent the defendant from disclosing or using the information that two specified ingredients might be used in combination in the manufacture of a drier for a printing ink and from manufacturing or arranging for the manufacture of printing inks containing therein a drier containing the two ingredients. The defendant had argued that this information, ie the knowledge that the combination of the two ingredients produced an effective drier could not be protected by an injunction since the knowledge of that combination was knowledge which the second defendant must inevitably have taken away from the plaintiffs when he left their employment and that he could not proceed to expunge that knowledge from his mind. Parker LJ rejected that submission by pointing out that there was no evidence that the combination of the two ingredients was commonly known or used in the trade. Moreover he pointed out that there is no principle in English law which says that anything which is inevitably in somebody's head when they leave their employment is something which they are free to use. In certain cases such information may well be confidential. This was such a case.

It is often said that there can be no confidence in iniquity. In general, however, the cases tend to view that the disclosure of iniquity is a just cause for breaking an obligation of confidentiality. Accordingly, these cases are examined in the context of breach of the duty of confidentiality.

2 Circumstances importing an obligation of confidence

The courts have found it difficult to determine a generally applicable test of the circumstances in which an obligation of confidence will arise. In part this difficulty may stem from the uncertain legal nature of the action for breach of confidence. In many cases the obligation has been held to arise out of an implied term of a contract between the parties. In others, where the courts have been unable to find any contract between the parties, the courts have had to rely on an equitable doctrine of confidence. However, in practice it is rare to find circumstances in which the court would be prepared to find that an obligation of confidence arises by virtue of an implied term of a contract but not by virtue of an equitable obligation (see for example *Marshall (Thomas) (Exporters) Ltd v Guinle* [1979] Ch 227). However a plaintiff should always plead both the equitable and the contractual duty for the remedies available are different: see Part VIII. The principles set out below for determining when an obligation of confidence will arise would therefore seem equally applicable to both equitable and implied contractual obligations.

Perhaps the most elegant formulation of principle was given in *Coco v Clark (AN) (Engineers) Ltd* where it was said that if a reasonable man standing in the shoes of the recipient of the information would have realised that upon reasonable grounds the information was being given to him in confidence then this should suffice to impose upon him the equitable obligation of confidence. Although this formulation has been referred to in subsequent cases it has not been adopted as laying down an all embracing test. The courts have instead tended to consider a number of factors which point to the existence of an obligation of confidentiality. These factors can be conveniently categorised under three headings.

2.1 Express indications of confidentiality

Where the person disclosing information expressly states to the recipient that it is being disclosed in confidence this will usually suffice to impose an obligation of confidence (assuming the information has the necessary quality of confidence). For example in *Dunford & Elliott Ltd v Johnson & Firth Brown* [1978] FSR 143 information supplied to investors under cover of a letter making express reference to its confidential nature was held to have been imparted in circumstances of confidence (although the action failed on other grounds). Similarly, where a product which contains a secret mechanism is supplied subject to a condition that the recipient should not examine the mechanism, this will establish confidence in the mechanism (see *Paul (KS) (Printing Instruments) Ltd v Southern Instruments (Communications) Ltd* and *EP Ellis (Male) (Trading as Ellis and Sons)* [1964] RPC 118). Unsolicited information gives rise to difficulties for it is not clearly established whether this may be made subject to an obligation of confidence. It is submitted that there is no good reason why an obligation of confidence should not arise if the supplier of the information clearly expresses it to be confidential. Provided the springboard doctrine is sensibly applied and injunctions granted only in the clearest of cases so that the recipient of the information is not effectively placed in a worse position than if he had not received it, the interests of both the supplier of the information and the recipient can be satisfied.

2.2 Mode of expression

Where no express indication of the confidentiality of the information disclosed has been given it is necessary to examine the circumstances surrounding the disclosure. This has frequently been necessary in the case of information obtained by employees in the course of their employment. The cases are discussed in Chapter 8 at p 76.

It would appear that an obligation of confidence may arise in relation to information which is overheard but it seems that this will only be the case where the recipient has used surreptitious means to put himself in a position to overhear the information. This question has achieved some notoriety in two cases concerning telephone tapping. In the first, *Malone v Commissioner of Police of the Metropolis (No 2)* [1979] 2 All ER 620, which concerned the use to which recordings of telephone conversations made with the authority of the Secretary of State for the Home Office, Megarry V-C said 'it seems to me that a person who utters confidential information must accept the risk of any unknown overhearing that is inherent in the circumstances of the communication'. In the second case, *Francome v Mirror Group Newspapers Ltd* [1984] 2 All ER 408, the Court of Appeal held that there was a serious issue to be tried on the question of whether information obtained by illegal tapping by private individuals was subject to confidentiality. It is however apparent from the judgment in that case that the Court of Appeal regarded information overheard as a result of accidents or imperfections in the telephone system as free from the obligation of confidence. *Francome* is important because the court recognised the possibility that information taken without anyone's consent, for example by espionage, might be held subject to an obligation of confidence. In *Attorney General v Guardian Newspapers Ltd (No 2)* [1988] 3 All ER 545 (part of the *Spycatcher* case) it was recognised that information which Peter Wright had unearthed by his own endeavours was clearly covered by an obligation of confidence even though one could not say there existed a 'confider' or 'confidant' in relation to that information. Whether the courts would extend this remedy to information in documents which were accidentally released as opposed to surreptitiously obtained was answered in *English and American Insurance Co Ltd v Herbert Smith* [1988] FSR 232. The papers of counsel acting for the plaintiffs in a pending action in the Commercial Court were mistakenly sent to the solicitors for the other side. The papers were entitled to legal professional privilege. Those solicitors, the first defendant, realised what had happened and did not at first read the papers. However, they considered it their duty to tell their clients, the second defendants, that they had them. Their clients instructions were to read the papers. They did so and informed their clients of what they had discovered; they then returned the papers. By notice of motion the plaintiffs claimed an interlocutory order restraining the defendants from making any use of any information derived from the privileged documents. Such an order would prevent the defendants using that information for any purpose of defending an action in the Commercial Court. The defendants, *inter alia*, submitted that the owner of confidential information could not restrain its use by a party to whom it had accidentally escaped and who had not himself undertaken the duty of confidentiality. Sir Nicolas Browne-Wilkinson V-C granted an order limited to overt use of the information. He held that an injunction could be granted against a stranger who had come innocently into the possession of confidential information to which he was not entitled. See also *Derby and Co Ltd v Weldon* (No 8) [1990] 3 All ER 762.

2.3 Limited purpose of disclosure

There is a large body of authority in support of the proposition that information which is disclosed for a limited purpose is received under an obligation of confidence and cannot be used or disclosed otherwise than for that purpose.

Business negotiations

Information disclosed by one party to another in the course of negotiations will be subject to the obligation of confidence where information relates to the subject matter of the negotiations and has the necessary quality of confidence. Thus in *Seager v Copydex Ltd* [1967] 1 WLR 923 details of an unpatented invention disclosed in the course of negotiations relating to a similar patented invention were held to have been disclosed under an obligation of confidence. Similarly in *Coco v Clark (AN) (Engineers) Ltd* [1969] RPC 41 Megarry J held that information concerning an engine supplied by the plaintiff in the course of negotiations was subject to an implied obligation of confidence. Megarry J suggested that the test of an officious bystander could be helpful: if the parties, when asked by an officious bystander whether their discussions were confidential, would have responded 'but obviously it is', that would establish the obligation.

Clearly there may be some negotiations where it would be unwise to assume that an obligation of confidence will arise. One example would be negotiations for settlement of litigation. Another example which recently came before the court concerned confidentiality in an offer made to a vendor of land. The vendor's agent disclosed the amount of an offer made by one potential purchaser to another. The offeror, who was unsuccessful in obtaining the property sued for breach of confidence. The court held on the facts that the vendor's agent was not under a duty of confidence *(Trees Ltd v Cripps* (1983) 267 EG 596).

Professional advisers and bankers

Information supplied by clients to their professional advisers will be received subject to an obligation of confidence. In the case of solicitors this is clearly shown in *Rakusen v Ellis, Munday & Clarke* [1912] 1 Ch 831 where it was said 'A solicitor can be restrained as a matter of absolute obligation and as a matter of general principle from disclosing any secrets which are confidentially reposed in him'. The obligation of confidence is of wider ambit than legal professional privilege. In *Weld-Blundell v Stephens* [1920] AC 956 it was held that an accountant owed a duty to keep a letter of instructions confidential. Bankers are under a similar duty of confidentiality to their clients (see *Tournier v National Provincial and Union Bank of England* [1924] 1 KB 461). Statutory regulation of the disclosure of confidential information in the banking sphere is found in ss 82–7 of the Banking Act 1987. Under this the Bank of England is permitted in certain circumstances to disclose information provided to it.

Information supplied to enable the performance of contracts

Information having the necessary quality of confidence which is supplied by one party of a contract to another for the purpose of enabling that other to perform a contract will usually be subject to an obligation of confidence so that the recipient may only use it for the purpose of that contract.

A common situation where such an obligation of confidence is likely to arise is in subcontracting arrangements where the prime contractor supplies detailed information relating to the products which are to be built to his subcontractor. This information may only be used by the subcontractor for the purpose of performing the agreement.

A typical example of this was the subject of *Saltman Engineering Co v Campbell Engineering Co* (1963) 65 RPC 203 where drawings of tools for the manufacture of leather punches were placed in the hands of subcontractors for the purpose of manufacturing the tools for one of the plaintiffs. The defendants used the drawings to manufacture tools which they sold on their own account. The court held that the defendants were guilty of a breach of confidence. (See also *Ackroyd v Gill* (1856) 5 E&B 808, *Tuck & Sons v Priester* (1887) 19 QBD 629 and *Prince Albert v Strange* (1849) 1 Mac & G 25.) *Schering Chemicals v Falkman* [1981] 2 WLR 848 provides perhaps the most extreme example of the obligation of confidence arising from disclosure for a limited purpose. In that case Schering employed Falkman Ltd to give its executives instruction in how to deal with the media regarding one of its products. Falkman employed a freelance expert to assist it. Schering disclosed what it regarded as confidential information to Falkman and the expert for this purpose. It was held that the expert was bound to maintain the confidentiality of the information and was accordingly not entitled to use the information for the purpose of making a television film. This was the case notwithstanding the fact that all the information which was given to the expert had in fact been previously published. As Templeman LJ put it:

> As between Scherings and [the expert] if [the expert] had obtained the information from sources other than Scherings, then it would of course not have been confidential in his hands, but, by agreeing to advise Scherings and by accepting information from them to enable him to advise Scherings, [the expert] placed himself under a duty, in my judgment not to make use of that information without the consent of Scherings in a manner which Scherings reasonably considered harmful to their cause.

This difficult case was discussed in *Attorney General v Guardian Newspapers Ltd* [1987] 3 All ER 376 at p 374 per Lord Oliver, and *Attorney General v Guardian Newspapers Ltd (No 2)* [1988] 3 All ER 545 at p 625 per Bingham LJ.

Considerable difficulties of construction can arise in licence and distribution agreements where confidential information relating to the products is supplied to the licensee or distributor. In *Regina Glass Fibre v Schuller* [1972] RPC 229 it was held that the licensee had the right to continue using improvement patents and know-how even after the end of the licence agreement. Conversely in *Torrington Manufacturing Co v Smith and Son (England) Ltd* [1966] RPC 285 it was held that a distributor's right to use drawings of products supplied by the manufacturer was limited to the purpose and duration of the agreement. It could not use them to manufacture its own products (see also *Peter Pan Manufacturing Corp v Corsets Silhouette* [1964] 1 WLR 96). What is required is an agreement which clearly addresses the point. For an example of the difficulties in proving what is confidential in such a case see *Suhner and Co AG v Transradio Ltd* [1967] RPC 329.

An obligation of confidence will usually arise as between partners. Thus in the case of *Morrison v Moat* (1851) 9 Hare 241 when one partner communicated a secret recipe of the partnership to his son who subsequently sought to exploit that recipe for his own account, an injunction was granted to restrain him.

Information disclosed on discovery in legal proceedings is clearly held under an obligation of confidence and may be used only for the purpose of those proceedings. See for example *Distillers Co (Biochemicals) Ltd v Times Newspapers* [1975] QB 613 and *Riddick v Thames Board Mills Ltd* [1977] QB 881.

3 Duration of the duty

It is difficult to lay down any general rule for determining the period for which an obligation of confidence will last. Much will depend upon the circumstances of the disclosure, the nature of the information itself and even whether it is capable of being protected by an implied obligation. In the case of an employment contract, Scott J, in *Balston Ltd v Headline Filters Ltd* [1987] FSR 330 at p 348, said that the implied obligation referred to in *Faccenda Chicken* of protecting trade secrets 'will always be unlimited in time' and probably in area as well. The question of the duration of the duty in cases where the 'springboard' doctrine applies has been discussed above. An example of the limited duration of an obligation of confidence in a 'springboard' case is found in *Fisher-Karpark Indusries Ltd v Nichols* [1982] FSR 351 where account was taken in determining the duration of an injunction of the extent to which the information was generally available from public sources. The obligation will usually last only for as long as the information retains the necessary quality of confidence. For example in *Franchi v Franchi* [1967] RPC 149 the obligation of confidence in information relating to a method of making stone tiles was held to have lapsed upon the publication by the plaintiff of the information in a patent application.

However, publication of the information will not always bring the obligation to an end. In *Schering Chemicals v Falkman* the fact that all the information which the defendant sought to use was already available in published material did not relieve the defendant of his duty. As Shaw LJ said 'It is not the law that where confidentiality exists it is terminated or eroded by adventitious publicity. Nor is the correlative duty to preserve that confidentiality'.

The pragmatic approach of the courts to the question of when publication brings the obligation to an end is shown in *Speed Seal Ltd v Paddington* [1985] 1 WLR 1327 where the publication of the plaintiff's secrets had been made by the defendant. Fox LJ pointed out that the purpose of the injunction was to protect the plaintiff. If the defendant was the only person other than the plaintiff using the information (or one of a few) then the injunction would be effective to protect the plaintiff and would be granted.

The following conclusions can perhaps be drawn from the authorities. Firstly, where the use to which the information is to be put is publication or sale of the information the courts will be less sympathetic to arguments that there can be no confidence. This is perhaps inevitable because in such cases it is not entirely illogical to argue that if the information was already publicly known why should anyone want to publish it or sell it? It is perhaps for this reason that the Court of Appeal in *Faccenda* left open the question as to whether an employee could sell the information which was comprised in the skills acquired in the course of employment which he could not be prevented from using himself. Secondly, that where information becomes publicly available through the actions of the plaintiff the courts will more readily find that the information no longer has the requisite quality of confidence than where publication is by a third party. It was in this context that Lord Denning in *Dunford and Elliott v Firth Brown* [1978] FSR 143 added a gloss to the analysis of Megarry V-C in *Coco v Clark (AN) (Engineers) Ltd* when he said that if the stipulation of confidence was unreasonable at the time of making it; or if it was reasonable at the beginning, but afterwards, in the course of subsequent happenings, it becomes unreasonable that it should be enforced: then the courts will decline to enforce it. In that case the plaintiff had made information relevant to evaluating a takeover bid for its shares available to 43 per cent of its shareholders. The information had also been disclosed in confidence to another shareholder who was using if for the purpose of making a bid for the plaintiff company. It was held that the widespread use of the information drove a hole in the blanket of confidence.

A further circumstance in which the obligation of confidence will come to an end is where an express provision of limited duration expires. In such a case it will be difficult to persuade a court to imply any further obligation: see the judgment of Lord Denning in *Potters Ballottini Ltd v Weston-Baker* [1977] RPC 202. Similarly the court in *Bullivant (Roger) Ltd v Ellis* took note of the duration of a restrictive covenant in a former employee's contract of employment in determining how long it would restrain the defendant from using an index of customers removed from his former employers. In *Systems Reliability Holdings Plc v Smith* [1990] IRLR 377. Harman J decided that the injunction restraining a breach of confidence should expire at the same time as a restrictive covenant.

Lastly, an obligation of confidence, at least where it is only equitable, will come to an end when public policy will no longer be served by upholding it. This principle is unlikely to be of great relevance in cases for the protection of business secrets. It is best illustrated by the Crossman Diaries Case, *A-G v Jonathan Cape Ltd* [1976] QB 752 where the court would not prevent the publication of diaries of cabinet discussions on grounds of confidentiality after a period of ten years.

4 Breach of the duty

The question of what constitutes a breach of the duty of confidentiality falls into two parts. There is the difficult issue of whether use as opposed to disclosure constitutes breach. In addition there are circumstances in which disclosure is permissible.

In general, it would appear that where an obligation of confidentiality arises, the courts will give relief, not only in respect of disclosure of the information, but also as to use of the information without the consent of the person to whom the duty of confidentiality is owed. This will be the case even where disclosure of the information is not an inevitable consequence of its use (see for example *Amber Size and Chemical Co Ltd v Menzel* [1913] 30 RPC 433). However the courts are often reluctant to grant injunctions against the use of information where such information could have been relatively easily acquired by the defendant through his own legitimate efforts (see *Seager v Copydex Ltd* and *Coco v Clark (AN) (Engineers) Ltd)*. Care must be taken in the drafting of express contractual restraints to ensure that they clearly cover both use and non-disclosure. In *Marshall (Thomas) (Exporters) Ltd v Guinle* [1979] 1 Ch 227 Megarry V-C held that an express contractual restriction on disclosure did not also prohibit use of the information (the plaintiff was, in fact, granted an injunction against use on the grounds of the defendant's duty of good faith but this duty will not exist in all cases). This point is discussed further at p 104.

5 Defences

5.1 Iniquity

In a long line of cases the courts have held that the disclosure of information relating to what was originally termed iniquity will not be restrained: see *Gartside v Outram* (1856) 2 LJ Ch 113, *Weld-Blundell v Stephens* [1920] AC 956; *Initial Services Ltd v Putterill* [1968] 1 QB 396; *Fraser v Evans* [1969] 1 QB 349; *Hubbard v Vosper* [1972] 1 All ER 1023; *Church of Scientology of California v Kaufman* [1973] RPC 635; *British Steel Corporation v Granada Television Ltd* [1981] 1 All ER 417; and *Lion Laboratories Ltd v Evans* [1984] 2 All ER 417. This doctrine has its roots in the equitable nature of the duty of confidence but can now be regarded as covering both equitable and contractual obligations of confidence (see *Initial Services Ltd v Putterill*). Although originally the doctrine was thought to be restricted to cases of iniquity or wrong-doing on the part of the party seeking to enforce the obligation of confidence, it is now clear that this is not so. The test is whether the public interest in disclosure outweighs the public interest in the preservation of confidence. As Griffiths LJ explained in *Lion Laboratories Ltd v Evans* 'I believe that the so-called iniquity rule evolved because in most cases where the facts justified a publication in breach of confidence the plaintiff had behaved so disgracefully or criminally that it was judged in the public interest that his behaviour should be exposed' and, as he aptly stated, 'there is a world of difference between what is in the public interest and what is of interest to the public'.

In *Re A Company's Application* [1989] 3 WLR 265 the plaintiff company carried on the business of providing financial advice and was subject to the regulatory scheme imposed by FIMBRA pursuant to the provisions of the Financial Services Act 1986. The defendant had been employed by the company as its compliance officer; his duty it was to supervise the procedures and practices of the plaintiff so as to secure fulfilment of the regulatory requirements imposed by FIMBRA. FIMBRA was entitled at its discretion from time to time to make spot checks on companies subject to its regulatory umbrella and therefore the details of the businesses carried out by the company might at any time have become known to it. In October 1988 the company gave the defendant one month's notice. On 12 December 1988 a telephone conversation took place between the defendant and one of the company's chief executives which the plaintiff's company interpreted as an attempt to blackmail, whereas the defendant contended that he had merely indicated his intentions to seek compensation for dismissal. The defendant also raised certain matters which in his view represented breaches of the regulatory scheme by the plaintiff or improprieties in regard to tax. The plaintiffs made an application for an interlocutory injunction to restrain the defendant from disclosing to the regulatory body or to the revenue its confidential information or documents. Scott J concluded that if this were a case in which there was any question or threat of general disclosure by the defendant of confidential information concerning the way in which the plaintiff carried on its business or concerning any details of the affairs of any of its clients there would be no answer to the claim for an injunction; but it was not general disclosure that the defendant had in mind. He desired to disclose only to FIMBRA and the Inland Revenue. He asked himself whether an employee of a company carrying on the business of giving financial advice and of financial management to the public under the regulatory umbrella provided by FIMBRA owes a duty of confidentiality that extends to barring disclosure information to FIMBRA. He answered that question in the negative and likewise in relation to the Inland Revenue. He granted an injunction restraining the defendant from using and/or disclosing confidential information but qualified it so that it did not apply to communications made by the defendant either to FIMBRA or the Inland Revenue in respect of the matters identified in the defence. In addition he accepted an undertaking by the defendant not to reveal other than to his legal advisers the fact that he had made communications to FIMBRA and the Inland Revenue.

In *W v Egdell* [1989] 2 WLR 689 Scott J had to consider the duty of confidentiality owed by a doctor to a patient. The plaintiff had applied to a Mental Health Tribunal to be transferred from a secure hospital. In support of the application he sought a report from the first defendant, an independant consultant psychiatrist. The first defendant's report was unfavourable to the plaintiff and it was sent by him to the plaintiff's solicitors. The plaintiff's solicitors withdrew the application to the tribunal. The first defendant learnt of this but also became aware that no copy of his report had been sent to the tribunal or was on the plaintiff's file at the hospital. The first defendant decided to supply a copy of it to the hospital and subsequently copies were sent to the Home Secretary and the Department of Health and Social Security. The plaintiff issued a writ against the defendant claiming that a breach of confidence had occurred. The judge was in no doubt that if the defendant had sold the contents of his report to a newspaper that would have been a breach of confidence. However the question in the present case was whether the duty of confidence which the defendant no doubt owed to the plaintiff extended so far as to bar disclosure of the report to the hospital or the Home Office. In order to answer that question the court had to balance the interest to be served by non-disclosure against the interest served by disclosure. Scott J concluded that it was in the public interest for there to have been disclosure to those two bodies.

5.2 Miscellaneous

It will be no breach of confidentiality to disclose documents on discovery in the course of litigation even if they are held subject to a duty of confidence owed to a third party. See for example *Chantry Martin & Co v Martin* [1953] 2 QB 286 and *Crompton (Alfred) Amusement Machines Ltd v Commissioners of Customs & Excise* [1974] AC 405. However in a proper case the court is prepared to balance the public interest in full disclosure on discovery against the public interest in honouring an obligation of confidence. Thus in *D v NSPCC* [1978] AC 171 the court was willing to permit the NSPCC to withhold the name of their informant but in *British Steel Corporation v Granada Television Ltd* [1981] 1 All ER 417 the defendants were ordered to disclose the name of the plaintiff's employee who had supplied them with confidential information belonging to the plaintiff.

Similarly an obligation of confidence may not be prayed in aid of a refusal to disclose secret information to a trustee in bankruptcy if it can be regarded as part of the bankrupt's property (see *Keene, Re* [1922] 2 Ch 475).

6 The question of detriment

It has been suggested in some cases (see eg *Coco v Clark (AN) (Engineers) Ltd* [1969] RPC 41) that an obligation of confidence will not be enforced unless the disclosure or use of the information results in a detriment to the plaintiff or an advantage to his competitors. As far as any remedy in damages is concerned this point will not be of any significance and it is most unlikely that any action would be brought in a business secrets case unless some damage or advantage to a competitor had occurred or was thought likely to do so. However in an application for an injunction it is of great significance. The matter was discussed in *Attorney General v Guardian Newspapers Ltd (No 2)* [1988] 3 All ER 545. Lord Keith at p 640 said, as a general rule it is in the public interest that confidences should be respected, and the encouragement of such respect may in itself constitute a sufficient ground for recognising and enforcing the obligation of confidence even where the confider can point to no specific detriment to himself. Information about a person's private and personal affairs may be of a nature which shows him up in a favourable light and would by no means expose him to criticism. The anonymous donor of a very large sum to a very worthy cause has his own reasons for wishing to remain anonymous, which are unlikely to be discreditable. He should surely be in a position to restrain disclosure in breach of confidence of his identity in connection with the donation. '. . . I would think it a sufficient detriment to the confider that information given in confidence is to be disclosed to persons whom he would prefer not to know of it, even though the disclosure would not be harmful to him in any positive way.' Lord Griffiths at pp 649–50 concluded that 'detriment or potential detriment' was necessary in order to obtain an injunction. Lord Goff at p 659 went further in saying 'I would . . . wish to keep open the question whether detriment to the plaintiff is an essential ingredient of an action for breach of confidence'. However, he pointed out that in most cases detriment will exist. This is certainly correct in commercial cases.

7 *Locus standi* (to whom is the duty owed)

Leaving aside the question of duties of third parties who receive confidential information which is dealt with below, the question of *locus standi* to bring a claim for breach of confidence has not often come before the courts. The leading case is *Fraser v Evans* [1969] 1 QB 349. That case concerned an article which *The Sunday Times* were proposing to publish. It was to be based on a report which the plaintiff had prepared for the Greek Government. The plaintiff's contract with the Greek Government placed him under an obligation of confidence but placed the Greek Government under no such obligation. It appeared that *The Sunday Times* had obtained their copy of the report from an unauthorised Greek Government source. It was said by the court that the plaintiff's case must fail because any duty of confidence which might exist was owed to the Greek Government and not to the plaintiff.

It therefore seems clear that in order to found an action for breach of confidence the defendant must have obtained the information as a result of a disclosure by the plaintiff in circumstances of confidence. Presumably it is also possible to acquire *locus standi* to bring a claim by means of an assignment, subject to the usual limitations on the assignment of bare causes of action.

8 Third parties

Without doubt the courts will in proper circumstances restrain a breach of confidence by third parties who have come by confidential information. The nature of those circumstances is unclear.

Two clear situations can be discerned. Firstly, if the defendant receives the information in the knowledge that it is being disclosed in breach of confidence he will be bound by an obligation of confidence (see for example *Albert (Prince) v Strange* (1849) 1 Mac & G 25, *Schering Chemicals v Falkman* [1981] 2 WLR 848). Secondly, if X discloses information in confidence to Y and Y then discloses the information in confidence to Z (but does not tell Z that he has obtained the information from X) then X will be able to proceed directly against Z if Z disregards the obligation of confidence (see *Saltman Engineering Co v Campbell Engineering Co* [1963] 65 RPC 203).

Greater difficulties arise where the defendant comes by the information without notice of any restrictions on its disclosure. In certain cases it might well be that the defendant's ignorance will not help him. In the *Argyll Group Plc v Distillers Co Plc* [1986] 1 CMLR 764 the confidentiality of documents produced on discovery was in issue. Talbot J said 'those who disclose documents on discovery are entitled to the protection of the court against any use of the documents by any person into whose hands they come unless it is directly connected with the action in which they are produced'. There was no suggestion that an innocent recipient should be permitted to use the documents (by the same token there was no suggestion that the recipients were innocent of the means by which the documents had been obtained).

In other cases an innocent recipient may be protected at least until he becomes aware of the confidential nature of the information. As Lord Denning said in *Fraser v Evans*:

> No person is permitted to divulge to the world information which he has received in confidence, unless he has just cause or excuse for doing so. Even if he comes by it innocently, nevertheless once he gets to know that it was originally given in confidence, he can be restrained from breaking that confidence.

However it should be recalled that even if an obligation of confidence is held to exist the grant of an injunction is in the discretion of the court. Where the defendant has innocently made a substantial investment on the basis of information innocently acquired it is most unlikely that an injunction would be granted to restrain him from making use of that information (although the fact that an injunction might drive the defendant into liquidation is not relevant if the tests in *American Cyanamid Co v Ethicon* [1975] AC 396 have been satisfied; per May LJ in *Bullivant (Roger) Ltd v Ellis* [1987] ICR 464). Thus, in *Seager v Copydex Ltd* [1967] 1 WLR 923 no injunction was granted to prevent the defendant's use of information supplied by the plaintiff in ignorance of the duty of confidence but the plaintiff had a remedy in damages. In *Attorney General v Guardian Newspapers Ltd (No 2)* [1988] 2 WLR 805 at p 873, Lord Donaldson MR stated that at first instance Scott J had come to the conclusion that the duty to maintain confidentiality was not necessarily in all circumstances the same in relation to third parties who became possessed of confidential information as it was in relation to the primary confident. He agreed with that proposition and stated:

> The reason is that the third party recipient may be subject to some additional and conflicting duty which does not affect the primary confidant or may not be subject to some special duty which does effect that confidant. In such situations the equation is not the same in the case of the confidant and that of the third party and accordingly the result may be different.

Even though this case went to the House of Lords no disagreement with that statement of principle is found in the judgments there.

9 Equity, law and property

There has been much academic discussion about the nature of the law of confidence. It is clear that one cannot own confidential information in the sense that one can own a car. This is because information is not the same sort of thing as a car. This is obvious when one considers that two identical copies of a blueprint clearly contain the same information, but two identical cars are not the same car. To talk of owning information is therefore misleading. All one may own are such rights as the law confers upon someone who holds confidential information.

These rights do not exist in the information itself but arise from its confidential nature and the circumstances in which persons other than the originator of the information come by it. As has been seen the courts prefer, where possible, to give these rights a contractual basis (see *Faccenda Chicken Ltd v Fowler* [1985] 1 All ER 729). However, where no express or implied contract exists, as for example will be the case where third parties come by confidential information, the rights are presumably equitable in nature. The judgments in *Attorney General v Guardian Newspapers Ltd (No 2)* [1988] 3 All ER 545 made no distinction between contract or equity as a basis for the duty of confidence. It should not however be supposed that because of the equitable nature of these rights a *bona fide* purchaser for value will be protected. Although the point is undecided (but see the Australian *Wheatley v Bell* [1984] FSR 16) the nature of information would seem to conflict with the existence of any legal estate. Equity only protects the *bona fide* purchaser for value of a legal estate and so the rule should be of no application. It is more probable that the whole matter lies in the discretion of the court as to the grant of an injunction (or damages in lieu). In one respect, however, confidential information can be regarded as property. It is possible to transfer it from one person to another so that the recipient can exercise such rights against third parties as may arise (see for example *Keene, Re* [1922] 2 Ch 475).

If this is the aim it will, by the agreement of transfer, be necessary to specify that the transferor will not further use or disclose the information himself, otherwise the transferee will simply be one further person who is aware of the information. The right of the transferee to sue, in his own name, persons who used information obtained from the transferor in breach of confidence before the date of the transfer is not clearly established. Any well-drafted transfer will therefore provide for the transfer of the right to sue for such breaches. In addition, it will be prudent for the transferee to join the transferor as a party to any such action.

10 Contractual rights

The courts adopt substantially the same rules when implying an obligation of confidence into a contract and when finding an equitable obligation of confidence. This is shown by the judgment of Lord Greene in *Saltman* where he said: 'If two parties make a contract under which one of them obtains for the purpose of the contract or in connection with it some confidential matter, even though the contract is silent on the matter of confidence the law will imply an obligation to treat that confidential matter in a confidential way as one of the implied terms of the contract; but the obligation of confidence is not limited to cases where the parties are in a contractual relationship'.

This passage also shows the clear preference of the courts to rely on an implied contractual obligation (see also *Faccenda*).

10.1 Relationship between copyright and confidentiality

It is important to remember that the actions for breach of confidence and breach of copyright are fundamentally different. Whereas copyright protects the form in which an idea is expressed but not the idea itself, confidence can protect both the form and the idea.

Part III

Employer and Employee

Chapter 6

The Classic Problems

There are two categories of case to which the restraint of trade doctrine has traditionally been applied: contracts between employers/employees and business sale agreements. In Chapters 10–12 we examine the latter and in the next four chapters the former. The general law relating to restraint of trade and business secrets is analysed in the first five chapters.

The usual difficulties which arise from restraint of trade and business secrets clauses in employment contracts occur because an employee has decided to set up as, or work for, a competitor of his employer. His former employer will quite clearly not benefit from this conduct and the courts are concerned with defining how far the employer can restrict such competition. It is important to divide the analysis between the position during employment and what happens once the employee has left because, generally, the courts are much more protective of the employer's interests during employments. During employment the employee may damage his employer's business in the following ways:

(a) working for a competitor during his hours of employment;
(b) working for a competitor in his spare time;
(c) making preparations in order to compete with his employer after he has left;
(d) disclosing or using the employer's business secrets; or
(e) failing to disclose information which may be of use to his employer and in some instances personally profiting from its use.

Once employment has terminated the employee may still damage his former employer's business by:

(a) competing with his former employer;
(b) canvassing or soliciting his former employer's business connections;
(c) using or disclosing his former employer's business secrets; or
(d) enticing his former colleagues away from his former employer to his new employer or business.

This part analyses the limits which the courts have placed on the freedom of an employee in the absence of express restrictive covenants and upon the ability of employers to restrain employees by contractual restrictions.

1 The attitude of the courts

The courts have developed a practice of viewing the position of an employee as particularly special and significant when dealing with restraint of trade claims by an employer. The reasons for this approach are clear. Traditionally the contract of employment was drawn up by the employer and there was little or no negotiation as to its contents. The employee was thought to lack bargaining power. In *M & S Drapers v Reynolds* [1956] 3 All ER 814 Denning LJ said:

> During the last 40 years the courts have shown a reluctance to enforce covenants of this sort. They realise that a servant has often very little choice in the matter. If he wants to get or to keep his employment, he has to sign the document which the employer puts before him and he may do so without fully appreciating what it may involve. Moreover if these covenants were given full force, they would tend to reduce his freedom to seek better conditions even by asking for a rise in wages; because if he is not allowed to get work elsewhere he is very much at the mercy of his employer. Whilst showing proper reluctance to enforce these convenants, the courts will, however, do so if they are shown to be reasonable . . . .

Another reason for this special approach is that the employer does not pay a premium for freedom from competition from his employee. On the other hand on the sale of a business the purchaser frequently does pay such a premium and the vendor correspondingly receives a price higher than if no restraint existed (see *Morris (Herbert) Ltd v Saxelby* [1916] 1 AC 688 per Lord Atkinson). Another reason for the special attitude of the courts in employment cases was given by Younger LJ in *Attwood v Lamont* [1920] 3 KB 571: the employer cannot prevent the employee from using skill and knowledge once he has left, but he frequently tries to do so. His attempts must be curbed.

In more recent times and in a case which did not strictly involve an employee, Lord Diplock said that the real concern of the courts was simply to ask whether the party with the greater bargaining power had exacted an unfairly onerous benefit (*Schroeder (A) Music Publishing Co v Macaulay* [1974] 3 All ER 616).

However, the existence of the special approach towards employees can be overstated and it is dangerous to assume its existence. Although a managing director will usually be an employee the courts sensibly view him in a different light from that of a manual worker. As Denning LJ said in the *M & S Drapers* case: 'A managing director can look after himself'. In other words the courts are not required to be so vigilant in his case as he is presumed to have negotiated the terms of his contract. It may also be thought that when an agreement is negotiated by a trade union inequality of bargaining power as understood in the cases is not often a relevant factor. However, there is no reported case in which this point has been taken by an employer in order to argue that the special approach is not always applicable; it may be that the special approach is so entrenched in judicial thinking that even an employer who is able to demonstrate that the factual bases for the special approach do not exist in the instant case will not succeed in persuading the court to abandon it. However it must be worth trying to do so especially if a senior employee has received independent legal advice before entering the agreement and has been specifically compensated (as is common in the USA) for accepting the restraint.

The courts have recently demonstrated a reaction against an absurdly over-generous approach to the construction of agreements in the employee's favour: see *Home Counties Dairies Ltd v Skilton* [1970] 1 WLR 526 in which the defendant was employed by the plaintiffs as a milkman and he expressly agreed that for a period of one year after his employment terminated he would not 'serve or sell milk or dairy produce' to any person who had been a customer of his employers and who had been served by him during the six months prior to his leaving. Harman LJ noted that the clause appeared to have been carefully limited to avoid the usual pitfalls associated with an employer trying to 'get too much'. The defendant did leave and worked as a milkman for a competitor of his former employer. At first instance, the court found that the restriction was unreasonable. It acceded to an argument that it would prevent the defendant being employed by a grocer in selling dairy products in his shop. This construction meant that the clause went beyond the protection of the goodwill of the employer's business. On appeal, the court took a much more sensible view of the clause: it allowed the appeal on the basis that the clause should be read in the context of the whole employment agreement. That agreement made it clear that the defendant was employed as a milkman and that the intention of the clause was to afford the employer protection only against the activities of an employee who worked as a milkman once his employment ended. The court was adamant in its rejection of fanciful interpretations of the clause so as to make it so wide as to be unreasonable. This case has been extensively cited and approved in more recent authorities: see for example *Littlewoods Organisation Ltd v Harris* [1978] 1 All ER 1026. Finally the courts do not appear to exhibit such a protective attitude towards the employee when asked to control his misuse of business secrets. The result of this dichotomy is that the employer who can rely on the right to protect his business secrets is much more likely to succeed in court than when he seeks to enforce a traditional restraint of trade clause.

Chapter 7

Implied and Express Duties during Employment

1 Implied duties

During employment the employee owes his employer a duty of 'fidelity', alternatively called 'good faith'. This general duty has been considered in many cases and is quite clearly based on what a person of ordinary honesty would consider honest/dishonest (see *Robb v Green* [1895] 2 QB 315; *Printers and Finishers Ltd v Holloway* [1964] 3 All ER 731 and Roger *Bullivant Ltd v Ellis* [1987] ICR 464 at p 475 per Nourse LJ). In *Robb v Green* Lord Esher MR justified the implication of such a term: 'It is impossible . . . that a master would have put a servant into a confidential position of this kind unless he thought that the servant would be bound to use good faith towards him; or that the servant would not know . . . that the master would rely on his observance of good faith . . .'.

However, as was recognised by Lord Greene MR in *Hivac Ltd v Park Royal Scientific Instruments Ltd* [1946] Ch 169, 'The practical difficulty in any given case is to find exactly how far that rather vague duty of fidelity extends'.

The general duty of fidelity will be examined in the next five sections.

1.1 Duty not to compete within the duration of the employment contract

This aspect of the duty of fidelity requires the employee not to work for any person who is or who might be in competition with his employer during the working day. In *Marshall (Thomas) (Exporters) Ltd v Guinle* [1978] 3 WLR 116 whilst managing director of the plaintiffs and without their knowledge or consent, the defendant placed orders for the benefit of himself and his own company with the plaintiffs' suppliers. He also sold goods for his own benefit to customers of the plaintiffs. His conduct was described by Megarry V-C as amounting to gross and repeated breaches of his implied obligation to be faithful to the plaintiffs. There could be no doubt that by competing with the plaintiffs both as regards supplies and customers he had placed himself in a position in which there was a conflict of interest and duty. Even though this case dealt with a managing director who was clearly in a fiduciary position, its principles are equally applicable to other employees (see *Sanders v Parry* [1967] 2 All ER 803).

This duty also prevents an employee from taking advantage of any approach which is initiated by a customer or supplier even though the employee did not seek or even encourage it, as happened in *Sanders'* case.

The degree of involvement which an employee has to demonstrate in order to fall foul of this duty need not always be very great. He may simply assist a competitor in any way which does or may have an adverse and material effect on his employer's business. As Brightman J said in *United Sterling Corp Ltd v Felton and Mannion* [1974] RPC 162 'This contractual obligation of fidelity . . . may prevent a skilled employee from giving his assistance to a competitor despite the fact that such assistance is provided by the employee in his own time and despite the fact that no information has been disclosed to the employees in confidence'.

However, it should not be thought that *any* assistance given to a competitor by the employee is necessarily a breach of his duty, for it may have been done with the employer's authority, though this will be a rare occurrence. In practice, an employer will not always rely on the implied duty of fidelity: there will often be an express clause in the employment contract which directs the employee to devote his time exclusively to the promotion of the employer's business.

1.2 The employee's duty not to compete in his spare time

As a general rule an employee cannot compete with his employer in his spare time without being in breach of his duty of fidelity. The basic question is: do the activities of the employee interfere with the employer's legitimate interests or are they likely to do so? If the answer is positive then the employer can seek redress.

In *Hivac Ltd v Park Royal Scientific Instruments Ltd* [1948] 1 Ch 169 employees of the plaintiffs who were highly skilled in assembling hearing-aid valves had Sundays off. The defendants who manufactured similar valves and were effectively competitors of the plaintiff company offered work to the plaintiff's employees on Sundays. The employees accepted. The defendants alone were sued for inducing/procuring the employees to breach their contracts of employment. There was no evidence that the employees had misused any of the plaintiffs' business secrets. The Court of Appeal concluded that this was a case of deliberate and secret action by the employees and the defendants in circumstances in which they must have known the exact result of what they were doing and must have known it was wrong. In addition to this breach of the moral duty of fidelity, the court appears to have been concerned with the risk of confidential information being passed to competitors, because it was satisfied that the plaintiffs did own certain business secrets of which the employees had knowledge.

The court also commented that a manual worker might owe a duty which did not extend outside his hours of employment and this seems sensible. On the other hand the very nature of the work may be such as to make it quite clear that the duties of the employee to his employer cannot properly be performed if he engages in certain activities in his spare time. Each case depends on its facts.

The court discussed the example of a solicitor's clerk and said that in such a case it would be improper for him to work for another solicitor in his spare time. There might be a real risk of embarrassment to his full-time employers if he were asked to act for a client in his spare time who was on the other side of a case in which his main employers were engaged.

The important points which emerge from this case are that the employer will be able to rely on this part of the duty of fidelity if it can be shown that the employee works for a trade competitor in his spare time and:

(a) knows of business secrets which may be of use to the competitor and/or
(b) occupies a position which makes it expedient to recognise the existence of his duty to work for the employer alone.

See also *Nova Plastics Ltd v Froggatt* [1982] IRLR 146 which concerned an 'odd-job' man.

1.3 The employee's duty not to make preparations in order to compete with his employer after he has left or to enable another to do so

The employee cannot make preparations during his employment, either during the working day or in his spare time, with a view to competing with his employer once his employment is over if such preparation may have a material effect on his employer's business. Obviously, an employee is free to apply for another position even with a rival of his present employer, or to find premises in which to set up a future business so long as in doing so he is not in breach of any valid express term in his employment contract: see *Searle (GD) & Co Ltd v Celltech Ltd* [1982] FSR 92. Certainly, the law will not imply a term which prevents him from doing so. What he cannot do without infringing the duty of fidelity is to make such preparations in his employer's time or use or disclose either the business secrets or trade connections of his employer. Only after he had left is he free, in the absence of express restraint, to make use of the latter though never the former. In *Marshall (Thomas) (Exporters) Ltd v Guinle* [1978] 3 WLR 116 the defendant was not simply competing with the plaintiff during his employment but was also taking steps to prepare to compete once he had left by dealing with customers and suppliers of his employer. This was a very clear example of breach but others are less obvious. Detection is a great problem as breach is frequently only discovered after employment ends. The employer may find it difficult when he becomes aware of the fact that his former customers are now dealing with his former employee to prove that preparation to entice them away or enticement did in fact take place during employment. The usual way in which this duty is breached is for the employee to mention to customers that he is leaving and either directly or indirectly suggest to them that he is available to meet their needs once he has left. He may also consciously memorise client's names and their particular requirements. In *Robb v Green* [1895] 2 QB 315 the defendant, employed by the plaintiff as the manager of his business, surreptitiously copied from the plaintiff's order book a list of names and addresses of customers with the intention of soliciting them after he had left employment and had set up a similar business on his own. Subsequently he did leave and did use the list. The Court of Appeal affirmed the existence of an implied duty not to prepare to compete and gave judgment for the plaintiffs. However, they did not deal with a suggestion made by Hawkins J at first instance that, in some circumstances, an employee could 'legitimately canvass, issue his circulars, have his place of business in readiness, hire his servants, etc' [1895] 2 QB 1. He was relying on the earlier case of *Nichol v Martyn* [1799] 2 Esp 732, but in *Wessex Dairies Ltd v Smith* [1935] 2 KB 80 Maugham LJ cast doubt on both those judgments and so far as the modern law is concerned they should not be relied on to the extent that they indicate the employee can canvass or issue circulars to customers of his employer before he leaves. Nor can the employee do anything else in Hawkins J's list in his employer's time. In the *Wessex Dairies* case, it was found that on the last day of his employment as a milkman the defendant, whilst on his round, informed customers that he would soon cease to be employed by the plaintiffs, that he was going to set up business on his own and could supply them with milk. The court said that he was plainly soliciting their custom at a time when he was under a duty of fidelity to his employer and awarded his former employers damages. A more recent example is *Sanders v Parry* [1967] 1 WLR 753 which concerned a solicitor's practice. After joining the plaintiff as an assistant solicitor the defendant entered an agreement with T, one of the plaintiff's clients. The agreement stated that the defendant would leave the plaintiff's employment and set up on his own in premises which T would lease to him and T would transfer his custom to the defendant. When the plaintiff heard of this, he dismissed the defendant, and sought an injunction to prevent him breaching his duty of fidelity. In his defence, the defendant claimed that it was T who had approached him and that he had not initiated the agreement. Havers J accepted this but said:

> ... there was a duty on the defendant at all times during the subsistence of [the employment] agreement to protect his master's interests, especially to do his best to retain Mr Tully as a client of his master. ... Now, in accepting Tully's offer, the defendant was not protecting his master's interests ... [he] was placing himself in a position in which there was a conflict of interests between him and his principal and he was looking after his own interests to the detriment of his master's interests. He was knowingly, deliberately and secretly acting, setting out to do something which would inevitably inflict great harm on his principal.

However, the dividing line between what is and what is not permissible is often difficult to draw, as Maugham LJ illustrated in the *Wessex Dairies* case:

> ... although the servant is not entitled to make use of information which he has obtained in confidence in his master's service he is entitled to make use of the knowledge and skill which he acquired while in that service, including knowledge and skill directly obtained from the master in teaching him his business. It follows, in my opinion, that the servant may, whilst in the employment of the master, be as agreeable, attentive, and skilful as it is in his power to be to others with the ultimate view of obtaining

the benefit of the customers' friendly feelings when he calls upon them if and when he sets up business for himself.

What he cannot do is anything more positive.

In *Island Export and Finance Ltd v Umunna* [1986] BCLC 460 it was held that a director's fiduciary duty did not necessarily come to an end when he ceased to be a director. A director was precluded from diverting to himself a maturing business opportunity which his company was actively pursuing even after his resignation where the resignation was prompted or influenced by a desire to acquire that opportunity for himself. However, on the facts of the case the plaintiff's claim failed as it had not proved:

(a) the existence of a 'maturing' business opportunity;
(b) that it was actively pursuing the business either when the defendant resigned or when he subsequently obtained the contracts; or
(c) that his resignation was prompted or influenced by the wish to acquire the benefit of the contracts for himself.

It is to be noted that even in the case of a fiduciary the ambit of his duty once he has ceased to be for example, a director, is circumscribed. A difficult question is whether in the case of an employee who is not a fiduciary the same principles also apply. It is submittted that, on the whole, most employees are under no such implied duty once employment has ceased. If the employer requires protection he should have the foresight to include an express covenant in the employment contract.

In *Balston Ltd v Headline Filters Ltd* [1987] FSR 330, H, the second defendant, on 17 March gave notice of termination of his employment as deputy managing director with Balston Ltd. It was agreed that his employment would end on 11 July. On 16 April he resigned his directorship of Balston Ltd and it was agreed that he need not attend work during the remainder of the notice period. In the period between 16 April and 11 July he bought H Ltd off the shelf, arranged premises for it and ordered materials preparatory to the start of trading on 11 July. H Ltd was to trade in direct competition with Balston Ltd. Scott J however did not criticise H for his activities during the notice period. It may be that the decisive factor in H's favour was the fact that H was effectively on 'garden leave'. It may be that if he had been actively working for Balston Ltd his activities might have been in breach of his implied duty of fidelity.

This subject has been recently considered by the Employment Appeal Tribunal in *Laughton v Bapp Industrial Supplies Ltd* [1986] ICR 634. In that case the employees, who were warehousemen employed by a company which supplied nuts and bolts, wrote to ten of their employers' suppliers informing them that they intended to start up in business on their own trading in nuts and bolts, and asking for details of their products. The employers learned of the letters and summarily dismissed the employees for gross misconduct. On their complaints of unfair dismissal an industrial tribunal found that the employers were justified in their decision that the employees were in breach of their implied duty in their contracts of employment that they should be loyal to their employers and that the dismissals were not unfair. The employees appealed and it was held, allowing the appeal, that the industrial tribunal had erred in law in holding that an intention to compete in the future with their employers expressed by the employees in letters to their employers' suppliers was in itself a breach of a duty of fidelity owed by the employees to the employers and that accordingly the dismissals had been unfair. Peter Gibson J said, at p 638:

> An employee with experience in a particular industry who is intending to leave, whether to join a competitor as an employee or to set up in competition on his own account, commits no breach of contract in doing so unless either there is a specific term of his contract to that effect which does not fall foul of the doctrine against restraint of trade or he is intending to use the confidential information of his employer otherwise and for the benefit of his employer.

See also *Ixora Trading Inc v Jones* [1990] 1 FSR 251 per Mummery J at p 262. There the evidence before him merely disclosed that the defendants whilst being employed by the plaintiffs simply made plans or preparations for their future post termination activities. This, he said, could not be characterised as having breached the duty of good faith which amounted to no more than a principle of fair and honourable dealing.

1.4 The employee's duty not to disclose or use his employer's business secrets

What constitutes a legitimate business secret has already been discussed earlier. However, given the existence of such a secret there is an implied duty that an employee will not disclose such secrets to another or use them himself. A general principle in the employment field was laid down in *Printers and Finishers Ltd v Holloway* [1964] 3 All ER 731 where Cross J said that employees are prohibited from using information which 'can fairly be regarded as a separate part of the employee's stock of knowledge which a man of ordinary honesty and intelligence would recognise to be the property of his old employer and not his own to do as he likes with'. (See also *Bents Brewery Co Ltd v Hogan* [1945] 2 All ER 570.)

Unfortunately, this test has proved somewhat difficult to apply to practical situations. However it was used in *Industrial Furnaces Ltd v Reaves* [1970] RPC 605. The defendant had been a director of plaintiffs for 13 years and had been in charge of the development and sales of a certain type of heater. On leaving the plaintiffs, the defendant set up another company which sold heaters of a similar type to some of the plaintiffs' previous customers. On being sued by the plaintiffs for breach of the implied duty of confidentiality, the defendant claimed that he had made all his calculations in designing the heater from information which had been published in a readily obtainable leaflet. Graham J found that such information was not readily available and went on to say that the information had been obtained as a result of considerable labour and expense on the part of the plaintiffs and was therefore valuable and, it followed, confidential.

A particular problem which frequently arises is a claim by an employee that even if he must have realised, in accordance with the principle laid down in the *Printers and Finishers* case, that he was under a duty to maintain a confidence, such duty was in fact overridden by the way in which his employer acted towards the information ie that the employer is estopped from now relying on confidence. An example of such a case is *Bjorlow (GB) Ltd v Minter* [1954] 71 RPC 321 in which the employer claimed that a process was secret and had been wrongfully used and disclosed by the defendant, a former employee. The plaintiff could not prove that the defendant knew it was a secret process either because of its nature or because he had been specifically told that it was and Vaisey J pointed out that if it were really secret it was surprising that the defendant's employment had brought him into contact with it; he had been to prison in the past. He said that the defendant had never been told he was being entrusted with secrets, there was no express covenant covering business secrets and the defendant never knew that he must not talk about his work outside his employment. Vaisey J went on to say that the employers had shown 'the utmost carelessness in allowing this defendant to get knowledge of what they knew was a very valuable secret . . . . People with valuable secrets ought not to allow subordinate employees . . . to obtain knowledge of this kind, and if they choose to do it without warning them they will find it very difficult to claim interlocutory relief successfully'.

Evershed MR said that 'the plaintiffs took no steps whatever . . . to impress upon anybody that there was here any important secret which they desired to preserve'.

This case shows neither that employers should refuse jobs to those who have a murky past nor that they should not entrust secrets to subordinate employees—that is impracticable—but that they should not simply rely on the implied duty of confidence; it can lead to misunderstandings and difficulties as to what is really secret. A prudent employer will always have an express contractual term protecting business secrets.

Whether the court's approach in cases such as *Bjorlow* would also be adopted even if the employee made use of or disclosed business secrets during employment has not been determined: in *Bjorlow*, the defendant made use of the information only after he had left. It is submitted that in the former case the approach would probably be modified by the basic duty of fidelity to the extent that confidentiality would be lost only if the employer could be said to have shown *wilful* disregard to the quality of the confidence, rather than having been merely negligent.

Recently, in *Faccenda Chicken Ltd v Fowler* [1985] 1 All ER 724; [1986] 1 All ER 617 Goulding J and the Court of Appeal considered information which was not protected by an express clause and which was clearly used by employees once employment had ended. In addition, comments were made about the ambit of the implied duty of fidelity and business secrets during employment. There is a full discussion of this case at p 76.

1.5 The employee's duty to disclose to his employer information which may be of use to that employer (and not personally to profit from it)

If, during the course of employment, an employee receives information which is or may reasonably be relevant to his employer's business then he is under a duty:

(a) to disclose all relevant information received to the employer; and
(b) not to use that information for his or another's benefit unless the employer consents.

The source of the information is irrelevant. Moreover, the information need not be confidential as is shown in *Sanders v Parry* [1967] 1 WLR 753 and *Swain v West (Butchers) Ltd* [1936] 1 All ER 224; 3 All ER 261; though it was in *Cranleigh Precision Engineering Ltd v Bryant* [1966] RPC 81. It need only be relevant to the wellbeing of the employer's business.

In *Sanders v Parry*, the defendant whilst in the plaintiff's employment as an assistant solicitor was told by another member of staff that she was dissatisfied with her employment. It seems that the other staff member had never spoken to her employer on the subject, though she had opportunity to do so. Moreover, an important client of the plaintiff told the defendant that he was dissatisfied with the plaintiff's conduct of his affairs. Instead of passing on this information, the defendant persuaded the other employee to leave and join his own business; the discontented client in the meantime had agreed with the defendant that he would use him as his legal adviser in the future. The result of the case—in which the defendant was found in breach of his duty of fidelity—was inevitable. The defendant had placed himself in a position where his duty and interest conflicted even though both the employee and client appear to have had no intention of remaining with the plaintiff. In *Swain v West (Butchers) Ltd* it was held that an employee, having learnt of detrimental behaviour of another employee, which was relevant to his employer's business, was under a duty to report that fact to his employers. Although there was an express clause in the employment contract by which the employee was under a duty 'to promote, extend and develop the interests of the company' the court would clearly have reached the same conclusion on the basis of the implied duty of fidelity. Obviously, what is or may be of importance to an employer's business is a question of fact; and it was no doubt significant in *Swain* that S was the general manager, the wrongful employee was the managing director, his conduct was dishonest and it could have had a material effect on the defendant's business (labelling meat as 'Empire Products' when it was not). Moreover, Greer LJ specifically said 'I do not decide that in every case where the relation of master and servant exists it is the duty of the servant to disclose, or to disclose upon inquiry, any discrepancies of which he knows of his fellow servants'. This caveat was echoed in *Sybron Corp v Rochem Ltd* [1983] 3 WLR 713 where it was said that if an employee were required to report each and every breach of duty by fellow employees this would ruin good industrial relations. The ambit of the duty must depend on the circumstances, especially the respective positions of those involved. Moreover that case established that the duty still exists even if by reporting the conduct the reporter incriminates himself. The Court of Appeal in *Sybron* were not in a position to criticise the House of Lords decision in *Bell v Lever Bros Ltd* [1931] AC 161 though they distinguished it. *Bell* says that a contract of employment is not a contract *uberrimae fidei* so as to require disclosure by the employee of his own misconduct, either before he is taken into employment or during the course of his employment. It seems to us that the House of Lords today might come to another conclusion. However, see *Horcal Ltd v Gatland* [1984] IRLR 288.

Cranleigh Precision Engineering Ltd v Bryant [1964] 3 All ER 289, is a particular example of the misuse of confidential information received by an employee for his employer's benefit. B was the managing director of the plaintiffs. However, he had, unknown to the plaintiffs, set up another business which was dormant until he left their employment. Whilst still employed by the plaintiffs, B was told by that company's patent agents of a foreign invention of a product similar to that of the plaintiffs. That invention had been awarded an English patent but B did not mention that fact to the plaintiffs, and after he left he acquired it. Roskill J said that B was in breach of an implied duty in:

(a) not communicating to the plaintiffs' board the information which he received from the patent agents and in taking no steps to protect the plaintiffs against possible consequences of the existence of the patent; and

(b) using information regarding the patent for his own benefit.

Moreover, as the patent specification was not published by the plaintiffs but by another party, its publication did not cause the information to lose its quality of confidence and therefore B was not released from his duty to the plaintiffs. B was enjoined from using the patent; see also *Industrial Development Consultants v Cooley* [1972] 2 All ER 192.

2 Express duties

In some instances all of the duties which are implied by law during the currency of an employment contract will be expressly included in such a contract. However, practice differs and it invariably happens that express provision is made only regarding two areas: non-competition/canvassing and non-disclosure/use of business secrets.

2.1 Non-competition/canvassing clauses

It is common to find in an employment contract an express clause which restricts competition/canvassing by an employee both during and after employment. Later we deal with how far a clause can legitimately restrict competition by a former employee: legitimacy is determined by whether the restriction is reasonable. However, it is important to decide at this stage whether that part of an express clause which seeks to control competition during employment is also subject to such a test. There is authority on this point. In *Esso Petroleum Co Ltd v Harper's Garage (Stourport) Ltd* [1968] AC 269 Lord Reid said:

Whenever a man agrees to do something over a period he thereby puts it wholly or partly out of his power to 'exercise any trade or business he pleases' during that period. He may enter into a contract of service or may agree to give his exclusive services to another: then during the period of the contract he is not entitled to engage in other business activities. But no one has ever suggested that such contracts are in restraint of trade except in very unusual circumstances. . . .

See also *Warner Bros Inc v Nelson* [1937] 1 KB 209; *Schroeder (A) Music Publishing Co Ltd v Macaulay* [1974] 1 WLR 1308 and *Davis (Clifford) Management Ltd v WEA Records Ltd* [1975] 1 WLR 61. These cases were discussed earlier.

2.2 Business secrets

The particular importance of an express clause covering business secrets during employment is that it avoids some of the problems encountered in *Bjorlow (GB) Ltd v Minter* (1954) 71 RPC 321. It creates certainty as it specifically defines what amounts to a business secret and brings its existence to the mind of the employee.

Chapter 8

Interests Protectable After Employment Ends

The end of employment is a critical and decisive event. The practical effect of it is to reduce the law's interest in implying duties largely for the reason that public policy demands that an employee be free to work for whom he chooses. This is reflected by the fact that, in the absence of express provision, it is now quite legitimate for the employee to compete with his old employer and to canvass his customers. However, the employee is still prevented from betraying his employer's business secrets. Put briefly, once employment ends he cannot, without a specific covenant, be prevented from doing anything unless his actions contravene what is perceived to be a proprietary right of his employer: *Morris (Herbert) Ltd v Saxelby* [1916] 1 AC 688.

Therefore, once he has left, the employee is allowed to pursue his own interests. How far he can go in the absence of restrictive covenants is dealt with later. However, first we must discuss when employment ends. This may be dealt with in some way in the contract in that a certain notice period may have been specified and this may have been adhered to by the parties. What if the situation is more complicated—as it was in *Marshall (Thomas) (Exporters) Ltd v Guinle* [1978] 3 WLR 116. Having decided that the doctrine of automatic determination (ie determination of a contract solely at the will of the party who was guilty of a wrongful repudiatory breach) did not exist, even in employment contracts, Megarry V-C concluded that as the breach had not been accepted by the innocent party then the contract subsisted and therefore for the period which it had to run—circa four and a half years—the defendant was bound by its terms. His status as an employee had ended but the continuing terms of the contract of employment subsisted. This meant, *inter alia*, that a provision in the contract which allowed him to solicit once employment was over did not come into effect until that contractual period was up. See also *Gunton v Richmond-upon-Thames LBC* [1981] Ch 448, especially the judgment of Brightman LJ. Therefore, if an employer wants to sue on the basis of a continuing obligation which lasts after determination and requires a remedy other than damages, he should not accept the repudiation but treat the contract as if alive.

In *Spencer v Marchington* [1988] IRLR 392 the plaintiff was employed by the defendant for a fixed period of one year. Just over two months before the expiry of that term the plaintiff was informed that her contract would not be renewed. Indeed she was asked to stay away from work for that remaining period. It was held that the defendant had not repudiated the plaintiff's contract of employment by refusing to allow her to carry out her duties until her fixed-term contract had expired. The request for her to stay away from work for two months out of 12 was not sufficient to amount to a fundamental breach. Moreover even if it had been, there was no evidence that the plaintiff had accepted the repudiation by electing to treat the contract as at an end. In staying away she was only doing what she had been asked to do and that was as consistent with her agreement to the request as her rejection of it.

What is the effect of dismissal? If an employee is wrongfully dismissed then whether a covenant is reasonable or not is irrelevant. A wrongful dismissal is a repudiation by the employer. Once accepted by the employee he will be discharged forthwith from any contractual duties including compliance with the restraint of trade clause (see *General Billposting v Atkinson* [1909] AC 118). However, it is quite clear that if an employee gives notice in accordance with the contract he is by so doing affirming the existence of the contract and not accepting any perceived repudiation by the employer: see *Normalec Ltd v Britton* [1983] FSR 318.

In *Briggs v Oates* [1991] 1 All ER 407 the plaintiff and his partner in a firm of solicitors employed the defendant as a solicitor for a period of five years. His contract of employment contained a restraint of trade clause. Following the dissolution of the partnership in August 1983 the defendant wanted to practice with other solicitors in *prima facie* breach of that clause. The plaintiffs sought to enforce the clause but Scott J dismissed the action for he found that on its true construction the employment agreement was a contract of employment of the defendant by the two partners, that the dissolution of that partnership within the term of the employment constituted a breach of the contract of employment and brought it to an end and that accordingly the restraint of trade clause ceased thereafter to be binding upon the defendant.

If an employee is justifiably dismissed then provided the restraint is reasonable it is still enforceable. An example where this happened is *White (Marion) Ltd v Francis* [1972] 1 WLR 1423. See also the novel case of *Foot DC v Easter Counties Timber Co Ltd* [1972] IRLR 83.

1 Implied duties

1.1 Competition with previous employer

The courts will not imply any duty which prevents competition with a previous employer or the canvassing of his customers: *Attwood v Lamont* [1920] 3 KB 571. Therefore, if an employer feels that such protection is necessary he must include express restrictions in the contract of employment. The plaintiff in *Diamond Stylus Co Ltd v Bauden Precision Diamonds Ltd* [1973] RPC 675 paid the price for not having an express covenant restraining employees from soliciting customers after employment ended and was forced to argue that solicitation could only have come about because of the misuse of business secrets. Graham J concluded that the defendants had simply remembered the names of clients, the number of whom was very small. They had not consciously memorised the names or done anything which an honest man would consider wrong.

However, what appears to be competition/soliciting which cannot be restrained without an express clause frequently amounts to a breach of the duty of fidelity. For example, it often happens that the ability to compete/canvass arises from a breach of duty committed *during* employment. In *Wessex Dairies Ltd v Smith* [1935] 2 KB 80 Smith breached his duty of fidelity by canvassing his employers' customers during his last day of employment when he made his last milk round. Subsequently, as a direct result of such canvassing, they became his customers. It would be absurd if the law did not recognise the causal connection between these events despite its refusal to imply a non-competition restriction post employment. In this case it did so recognise that connection and Smith had to pay damages. Similarly, the ability to compete may arise from the use and disclosure of business secrets. Even if these are used only after employment ends the implied duty not to use or disclose them will mean that the employer can effectively prevent any competition based on breach.

It is therefore vital that what appears to be a non-restrictable act is examined in order to find what really lies behind the employee's ability to compete/ canvass.

1.2 Business secrets

The implied duty to maintain confidence in the employer's business secrets continues after employment ends. The most common example of breaches of this duty are the use or disclosure of a former employer's client list or of a secret process belonging to him. See *Under Water Welders and Repairers Ltd v Street and Longthorne* [1968] RPC 498.

A recent case, which has authoritatively reviewed the implied duty of fidelity as it applies to the use of confidential information once employment has ended, is *Faccenda Chicken Ltd v Fowler* [1985] 1 All ER 724; [1986] 1 All ER 617 (CA). The company claimed that Fowler, a former senior employee and eight other former employees and a new company set up by Fowler had wrongfully made use of confidential information which had been acquired during employment. The information was:

(a) the names and addresses of customers;
(b) the most convenient routes to be taken to reach the individual customers;
(c) the usual requirements of individual customers, both as to quality and quantity;
(d) the days of the week and the time of the day when deliveries were usually made to individual customers;
(e) the prices charged to individual customers.

It was argued that all of the information, as a package, was confidential and that (e) was itself secret. Goulding J found as a fact that all parts of the sales information had been used for the purposes of the defendant's business and he divided information into three categories where it was not the subject of any express provision:

(1) Information which because of its triviality or public accessibility was not confidential at all.

The employee, either during or after employment was free to impart it to anyone—including his employer's competitor.

(2) Information which was confidential in the sense that the employee had been told it was or because from its character it was obviously so. Goulding J was in fact referring to the employee's skill and knowledge acquired in the course of his present employment.

During employment the employee could not use or disclose this information without breaching the duty of fidelity. However once employment had ended it could be used or disclosed by an employee in competition with his former employer. The employer could only be protected by an express stipulation. The Court of Appeal specifically disagreed with Goulding J on the ability of the employer to prevent use of such information once employment had ended.

(3) Information which was confidential, such as details of a secret process; this type was so confidential that it could not be used by the employee at any time for the benefit of anyone but the employer.

He concluded that the information in the case came within category (2). As it had been used after employment it could only have been protected by an express term. The absence of such a term meant that there had been no breach of duty and therefore he dismissed the plaintiff's claim. The plaintiff appealed.

The Court of Appeal decided to undertake a review of the basic principles of the law in this area and as this has not been done for some time we now set out in detail what they held. Neill LJ giving the judgment of the court said:

(1) Where the parties are, or have been, linked by a contract of employment the obligations of the employee are to be determined by the contract between him and his employer. (No mention is made here of express terms which are defective and if in that event the court is free to imply terms, though as we suggest below, there is such power.)

(2) In the absence of an express term, the obligations of the employee in respect of the use and disclosure of information are the subject of implied terms.

(3) While the employee remains in the employment of the employer the obligations are included in the implied term which imposes a duty of good faith or fidelity on the employee. It is to be further noted:

(a) That the extent of the duty of good faith will vary according to the nature of the contract;

(b) That the duty of good faith will be broken if an employee makes or copies a list of the customers of the employer for use after his employment ends or deliberately memorises such a list, even though, except in special circumstances, there is no general restriction on an ex-employee canvassing or doing business with customers of his former employer.

(4) The implied term which imposes an obligation on the employee as to his conduct after the determination of the employment is more restricted in scope than that which imposes a general duty of good faith. It is clear that the obligation not to use or disclose information may cover secret processes of

manufacture such as chemical formulae, or designs or special methods of construction, and other information which is of a sufficiently high degree of confidentiality as to amount to a business secret. The obligation does not extend, however, to cover all information which is given to or required by the employee while in his employment, and in particular may not cover information which is only 'confidential' in the sense that an unauthorised disclosure of such information to a third party while the employment subsisted would be a clear breach of the duty of good faith. Therefore, in this context there are clearly two classes of confidential information when the employer is having to rely on the implied duty in order to protect his business secrets. The first class is of wider ambit than the second and exists only during the period of employment. The second class is apparently restricted to what, the judgment calls a 'business secret', eg a secret process. In the absence of any express provisions once employment has ended the law will only protect information within the second class. It is submitted that the only way for an employer to protect all forms of confidential information post employment is to have an express contractual provision relating to confidentiality. *Faccenda* had made the mistake of not having such an express term in their employment contracts.

(5) In order to determine whether any particular item of information falls within the implied term so as to prevent its use for disclosure by an employee after his employment has ceased, it is necessary to consider all the circumstances of the case.

The Court of Appeal was satisfied that the following matters were among those to which attention should be paid:

1 The nature of the employment

Employment in a capacity where 'confidential' material is habitually handled may impose a high obligation of confidentiality because the employee can be expected to realise its sensitive nature to a greater extent than if he were employed in a capacity where such material reaches him only occasionally or incidentally. (This is no doubt in some way concerned with the employee's honesty.)

2 The nature of the information itself

Information will only be protected if it can properly be classed as a business secret or as material which, while not properly described as a business secret is, in all the circumstances, of such a highly confidential nature as to require the same protection as a business secret *eo nomine*. The restrictive covenant cases demonstrate that a covenant will not be upheld on the basis of the status of the information which might be disclosed by a former employee if he is not restrained, unless it can be regarded as a business secret or the equivalent of a business secret. The court appeared to disagree with Goulding J at first instance in that it seemed to say that confidential information which cannot be described as a 'business secret' (in the narrow sense of that phrase) could not be protected by an *express clause*. This difficulty in the court's approach was addressed by Scott J in *Balston Ltd v Headline Fitters Ltd* [1987] FSR 330 who stated that

Faccenda was not authority for the proposition that confidential information that could not be protected by an implied term *ipso facto* could not be protected by express agreement. Scott J pointed out that an implied obligation may involve different considerations from an express one in that an implied obligation will be unlimited in time.

The court then went on to say that it was impossible to provide a list of matters which will qualify as business secrets or their equivalent. Secret processes of manufacture provide obvious examples, but innumerable other pieces of information are capable of being business secrets, though the secrecy of some information may only be short lived. In addition, the fact that the circulation of certain information is restricted to a limited number of individuals may throw light on the status of the information and its degree of confidentiality.

3 Whether the employer impressed on the employee the confidentiality of the information

Thus, though an employer cannot prevent the use or disclosure merely by telling the employee that certain information is confidential, the attitude of the employer towards the information provides evidence that may assist in determining whether or not the information can properly be regarded as a business secret. (This is obviously correct; one does not make something a business secret by simply describing it as such. It needs to have the necessary quality of confidence about it.)

4 Whether the relevant information can be easily isolated from other information which the employee is free to use or disclose

This to some extent relies on the intelligence and honesty of the employee. The court said that it would not regard the separability of the information in question as being conclusive, but the fact that the alleged 'confidential' information is part of a package and that the remainder of the package is not confidential is likely to throw light on whether the information in question is really a business secret. (This perhaps indicates that it was tactically inept in this case for the plaintiffs to seek to persuade the court that the whole package of information was confidential.)

5 Whether additional protection should be afforded to an employer where the former employee is not seeking to earn his living by making use of the body of skill, knowledge and experience which he has acquired in the course of his career, but is merely selling to a third party information which he acquired in confidence in the course of his former employment

Goulding J drew no such distinction. The distinction is an interesting and telling one. Although the Court of Appeal expressed no opinion on it, the court was

79

clearly concerned that the employer might possibly be able to protect himself from the use of the employee's skill and knowledge post employment by means of express provision if the employee were simply to sell that knowledge as a commodity (ie not use it as a means to gain further employment). Presumably this could happen if the employee retired and sold the information or if he joined company X and yet sold the information to company Y. It may be a recognition by the Court that the attitude of the courts generally towards employees since 1913 has, in some cases, been over generous. The correct answer to the question seems unclear. If one accepts, as so many cases do that the skill and knowledge of the employee has become part of himself then it is difficult to see why any distinction should be made as postulated in the question. He should be free to use or disclose or sell his skill and knowledge after the end of employment in any way he thinks fit. However that theory has to a certain extent been undermined by the ratio of this judgment which says that during employment the employee may not disclose or use his skill and knowledge to the detriment of his employer without being in breach of his duty of fidelity. The alternative view is that the reason for the present rule regarding skill and knowledge is that without it the employee might well be prevented from earning his living in the area in which he has the greatest experience. This is clearly not in his interests and is clearly contrary to public policy as well. If one then takes away the element of his ability to earn his living by the use of his skill and knowledge and supplants it with the notion of the employee selling that skill and knowledge as some commodity to a competitor of his former employer does that significantly change the situation? It could be said that by doing so he was simply in some way earning his living.

The court then went on to apply the law as it saw it to the facts of the case. It decided that the information about prices or as to sales information as a whole was not a business secret in this case. It did so despite the fact that Goulding J had found that an experienced salesman quickly acquired a good idea of the prices obtained by his employer's competitors, but that such knowledge was usually only approximate and that in this field accurate information was valuable, because a difference of even one penny a pound might be important. The court accepted that in certain circumstances information about prices could be invested with a sufficient degree of confidentiality to make that information a business secret or its equivalent but in the present case it found factors which led it to the conclusion that neither the information about the prices nor the sales information as a whole had the degree of confidentiality necessary to support the plaintiff's claim. These factors were as follows:

(1) The sales information contained some material which the plaintiff conceded was not confidential if looked at in isolation. (The concessions related to the defendant's entitlement to make use of any recollection they might have of the names and addresses of the plaintiff's customers as well as the most convenient routes by which the premises of such customers could be reached. There was a muted concession made regarding the requirements of the plaintiff's customers and the times when deliveries were made to them.)

(2) The information about the prices was not clearly severable from the rest of the sales information.

(3) Neither the sales information in general, nor the information about the prices in particular, though of some value to a competitor, could reasonably be regarded as plainly secret or sensitive.

(4) The sales information, including the information about prices, was necessarily acquired by the defendants in order that they could do their work. Moreover, as Goulding J had found, each salesman could quickly commit the whole of the sales information relating to his own area to memory.

(5) The sales information was generally known among the van drivers who were employees, as well as secretaries, at quite a junior level. This was not a case where the relevant information was restricted to senior management or to a specific category of staff.

(6) There was no evidence that the plaintiffs had ever given any express instructions that the sales information or the information about prices was to be treated as confidential.

1.3 Problems caused by the judgment in *Faccenda Chicken*

The judgment of the Court of Appeal in the *Faccenda* case has been perceived to cause as many problems as it has solved. The real area of difficulty is based on whether an express clause can validly protect information which does not fall within the Court of Appeal's narrow definition of a trade secret. It is claimed that the Court of Appeal said that information that came within Goulding J's second category cannot be protected by an express clause and that that is the wrong approach. We are sure that that reading is incorrect because we think the second category was meant to relate only to the skill and knowledge of the employee acquired during employment and that the Court of Appeal's approach is consistent with authority and is correct. However, others have not read the judgment in that way. They have seen the Court of Appeal's judgment as stating that even an express clause cannot validly protect confidential information unless it is a narrow trade secret or its equivalent.

The first reported expression of dissent occurred in *Balston Ltd v Headline Filters* [1987] FSR 330 where Scott J at pp 347 and 348 said, having quoted from the judgment of Neill LJ in *Faccenda*,

> both counsel before me express some reservations about that passage insofar as it suggests that confidential information cannot be protected by a suitably worded restrictive convenant binding on an ex-employee unless the information can be regarded as trade secret in the third of the categories described by Goulding J. I am bound to say that I share these reservations. I do not however think the Court of Appeal can have intended to exclude all information in Goulding J's second category from possible protection by a restrictive covenant.

He pointed out that trade secrets falling in to the third category would subsequent upon the judgment of the Court of Appeal, be protected under an implied term of the contract and therefore an expressed restrictive covenant would not be needed to protect trade secrets or their equivalent. Therefore Neill LJ must have been contemplating protection by an express restrictive covenant of confidential information in respect of which an obligation against use or disclosure after the determination of the employment could not be implied. He concluded that he declined to read the *Faccenda* case as holding that confidential information which could not be protected by an implied term *ipso facto* could not be protected by a suitably limited express covenant.

The concerns of Scott J were echoed by Harman J in *Systems Reliability Holdings Plc v Smith* [1990] IRLR 377 where the judge concluded (in a case where he was concerned with an express restriction on the use and disclosure of, in particular the knowledge acquired by the defendant during his employment of the ability to modify an old computer by a small addition so as to make a new product of significant commercial value) that the controversial part of Neill LJ's judgment did not bind him to hold that there cannot be in an express restrictive of covenant any restriction on information held by an ex-employee which is not a trade secret or something similar. He distinguished *Faccenda* on two bases; the first was that the case was clearly dealing with implied covenants and therefore any observations made by the court relating to express restrictions were clearly obiter. Secondly, that he was in fact dealing with a purchaser/vendor agreement and not with an employer/employee one. However these two bases are distinct and it is clear from Harman J's judgment that even if he had been dealing with an express confidential information clause in an employment agreement he would have declined to have followed *Faccenda*.

In *Lansing Linde Ltd v Kerr* [1991] 1 All ER 418, CA Staughton LJ discussed (a) the definition of trade secrets and (b) whether and if so how, trade secrets differ from confidential information. He defined trade secrets (at p 425 a–j) as:

   (a) information used in the trade or business;
   (b) of which the owner limits the dissemination or at least does not encourage or permit widespread publication;
   (c) and which if disclosed to a competitor would be liable to cause real or significant harm to the owner of the secret.

He said that was his preferred view of the meaning 'in this context' by which he seems to have meant that it was not an exhaustive definition. He continued 'it can thus include not only secret formulae for the manufacture of products but also in an appropriate case, the names of customers and the goods which they buy'. He anticipated that some might say that not all such information is a trade secret in ordinary parlance but if that were correct then 'the class of information which can justify the restriction is wider and extends to some confidential information which would not ordinarily be called a trade secret'. His approach is a clear indication that the apparent rigours of *Faccenda* are now being mitigated by judges because the definition of trade secrets given in that case has been found to be too narrow to be workable. Staughton LJ said that in this case plans for development of new products and for the discontinuance of existing products were likely to qualify as trade secrets or as confidential information which could be protected. The evidence showed that the defendant was aware of the timing of the fading out of old products, the timetable for the development of a prototype, the commencement of the production and of the sales of new products. Knox J at first instance had assumed that this information was confidential as he did prices and discounts allowed to customers. The Court of Appeal accepted his assumption. Butler-Sloss LJ said that the meaning of the words 'trade secrets' had developed since *Herbert Morris v Saxelby* and was now interpreted in the wider context of 'highly confidential information of a non-technical or non-scientific nature . . .'.

1.4 The employee's skill and knowledge

Although the courts are anxious to uphold the employer's right to have his business secrets protected they have ensured that the employee is not prevented from using, once he has left his employer, the general skill and knowledge which he has acquired during employment even though this may have been acquired at some cost to the employer. Frequently, a claim by an employer based on breach of confidence has failed as it was perceived to be an attempt to prevent the employee from working in the same field by offering his skill to another employer. Even in such an early case as *Morris (Herbert) Ltd v Saxelby* [1916] 1 AC 688 the plaintiffs abandoned a claim based on an express restraint because, as Lord Atkinson said, the clause prevented the defendant using '. . . in the service of some other employer that skill and knowledge which he had acquired by the exercise of his own mental faculties on what he had seen, heard, and had experience of in . . . employment . . .' (see also *Leng (Sir WC) & Co Ltd v Andrews* [1909] 1 Ch 763 where it was held, *inter alia*, that the defendant was entitled to use his acquired skill and knowledge for the benefit of himself and the benefit of the public who gained the advantage of him having had such admirable instruction). The courts have said that the general skills of an employee are his property and the employer can only protect *his* property—business secrets. The matter was discussed in *Commercial Plastics Ltd v Vincent* [1965] 1 QB 623 where it was said:

> It is clear from the authorities that the plaintiffs were not entitled to impose a restriction which would prevent the defendant from using in competition with the plaintiffs the skill and aptitude and general technical knowledge acquired by him in his employment by the plaintiffs. The restriction has to be justified in this case as being reasonably required for the protection of the plaintiffs' trade secrets by preventing the defendant from disclosing confidential information imparted to him by the plaintiffs in the course of his employment . . . . The defendant has no doubt gained much skill and aptitude and general technical knowledge with regard to the production of PVC calendered sheeting in general and particularly for the production of such sheeting for adhesive tape. But such things have become part of himself and he cannot be restrained from taking them away and using them.

A good example of general skill and knowledge was given by Younger LJ in *Attwood v Lamont*. There, a former customer of the plaintiffs gave evidence that he had met the defendant in the street and mentioned to him that he had heard he had set up his own business and wanted the defendant to cut him a suit. Younger LJ said 'The appellant is a dangerous rival of the plaintiff . . . not by reason of any knowledge of the plaintiff's connection or customers possessed by the appellant, but by reason of his own skill'.

Although the cases lay down the rule that a distinction between general skill and knowledge and business secrets must be maintained, it is impossible to formulate any general test. Each case turns on its own facts but once the boundary between protectable secrets and general skill and knowledge is crossed the employer cannot, even by way of express covenant, restrict the employee's ability to use those skills once employment has ended (*Faccenda Chicken Ltd v Fowler* [1985] 1 All ER 724).

Whilst it is clear that an employee cannot be prevented from using his general skill and knowledge once employment is over, there has been some doubt until recently as to whether the employer could exert any control over such use during employment or whether the law would imply such control. Brightman J in *United Sterling Corporation Ltd v Felton and Mannion* [1974] RPC 162 suggested that such control would be implied. However, in *Strange (SW) Ltd v Mann* [1965] 1 All ER 1069 Stamp J said that it was against public policy to allow an employer to exercise control by way of contract over an employee's skill and knowledge. It seems that he would have come to the same conclusion regarding the implication of such control. However, there is no doubt that many express terms which bind the employee to devote his time to his employment and to devote his energies to furthering his employer's business contemplate control over his skill and knowledge. Now, there is no doubt that the law will imply control over skill and knowledge during employment as being relevant to the general duty of fidelity (see *Faccenda Chicken*).

However, the fact that an employer may have evidence to support his claim does not preclude the employee from arguing that the employer has conducted himself in such a way that despite an express clause confidentiality no longer exists. For example, an employer who has allowed all his employees access to information or has entrusted it to the least skilled may find the court unsympathetic. Likewise, if visitors have been allowed to walk around his premises without restriction then the court will take this into account in its examination of the claim. This is especially so in the case of visiting competitors. If an employer does not prevent them availing themselves of the opportunity to learn business secrets how can he later seek to restrain an employee from using the same information. The existence of any secrecy which might have existed will have been destroyed by the indifference of the employer (see for example *Sun Printers Ltd v Westminster Press Ltd* [1982] IRLR 292). Mere negligence on the part of the employer may be sufficient to defeat confidence.

In practice, unless the employer can show that the employee has copied or physically removed a list of names or the details of a process then it may be very difficult to establish that the knowledge of the employee is exclusively due to confidential information. If the court is left in doubt as to whether the information might not have been acquired wholly or partly from the general experience gained by the employee then the employer will fail. A simple process may become part of his general knowledge but the more complex it is the less reasonable will be his claim that knowledge of it is part of his general skill and knowledge; the difficulties can be illustrated in *United Indigo Chemical Co Ltd v Robinson* [1931] 49 RPC 178. The plaintiffs were manufacturers of a boiler disincrustant and claimed that it had been produced by a secret process. They sought to restrain the defendant, who had been employed as their works manager, from using or disclosing information obtained in their service. They alleged that the product marketed by his company could only have been made by his wrongful use of their business secrets. They claimed that he had made and taken away copies or had memorised extracts from a book of secret formulae. The plaintiffs conceded that their product was not made of secret materials but secrecy arose from the way in which the materials were mixed, the temperature employed in various stages of manufacture and the method of testing the consistency of the product. The defendant denied that any secret process existed or that he had taken and used any information. Bennett J found that the defendant had not copied any formulae from the book; that he had not been warned as to secrecy when he entered his employment and that he was able to learn the relevant processes without difficulty; indeed this was information which he could not help acquiring in the course of his work. That knowledge had become his own and he had acquired it honestly and not surreptitiously. The plaintiff's claim failed.

There is no doubt that dishonest or surreptitious acquisition of information is usually overwhelming evidence that information was confidential and not part of the defendant's skill and knowledge. Indeed, the courts will take a pragmatic view of the complexity of the information and the employee's ability to remember it as a test of whether it has been wrongfully used/disclosed by him. In *Morris (Herbert) Ltd v Saxelby* there was no doubt that the defendant knew of business secrets but the court decided they were far too complicated and detailed for the defendant to have been able to carry them away in his head and as there was no evidence of actual copying, this part of the claim failed.

Another problem which frequently arises in practice is the claim by the employee that, after the end of his employment, he only used information which was already in his memory. This claim is then used as evidence of the fact that the information has become part of his general skill and knowledge and is not a business secret. The employee will further claim that he made no conscious effort to memorise the information. In *Printers and Finishers Ltd v Holloway* [1964] 3 All ER 731 Cross J made a distinction between the two concepts of remembering something and conscious memorising: 'The mere fact that the confidential information is not embodied in a document but is carried away by the employee in his head is not . . . of itself a reason against the granting of an injunction to prevent its use or disclosure by him'. He then went on to discuss whether an employee could use his recollection of any features of the plaintiff's plant, machinery or process which they claimed were peculiar to them even though they admitted that their competitors used similar machinery. Cross J in dismissing the claim, went on to say: 'Recalling matters of this sort is . . . quite unlike memorising a formula or list of customers or what was said (obviously in confidence) at a particular meeting'.

In order to show conscious memorising the employer will have to demonstrate that the complexity of the process or that the list of trade connections was so lengthy or important that an honest employee would have realised that these were the property of his employer. If however, it can be said that the employee had reasonable grounds for believing the information to be part of knowledge properly acquired during his employment then his defence will succeed. In the *United Sterling* case the basis for dismissing the motion was that there was no evidence that the defendant was given any special information which he ought to have regarded as a separate part of his stock of knowledge which an honest employee would have recognised as property of the employer.

1.5 Business methods

A further problem which frequently arises in practice is the ability of an employer to claim that information about 'business methods' or 'business organisation' constitutes a business secret which is protectable. The main problem with such a claim in the employment context is the difficulty of separating knowledge of business methods from the general skills etc of the employee. A claim in *Morris (Herbert)* regarding general business methods was defeated because of this difficulty. A similar view was taken in *Leng (Sir WC) v Andrews*. More recent authority has come to the same conclusion: see *Commercial Plastics Ltd v Vincent* [1965] 1 QB 623 per Pearson LJ and *Littlewoods Organisation Ltd v Harris* [1978] 1 All ER 1026 per Megaw LJ. Megaw LJ in *Littlewoods* however gave examples of what went beyond mere knowledge of the way in which the plaintiffs ran their business. These were the trends of mail order sales, the percentage and identity of the returns, the sources of manufacture, market research results, plans for mail order catalogues in the future and that Harris knew intimately the chairman of the manufacturers. See also *Greer v Sketchley Ltd* [1979] FSR 197. In *Amway Corporation v Eurway International Ltd* [1974] RPC 82 Brightman J described 'business methods, and paperwork' as 'mere know-how'. However, this case was an extreme example of disregard by the plaintiffs towards the quality of confidence (a tape recording was provided to, *inter alia*, the defendants, saying that the plaintiff's sales and marketing plan was available to anyone and could be copied by them: the tape gave details of the plan).

In *Under Water Welders* and *Repairers Ltd v Street and Longthorne* [1968] RPC 498 Buckley J, on motion, said nothing adverse about a clause which sought to make 'the policy' of the company a business secret.

The conclusion must be that it will be unusual, though not impossible to envisage, that business policy etc will be protectable. Relevant factors will be the type of business, the attitude that the employer has demonstrated towards the information and the precise type of information. If blanket assertions regarding business methods can be broken down into categories then a claim of confidence may succeed. For example information about prices can, in certain circumstances, constitute a business secret: see the discussion in *Faccenda Chicken Ltd v Fowler* [1985] 1 All ER 724 and *Lansing Linde Ltd v Kerr* [1991] 1 All ER 418.

2 Express duties once employment has ended

By including express restrictive covenants in an employment contract an employer will seek to achieve three goals once employment is over:

(a) to prevent the ex-employee canvassing orders from the employer's customers;

(b) to prevent the ex-employee competing with his business (usually within a defined geographical area);

(c) to prevent the ex-employee from using/disclosing any legitimate business secrets.

Note that (a) and (c) alone are not enough: neither would prevent an employee from serving those customers of his ex-employer who approached him. Similarly (b) alone may not be sufficient as the courts have laid down principles which effectively restrict the time for which any such covenant can run and also the geographical area it can cover. A clever employee would be able to set up business outside the restricted area and be able to serve former customers from there if (a) did not exist.

In summary, the law is that the courts will not enforce any post employment restraint on the activities of an employee unless the restraint is reasonable. What amounts to reasonableness is a question of fact and any answer approaching certainty can only be given after examining the circumstances of each case. However, what generally amounts to reasonableness can be examined by reference to three criteria although they inevitably overlap. The theoretical difference between the categories may well come down to a question of the burden of proof, though in practice a party seeking to uphold the validity of the restrictive covenant—usually the employer—has to make all the running. The three criteria are:

(a) Does the employer have an interest which merits protection?

(b) Is the restraint reasonable as between the parties?

(c) Is the restraint reasonable in the public interest?

One can sum up the position as being that a restraint will be invalid if it is imposed in order to prevent competition simpliciter or the use of personal skill and knowledge of the employee.

3 The existence of an interest which merits protection

The employer will be required to show that the restraint protects a valid interest: see *Morris (Herbert) Ltd v Saxelby* [1916] 1 AC 688 'a proprietary right'. There are generally two possible valid interests on which he may rely; special trade connections and business secrets. He is entitled to protect both of these: see *Morris (Herbert)* and *Attwood v Lamont* [1920] 3 KB 571.

3.1 The employer's special trade connections

The employer is entitled only to protect his business against use of his special trade connections by others but not to protection from competition from his former employee: see the *Morris (Herbert)* case. Protection from pure competition is known as 'a covenant in gross' and has always been rejected by the courts.

We use the phrase 'trade connections' rather than 'customer connections' because the interest is not limited to customers of the employer; it can in certain cases extend to potential customers and also to suppliers: see *Gledhow Autoparts Ltd v Delaney* [1965] 3 All ER 288 and *Marshall (Thomas) (Exporters) Ltd v Guinle* [1978] 3 WLR 116.

In practice the employer must show two things:

(a) the existence of trade connections which are to an extent 'special' to him; and

(b) that the employee is or will be in a position to take advantage of those special trade connections.

The first requirement will usually be simple to establish. The customers on a milk round are an obvious example of a special trade connection; see *Home Counties Dairies Ltd v Skilton* [1970] 1 All ER 1227 and *Wessex Dairies v Smith* [1935] 2 KB 80; so are the clients of a solicitor: see *Sanders v Parry* [1967] 1 WLR 753; as is a person who uses an estate agent's services: see *Scorer v Seymour-Johns* [1966] 3 All ER 347. All of these examples concerned customers who had or were likely to use the employer's services on more than one occasion. This is what made them 'special'. However, it is not necessary for an employer to prove that the connections are exclusive to him and they need not be long established. A customer may buy from several competitors in a given field; a supplier will invariably supply to more than one business and yet, depending on the facts, the employer may be able to argue that these connections are sufficiently special. Obviously, the more widely dispersed the loyalty of customers or suppliers, the less likely the employer will be able to succeed in claiming the speciality required. If a customer is known to buy from nearly every producer in the field then it will be very difficult to establish speciality.

In order to establish whether an employee was or is in a position to take advantage of his employer's special trade connections, it is necessary to examine the quality of the contact between the employee and those connections: 'the character of the work done' per Younger LJ in *Attwood's* case. It is usually not sufficient for the employer to demonstrate that *some* contact has taken place. It is suggested that there must usually be a special element in the employee/connection contact which creates a reasonable risk that the employee will be able to appropriate some part of the business when he leaves because of the chance that customers would seek him out on account of his knowledge of their requirements. A milkman who serves the same customers every day and who is usually known to them personally will clearly have sufficient contact. It was said in *Scorer v Seymour-Johns* [1966] 3 All ER 347 per Salmon LJ that the special element can be characterised as the connection relying on the employee to the extent that they regard him as the business rather than his employer: in that case the employer's business had many recurring customers (*cf Fellowes & Son v Fisher* [1975] 2 All ER 829). He said 'When the employee was in the Kingsbridge office he *was* in effect the Kingsbridge office. Every customer who came into that office dealt with him. He was in a position in which he would have every opportunity of gaining knowledge of the customers' business and influence over the customers'. Moreover, he was in sole charge of a relatively new branch office. However, it is important to realise that it is not always necessary to be able to characterise an employee 'as the office'. The factual question is whether sufficient quality of contact has been demonstrated. A clear example of an employee who was not in a position to influence customers is found in *Morris (Herbert) v Saxelby*. The real question is whether the employee has any power over customers. See also *Stenhouse Australia Ltd v Phillips* [1974] AC 391 (insurance brokers), and also *Routh v Jones* [1947] 1 All ER 758: '. . . the character of a general medical practice is such that one who is employed therein as a medical assistant, necessarily acquires such a special and intimate knowledge of the patients of the business that the employers . . . are entitled to protect themselves against unfair competition on the servant's part', per Evershed J.

Can mere contact ever be enough? In *Gilford Motor Co Ltd v Horne* [1933] Ch 935 Romer LJ suggested that mere contact between an employee and a customer was sufficient. Whatever may have been said in the 1930s—even if it reflected current views then—cannot be correct today. If mere contact were always enough then manifest injustice would be done in many cases. For example, a telephonist in a large company may have contact with a customer by answering his calls but this cannot be a reasonable basis for preventing that person from working for a trade competitor. Even employees who come into personal, face to face contact with the employer's trade connections, cannot always be said to have sufficient quality of contact. For example, a receptionist at a solicitor's office will no doubt meet clients but it would be most unusual for her to be in a position to take advantage of that connection to the detriment of her employer once she has left his employment.

The case of *Strange (SW) Ltd v Mann* [1965] 1 All ER 1069 is an example of frequent contact still not being sufficient. The defendant who was employed as the manager of a bookmakers only met customers once (if at all) as most business was done by telephone and was of a credit nature. It was immaterial to the customers who dealt with them on the telephone. Even though the defendant knew the names and addresses of all customers, the quality of contact was not of the degree required in order to establish that he was ever regarded as 'being the business' or even had any influence over the customers.

What of special trade connections introduced by an employee; can he freely take these with him when he leaves? It often happens that when an employee enters new employment he legitimately brings with him trade connections of use to his new employer. When he eventually leaves that employer how far can the latter control the ex-employee's ability to deal with the clients which he brought with him. Such a problem was analysed in *M & S Drapers v Reynolds* [1956] 3 All ER 814 when Denning LJ said:

> I do not . . . see why the employers should be able to forbid him to call on the people whom he already knew before he worked for them . . . . His knowledge of these people and his influence with them, was due to his own efforts—or at any rate they were nothing to do with these employers. His goodwill with those customers belonged to him and cannot reasonably be taken from him by a covenant of this kind.

Moreover, Hodson LJ said that as well as the period of restriction, an added circumstance which has to be taken into account in assessing reasonableness was the fact that many of the customers covered by the covenant had been introduced by the defendant. The other members of the court were of a similar view.

Although there is no example in the cases, it seems possible for an employer to appropriate the goodwill which an employee brings with him by express provision. Such is common in partnership agreements.

The final point to consider in this section is the ability of an employer to seek protection for the trade connections not only of his own company but also of other associated companies. In *Leetham (Henry) & Sons Ltd v Johnstone-White* [1907] 1 Ch 322 Farwell LJ commented:

> ... a man whose business is a corn miller's business, and who requires to protect that, cannot, if he has also a furniture business, require the covenantee who enter into his service as an employee in the corn business to enter into covenants restricting him from entering into competition with him in the furniture business also, because it is not required for the protection of the corn business in which the man is employed, however much it may be beneficial to the individual person, the owner both of the corn business and of the furniture business.

That is a clear example where there was no real common interest between the businesses. But, it did not accord with the facts of the case before him in which all companies within a group were millers. The Court of Appeal decided however that the defendant had really only contracted with one company within the group and that regarding the area in which it did its business a countrywide restraint was unreasonable. It rejected the idea that the associated companies which together did have a countrywide business were in any way relevant. By applying a strict rule of corporate personality it decided that a restriction which benefited any person other than the contracting parties was 'in gross' and therefore unenforceable. In *Stenhouse Australia Ltd v Phillips* [1974] AC 391 the Privy Council chose to ignore strict rules of corporate personality between different companies in a group because of the existence of a patent identity of interest. It now seems that only in those cases where there is no identity of interest will the problem of other businesses gaining the benefit of a restrictive covenant be at all important and the courts will not take account of the doctrine of incorporation or of privity of contract if such an identity exists. This is further demonstrated by the decision in *Littlewoods Organisation Ltd v Harris* [1978] 1 All ER 1026.

3.2 Business secrets

There is no doubt that business secrets are recognised as constituting an interest meriting protection. In the *Littlewoods* case in which the court upheld a 12 month restraint allied to protectable business secrets, Lord Denning MR said that the information acquired by Harris was confidential: 'It has been acquired at great expense and by great expertise by Littlewoods. No servant should be at liberty to carry it off to a rival in trade and thus save him the expense and expertise of doing it himself'.

The employer is entitled only to adequate protection for his business secrets: the concept of adequacy prevents the employee being restricted from using his general skills and knowledge.

The only doubt about this was raised by the Court of Appeal in *Faccenda Chicken Ltd v Fowler* [1985] 1 All ER 724 where the court specifically left open the question whether additional protection should be afforded to an employer where the former employee is not seeking to earn his living by making use of the body of skill, knowledge and experience which he has acquired but is merely selling the knowledge to a third party (see p 79 above).

In *Commercial Plastics Ltd v Vincent* [1965] 1 QB 623 the restrictive covenant read: 'In view of the highly technical and confidential nature of this appointment you have agreed not to seek employment with any of our competitors in the PVC calendering field for at least one year after leaving our employ'.

Therefore, the basic question was: what were business secrets? There were none in the general field of PVC calendering but only in the special field of PVC for adhesive tape. As the restriction sought to prevent the defendant from taking employment with a competitor in the general PVC calendering field it was held to be too wide.

4 Reasonableness between the parties: competition and canvassing

The fact that an employee has agreed to be bound by a restrictive covenant does not in itself make that restriction reasonable between the parties. Instead, the courts will subject the clause to the objective test of reasonableness. But remember the words of Glidwell LJ in *Rex Stewart Jeffries Parker Ginsberg Ltd v Parker* [1988] IRLR 483: 'in the end, whether a particular provision is or is not reasonable to protect the employer's legitimate interest is a matter of impression'.

In the area of competition and canvassing there are three general headings under which the courts will examine the existence of reasonableness of a restraint:

4.1 Restricted activities

If the employer seeks by contractual restraint to restrict the activities of a former employee by proscribing the types of business in which the employee may become engaged once employment is over then he can only do so if he can establish a close connection betwee the restriction and the work done by the employee prior to leaving. Moreover, the employer can only protect himself from activities by his employee which might reasonably affect the customer connection which has been built up.

The first question which has to be answered is: what is the employer's business? This is a question of fact but it is crucial. See *Routh v Jones* [1947] 1

All ER 758. The defendant was prohibited from practising 'in any department of medicine, surgery or midwifery'. This clause was construed by both Evershed J and the Court of Appeal to include acting as a consultant. Therefore, the plaintiffs, a partnership in general medical practice, were seeking to prevent an employee once he had left, from, *inter alia*, practising as a consultant within a certain area and for a certain time. The court found that as practice by the defendant as a consultant could not injure the plaintiffs' professional business, the clause was too wide in that it sought to encompass activities in which the plaintiffs did not have a legitimate interest. Moreover, the covenant went on to restrict the defendant's ability to accept any professional appointment. This was held to be reasonable during employment but was construed as being too wide post employment as it would prevent the defendant becoming a medical officer of health in which capacity he could not prejudice the plaintiff's goodwill. See also *Jenkins v Reid* [1948] 1 All ER 471. Moreover, it may not be enough for an employer to say 'I'm a wine merchant and my ex-employee is now working as a wine merchant and so I am entitled to enforce an express restriction'. It may be that the ex-employee is now working in an entirely different area of that business, such as wholesale, whereas his former employer's business is retail. The distinction between the wholesale and retail sides of a business was discussed in *Rogers v Maddocks* [1892] 3 Ch 346.

Once it has been established what the relevant scope of the employer's business is, the next question is whether the restriction does no more than protect any existing customer connection. In *Technograph Printed Circuits Ltd v Chalwyn Ltd* [1967] RPC 339 a restrictive covenant prevented the employee for a period of two years after the end of his employment from being associated with any company in the UK concerned with manufacture of 'printed electrical circuits'. It was found that such a restriction would prevent employees from being associated with a manufacturer of single-sided printed circuit boards and yet it was only in relation to multi-layered printed circuit boards that the plaintiff had any interest. Therefore the restrictions went beyond what was necessary.

Some restrictions go too far in their precision and thus are judged unreasonable whilst others are struck down as being too imprecise and/or wide. An example of the first type is found in *Morris (Herbert) Ltd v Saxelby* [1916] 1 AC 688 where the defendant was bound for seven years after employment not to work in the UK or Ireland in the sale or manufacture of pulley blocks, hand overhead runways, electric overhead runways or hand overhead travelling cranes. The court found that all his experience had been in these areas; he had always worked for the plaintiffs and therefore the clause rendered him unemployable over a very wide area for a significant time. The clause was held to be unreasonable. Later cases have also insisted that if an employee is to be prevented from working in that area in which he has gained great expertise then the covenant is unlikely to be upheld. See *Commercial Plastics Ltd v Vincent* [1965] 1 QB 623.

Examples of the second type are cases such as *Davies, Turner and Co v Lowen* (1891) 64 LT 655 in which a clause sought to prevent an employee entering any business similar to that 'now or hereafter to be carried on' by the employer; or *Perls v Saalfeld* [1892] 2 Ch 149 in which a clause preventing an employee from accepting 'another situation as clerk or agent' was struck down.

4.2 Geographical and similar restrictions

The geographical area covered by the restrictive covenant must have a reasonable nexus with the need to protect the employer's trade connections. It is usually the case that the more extensive the area sought to be covered the less likely it is to be reasonable. It is clear that if no space limit is expressed in the covenant it will be construed to impose a worldwide ban: see *Dowden and Pook Ltd v Pook* [1904] 1 KB 45 and *Commercial Plastics Ltd v Vincent*, but *cf Littlewoods Organisation Ltd v Harris* [1978] 1 All ER 1026.

In the *Nordenfelt* case a clause which included a worldwide restriction was upheld: however that was a very special case and in any event dealt with a business sale and not with employment. In *White, Tomkins and Courage v Wilson* (1907) 23 TLR 469 a worldwide restriction lasting five years on a brewery manager was upheld. However, in that case there may have been protectable business secrets belonging to the plaintiffs, although the report is unclear on this. The more usual attitude to such restrictions in employment cases is set out in *Vandervell Products Ltd v McLeod* [1957] RPC 185 at 191 per Lord Evershead MR: 'This is not a case of the sale of goodwill but of a master and servant, and it must be rare . . . to find an ex-servant restrained from exercising his trade in a competing business anywhere in the world . . .'. In *Commercial Plastics* it was argued that although the restriction was of worldwide ambit that width was cut down by a reference to 'competitors' of the plaintiffs and that such limitation made it reasonable. Pearson LJ said in response to this: 'There would have been considerable force in that argument if the evidence had supported it'; however he concluded that there was no evidence to prove that the plaintiffs needed the potentially worldwide restriction.

In *Scorer v Seymour-Johns* [1966] 1 WLR 1419 Dankwerts LJ said 'in present day conditions a radius of five miles is not a great distance, particularly in a district which is mainly rural'. This highlights two points: the first is that the ease of travel is relevant—a distance of five miles in the 19th century was effectively a much greater restriction than the same distance today. Secondly, it shows that the same distance in a town or city will usually be much more restrictive than in the country: quite simply, the potential market is much greater in the town or city and therefore the likelihood of the employer having protectable trade connections over the whole city is less likely. However, these points are subject to the facts: if an employer is a seed merchant or feed supplier a comparison between country and town may well be irrelevant.

It is generally true to say that preventing an employee from working or canvassing in a certain area is often a crude way for an employer to obtain protection for his trade connections and this crudeness has often resulted in an area covenant being held unreasonable: see *Attwood v Lamont* [1920] 3 KB 571. In many cases if a pure geographical restriction had been supplanted by a restriction preventing the employee from soliciting certain customers then it would have stood a greater chance of success. However, there are situations in which a geographical restriction is necessary, especially if the customers cannot be readily identified—thus making detection and enforcement very difficult. See *Empire Meat Co Ltd v Patrick* [1939] 2 All ER 85 and *White (Marion) Ltd v*

Francis [1972] 1 WLR 1423. In *Strange (SW) Ltd v Mann* [1965] 1 All ER 1069, Stamp J rejected the defendant's argument that an area restriction is always inappropriate in the case of an exclusively credit business. The reason for this was that a covenant not to deal with those who were customers during employment is not always sufficient for the employer. He may want to guard against the danger of the employee joining a business rival. However, he found on the facts that although a non-solicitation covenant would have been reasonable an area covenant which included both Cheltenham and Gloucester was too wide.

Covenants which restrain an employee from competing in any area in which his employer has customers, were frequently regarded as reasonable in a number of 19th and early 20th century cases. It is submitted that such clauses are unlikely to be upheld today unless there are exceptional circumstances. An example of such a case is *Standex International Ltd v C B Blades* [1976] FSR 114 in which the Court of Appeal upheld a restraint which lasted for five years and which prevented the employee from being engaged in or concerned with the business of mould engraving within Great Britain and Northern Ireland. The particular feature of this case was that the plaintiffs were the only manufacturers in the field. It is submitted that market share is the key to this decision. A pure geographical restriction limited to a five mile radius from the employer's place of business was upheld in *Scorer*, but Salmon LJ stated that he was troubled as to whether the employer's interests might not have been adequately protected by a restraint which prevented the defendant from doing business with persons who had been customers of the employer at the office of which the defendant had been in charge. He concluded that such a covenant might be impractical because breach might be very difficult to prove. In our submission, in most cases a pure area covenant related to the prevention of solicitation/canvassing by a former employee will invariably be indefensible unless the employer can demonstrate that a less oppressive clause would result in great difficulties regarding the detection of breach.

In *Spencer v Marchington* [1988] IRLR 392 the defendant in a counter claim sought to enforce a clause which read:

> Upon termination of this employment you shall not for a period of two years after such termination, either alone or in partnership with any other person or persons, or as servant or agent or officer of any person, concern or company, carry on or in any way be engaged or concerned or interested in the business of any employment agency within a radius of 25 miles of the Banbury office and 10 miles of the Leamington office.

The judge pointed out that 25 miles from Banbury in all directions is an area of nearly 2,000 square miles. He found that the great majority of the defendant's customers were in Banbury itself or at Bicester which was under 14 miles from Banbury. The judge concluded that it was not necessary to extend the area beyond 20 miles at the most from Banbury especially as the defendant's goodwill could have been as effectively protected by a clause which would have prevented the plaintiff from dealing with the defendant's customers. He pointed out that the object of the rule of public policy against too wide an area on a former employee's future activities is not primarily to protect the employee but to keep the market open to prospective customers, to maximise the number of, in the present case, employment agencies available to them and to promote competition among them. See also *Office Angels Ltd v Rainer-Thomas* (1991) *The Times*, 11 April.

Another type of crude geographical covenant is one which seeks to restrain an employee from competing in any area in which he was active. This is generally preferable to the first example, however it seems a very heavy handed way of providing protection. The existence of such a provision was the only reason why the employer failed in *Gledhow Autoparts Ltd v Delaney* [1965] 3 All ER 288 and in *Marley Tile Co Ltd v Johnson* [1982] IRLR 75. Take the example of a salesman who visits customers regularly in Dorset. His employer has only a small market share there. When he leaves the employer the latter may claim that his former employee should not canvass or deal with those customers, but we can see no reason why he cannot canvass others in Dorset. Obviously if that employer can demonstrate substantial and extensive goodwill in the area he will be able to rely on this type of clause though he does not need, as Dankwerts J said in *Kerchiss v Colora Printing Inks Ltd* [1960] RPC 235, to go so far as to prove sales in every part of the area in question. Indeed, in that case the defendants succeeded even though they could not show any business in one particular country at all; however, they did have clients in the remaining 15 countries covered by the clause. It must be remembered that the particular product and the nature of the customers can be crucial. In *Kerchiss*, although a wide geographical restraint was upheld, the company was not selling to the general public—if it had been the restriction would certainly have been too wide—but to printers who wanted particular types of ink.

Other problems associated with crude geographical restraints are that the size of the area and its character may have been drawn too widely as in *Mason v Provident Clothing and Supply Co Ltd* [1913] 1 KB 65, and also the difficulty encountered when the prohibited areas are defined by reference to the employer's places of business. In *Clarke, Sharp and Co Ltd v Solomon* (1921) 37 TLR 176 the restriction sought to prevent the defendant from working in the same trade as his employers for a period of five years in an area within a five mile radius of any railway station or port from which the employers then or at any future time during employment delivered coal. The Court of Appeal held that the restriction was clearly unreasonable: not only was there not sufficient contact between the defendant and customers to warrant protection, but the result of upholding the covenant would have been to restrict the defendant even if the plaintiffs had supplied only a single ton of coal from any station or port.

A problem can arise when dealing with branch offices. In *Scorer's* case, the branch in Dartmouth was effectively run as a separate entity from the one in Kingsbridge. The defendant worked at the latter office and had no real connection with the former. The covenant which restricted him working within ten miles of both offices was held to be too wide; fortunately for the employer the restriction was severable and that part applicable to Kingsbridge enforced.

However, there are more sophisticated types of restraint which because they are limited to a specific category of persons—usually customers—necessarily import a geographical element, though as Harman LJ said in *Plowman (GW) & Son Ltd v Ash* [1964] 1 WLR 468, they do not usually mention an area. They are usually called non-solicitation clauses.

The first type concerns a promise not to solicit any of the employer's customers with whom the employee dealt either generally or within a certain time period before employment ceased. This type of clause is the most acceptable to courts because it covers only the employer's trade connections; it also has the merit of certainty so far as the employee is concerned (see *Gledhow's* case). The clause may be limited to actual solicitation and therefore it is not breached by an employee who is approached by a customer. In order to cover that possibility the clause should include words such as 'or deal with'. However, there are objections to the use of such a wider term and, although these may come under the heading of the public interest, it is convenient to discuss them here. The basic objection is that a customer should be free to buy where it best suits him: unencumbered by an agreement between others. Moreover, there may be a very good reason why the customer has decided to do business with the former employee: he may be more efficient and/or provide goods at a lower price. To deny a customer the ability to take advantage of these matters cannot be in the public interest. Also, if the employee were found to be in breach even if the customer had approached him then he would be in the embarrassing position of turning the customer away—this is of benefit to neither and there is no guarantee that the customer will go back to the former employer. Moreover, a prohibition on dealing may encourage further breaches which the employer may find difficult and costly to detect. That leads to another waste of resources. However, it has to be stated that these worries do not appear to reflect current judicial thinking and it seems safe to rely on the wider version of this clause although there will always be the residual problem of detection.

Can a non-solicitation clause legitimately extend beyond actual customers and seek to cover those with whom the employee came into contact in order to get business for his old employer? In theory, we see no reason why such a clause should not be reasonable. The answer will depend on the facts of each case: relevant matters will be the type of business, whether the employee knew about the precise requirements of the contact and how long ago the enquiry was made. In *Gledhow's* case both Sellers and Diplock LJ indicated that it may be possible to have such a clause. A restraint of this type sometimes encompasses former customers of the employer (ie those who are no longer his customers). What interest the employer can have in this connection, apart from the chance that they may return, is unclear. However, in *Plowman's* case, after some hesitation, Harman LJ held that a clause which did not exclude people who had ceased to be customers of the employer and therefore formed no part of the present goodwill of his business, was still valid. He did so on the basis that hope of them becoming customers again of the employer should not be abandoned. This is not very convincing. There is, though, little doubt that an argument which claims that a clause is unreasonable simply because it includes some former customers is unlikely to succeed. Indeed an injunction may be granted to cover customers who apparently have no intention of doing business in the future with the plaintiffs. In *John Michael Design Plc v Cooke* [1987] 2 All ER 332 the facts were that towards the end of 1985 the defendants, an associate director and a senior designer employed by the plaintiffs, left to set up business on their own. Their contracts of employment with the plaintiffs contained a covenant not to canvass, solicit or accept from any client of the plaintiffs any business in competition with or similar to that of the plaintiffs for a period of two years from the termination of the contracts. In December 1986 the plaintiffs learnt that clients of theirs were proposing to place a contract with the defendants' firm and were not, in any event, going to do further business with the plaintiffs. The plaintiffs sought an injunction to restrain the defendants from acting in breach of their covenants. The judge found that the covenants were *prima facie* enforceable and that the plaintiffs were entitled to an interlocutory injunction pending trial in general form, but on the balance of convenience he excluded the particular contract from the scope of the injunction. The plaintiffs successfully appealed. It was held that although a covenant restraining competition by an ex-employee would always be looked at closely, if the court decided that it would be just to grant an interlocutory injunction pending trial by way of enforcement of that obligation, the plaintiff was *prima facie* entitled to protection in respect of all his customers who fell within the ambit of the covenant and, in granting the injunction, it was wrong in principle to try to exclude some customers or some parties on whom it would otherwise bite. The fact that a particular customer would not do any further business with a plaintiff was not *per se* a reason for excluding that customer from the scope of the injunction since such an eventuality was the very thing against which the covenant was designed to give protection.

Another version of the more sophisticated covenant is one which seeks to prevent solicitation of any of the employer's customers irrespective of whether the employee dealt with them. However, it is important to remember than an employer is *not* entitled to be protected by a covenant which restricts the employee in relation to customers over whom he had no control. The reason is because the employer is only entitled to restrictions which are necessary (ie without which his business might or would be endangered). Typically, this covenant usually restricts the employee from dealing with those who were the employer's customers at any time in the past or future (ie not merely during employment). Unless it can be construed so as to refer to the period of employment and only to those customers over whom the employee had any control (which is unlikely), the clause is bad. It gives excessive protection to the employer and is embarrassing to the employee: see *Plowman (GW) and Son Ltd v Ash* [1964] 2 All ER 10. An even more limited version—restricting the employee from dealing with any of the employer's customers during the period of employment irrespective of contact—may be too wide in most cases: see *Marley Tile Co Ltd v Johnson* [1982] IRLR 75. However, in *Plowman's* case, it was upheld by the Court of Appeal. Harman LJ dealth with an argument that the clause, which precluded canvassing of any persons who were at any time customers of the employer during the period of employment, was too wide because it was not restricted to customers with whom the employee had come into contact and did so by relying on *Gilford Motor Co Ltd v Horne* [1933] Ch 935 in which the Court of Appeal, overruling Farwell J at first instance, had come to the conclusion that such contact was not necessary. However, he gave no reasons for so doing and we are of the opinion that the prudent draftsman will not seek to include this type of covenant. It is inherently vague and potentially embarrassing to the employee as was recognised by Edmund Davies

LJ in *Plowman's* case. An even more extreme version of this clause which seeks to prevent the employee 'dealing' with such customers, is in our view, *a fortiori* even more objectionable. See also the *Marley Tile Co Ltd v Johnson* [1982] IRLR 75 in which *Plowman* was distinguished. Lord Denning MR pointed out that in *Plowman* the firm's customers were all situated around Spalding, it only employed five salesmen and it might well have been that Ash knew all of the customers. However, in the instant case the relevant customers numbered 2,500. Johnson could not have had influence over more than a small percentage of them. The clause was therefore unreasonably restrictive (see also *Spafax Ltd v Dommett* (1972) 6 July (unreported)). In *Spafax Ltd v Harrison* [1980] IRLR 442 a narrower clause was upheld. It prevented the employee, a branch manager, from soliciting any person 'to whom during the period of 12 months prior to . . . termination of his employment the manager or to his knowledge any member of his staff shall have sold such goods on behalf of the company'.

    Plowman v Ash has been recently applied by Millett J in *Business Seating (Renovations) Ltd v Broad* [1989] ICR 729. In that case the plaintiff carried on the business of repairing or renovating office furniture and commercial seating. It had an associated company with the same directors and shareholders which carried on the business of manufacturing and selling new office furniture and commercial seating. The two companies shared many customers but there were also customers of each which were not customers of the other. The defendant was employed by the plaintiff as a sales representative. Having worked for the plaintiff for just over two years he resigned and within a few days took employment with a company which supplied office furniture and fittings and had a rather wider and larger range of activities than either the plaintiff or its associated company. One per cent of the turnover of his new employer was concerned with re-upholstering and renovating office chairs and other furniture so that to a small extent it appeared to compete with the plaintiff and to a larger extent with the business of the plaintiff's associated company. The plaintiff sought an injunction to prevent the defendant from breaching clause 13 of his contract of employment. That stated:

> For a period of one year after the termination of the agreement for any cause whatsoever the employee shall not canvass, solicit or endeavour to take away from the company or any associated employer the business of any customers or clients of the company or any associated employer who have been customers or clients of the company or an associated employer during the period of one year immediately preceding the termination of the employment.

It was argued by the defendant that this clause was in unreasonable restraint of trade and therefore invalid. It was complained that the clause was not limited to customers who were known to the defendant whilst he was employed by the plaintiff or with whom he had had any contact. Moreover it was said that it included discontinued customers and was not limited to the areas within which the defendant had worked for the plaintiff. He worked only in two areas and the plaintiff's business was nationwide. Millett J found that the principles set out by Harman LJ in *Plowman's* case applied here and that these arguments were unsustainable. However he went on to accept the defendant's objection that the clause was unreasonable to the extent that it extended to prohibiting canvassing or soliciting customers or clients of the associated company of his employer. The judge pointed out that insofar as any customer was a customer of both companies then soliciting of his custom would be within that part of the clause which he had already held to be reasonable. He stated that he was concerned with the position of the defendant in relation to customers or clients of the associated company who were not customers or clients of the plaintiff company during the relevant period with whom the defendant had no contact and of whose existence he might have been wholly unaware. He found that the plaintiff had no connection at all with the associated company itself or any of its customers who were not customers of the plaintiff. He said that so far as the plaintiff was concerned its only interest in customers of the associated company was as potential customers of its own. He regarded it as an unwarranted extention of *Plowman* to uphold the validity of a non-solicitation covenant which prohibited solicitation of potential customers of the plaintiff notwithstanding that they are defined as existing customers of some other connected business. It is our view that if they had been potential customers of the plaintiff in the sense that they had made enquiries of the plaintiff or had responded in some positive way to canvassing by the plaintiff then the plaintiff could have legitimately protected that connection. See also *Hinton & Higgs (UK) Ltd v Murphy* [1989] IRLR 519 (Court of Session).

4.3 Time

Time and area are often very closely connected. When considering whether the area is too wide the court is bound to consider the duration of the restraint. It, therefore, follows that if it is felt necessary to have a wide or pure area restraint this may only be perceived to be reasonable if the period of the restraint is short. The Court of Appeal in *Plowman's* case seem to have found in the plaintiff's favour, in spite of many misgivings because the restraint lasted for two years. There is no mean reasonable time, though Lord Denning MR was frequently keen on 12 months (see *Fellowes & Son v Fisher* [1975] 2 All ER 829; *Office Overload Ltd v Gunn* [1977] FSR 39).

The length of time is only reasonable if it does no more than is necessary to protect the employer. This has been characterised as the period in which it takes an employer to start a new employee at the task and for the latter to have a reasonable opportunity to demonstrate his effectiveness to customers. In general, life-long restrictions are bad, see *Attwood v Lamont* [1920] 3 KB 571 and *Leng (Sir WC) and Co Ltd v Andrews* [1909] 1 Ch 763 for the courts will not allow a person who has been trained or gained some aptitude in an area to be deprived of using that ability for the rest of his life. In *Jenkins v Reid* a lifetime restriction on a medical practitioner was held unreasonable (*cf Fitch v Dewes* [1921] 2 AC 158 which is surely wrong on this pont). In *Wyatt v Kreglinger and Fernau* [1933] 1 KB 793 a similar view was taken even though the plaintiff was aged 61. This seems to have been an extreme case and of doubtful weight now.

In *Stenhouse Australia Ltd v Phillips* [1974] AC 391 a five year restriction on an insurance broker who had been the managing director of various companies within a group was upheld by the Privy Council and an indication was given on how to approach questions of time. Lord Wilberforce said:

> The question is not how long the employee could be expected to enjoy by virtue of his employment, a competitive edge over others seeking the client's business. It is, rather, what is a reasonable time during which the employer is entitled to protection against solicitation of clients with whom the employee had contact and influence during employment and who were not bound to the employer by contract or by stability of association. This question . . . [we] do not consider can advantageously form the subject of direct evidence. It is for the judge, after informing himself as fully as he can of the facts and circumstances relating to the employer's business, the nature of the employer's interest to be protected, and the likely effect on this if solicitation to decide whether the contractual period is reasonable or not.

In *Dairy Crest v Pigott* (1989) ICR 92 the court was concerned with an application to enforce a clause which read:

> Not at any time within two years after the termination or cessation in any manner of the service hereby created, either as master or servant to canvass, solicit or serve or cause to be served with milk or dairy produce, any person, firm or company who during the employee's service with the board and within one year prior to such termination or cessation has been so supplied by the employee on behalf of the board, and at the time of such soliciting or alleged soliciting continues to reside or carry on business at any address at which milk was supplied by the employee on behalf of the board.

The defendant was a milkman. The Court of Appeal having considered the judgment of Lord Wilberforce in Stenhouse and applying *American Cyanamid* granted the injunction. Balcombe LJ said that he shared some of the doubts of the judge at first instance about whether a two year period was or was not reasonable but that he could not say that there was no issue of law here to be decided. There was therefore a serious question to be tried. The injunction was granted. In *Rex Stewart, Jeffries, Parker, Ginsberg Ltd v Parker* [1988] IRLR 483 the Court of Appeal at the interlocutory stage held that a clause which operated to restrain a managing director who had been with the plaintiffs for seven years from soliciting customers for a period of 18 months was not unreasonable. It was pointed out that he had had opportunities to develop relationships with customers.

In *Lawrence David Ltd v Ashton* [1989] IRLR 22 the Court of Appeal granted an injunction in the terms discussed below in Chapter 21 in relation to a clause which sought to restrain the defendant for a period of two years from the determination of his contract of employment from carrying on or being employed in the business of manufacturing certain products.

4.4 Miscellaneous criteria

A number of cases have also pointed out that it is important to examine:

(a) the employee's position;
(b) the type of business; and
(c) the notice period under the contract

in order to gauge what is reasonable.

The employee's position

In *Kores Manufacturing Co Ltd v Kolok Manufacturing Co Ltd* [1957] 3 All ER 158 it was said that a restriction of five years was too long for a manual worker and for all categories of employee up to assistant works manager. Whilst a similar view will be taken in nearly all cases involving manual workers, it is unwise to assume that the latter part of this judgment will always be followed: it all depends on the facts of the case; particularly the type of business. In *M & S Drapers v Reynolds* [1956] 3 All ER 814, the Court of Appeal had to examine a restrictive covenant which gave the employer protection from competition/ canvassing for five years after the end of employment. During that period a former employee was forbidden from soliciting any person whose name had been on the books of the company and upon whom the employee had called during a period of three years before the end of employment. The defendant had been employed as a credit draper and, as he had called on customers, had considerable personal contact and influence over them, however the court held that five years was too long for a man in the defendant's position, especially as he received only a modest wage. The point was highlighted by Hodson LJ when he said 'The managing director is not regarded in the same light as the traveller or canvasser' (ie the latter is not as great a threat to the employer as the former and therefore any time restriction should reflect this). It is not only employees who are protected by the vigilance of the courts regarding periods of time. In both *Schroeder* and *Clifford Davis*, contracts which were to run for ten years were struck down as unreasonable as was 21 years in *Esso Petroleum Co Ltd v Harper's Garage (Stourport) Ltd* [1968] AC 269.

The type of business

In *M & S Drapers* this point was crucial to Morris LJ's judgments:

> ... the customers of one credit draper are likely to be canvassed by other credit drapers. In a sphere where competition is normally free, since every householder is a potential purchaser, and where successful selling must to some extent depend on the personal abilities of particular salesmen and also to some extent on the quality or attractiveness of the goods which the salesman's employer can offer. ...

A five year restriction was too long.

Length of notice

In *Gledhow Autoparts Ltd v Delaney* [1965] 3 All ER 288, two members of the Court of Appeal commented on how length of notice can be an indication of reasonableness regarding time. Diplock LJ pointed out that the defendant's employment could have been terminated only two weeks after it started and yet according to the clause, he would have been restrained from seeking any orders in similar goods, in any district he had operated (even though he may have called on very few customers) for a period of three years. The clause was struck down on other grounds, so this comment was *obiter* but it is submitted that it has much force. The shorter the period of notice the less important to the company the employee's services would appear to be and the more lowly his position is likely to be. Accordingly, the perceived need for protection is diminished. An alternative view, found for example in the judgment of Hodson LJ in the *M & S Drapers'* case that the period of notice is really within the ambit of consideration, the adequacy of which is not a concern of the court, is, it is submitted, unduly restrictive and technical. The practical and better view is that there is an inextricable link between reasonableness and the adequacy of consideration.

Soliciting/enticing away/employing former colleagues

It is not uncommon now to see in employment contracts a provision which restrains the employee from soliciting or enticing away from his former employer other employees. Apparently an injunction was granted to prevent an employee from doing this at first instance in *Rex Stewart etc v Parker* [1988] IRLR 483 however the case is not reported on this point; the Court of Appeal only considered the non-solicitation of customers part of the clause as the period applicable to the non-encitement of employees had expired by the time of Court of Appeal hearing. However there is doubt as to whether such a restraint can be valid. There is no authority on the point but the competing arguments for and against whether an employer has an interest meriting protection which relates to his current employees are obvious. The employer will argue that he has a legitimate interest in maintaining a stable workforce. He will point out that in order to recruit new staff he may have to spend money in advertising the post or employing an employment agency and that once those staff arrive they will have to be trained. There will therefore be a period during which they will be relatively unproductive. On the other hand, it could be argued that such a restraint is an indirect restraint on the remaining employees who might be open to enticement or solicitation by the employee who has left. This matter is bound to come before the courts before long. A restraint which seeks to prevent a defendant from working with or employing former colleagues is highly unlikely to be upheld by the courts. This version of the covenant is particularly objectionable as it attempts to prevent former colleagues from approaching the defendant even if he has not solicited them.

Potential customers

Can a plaintiff claim to protect itself against solicitation etc of 'potential customers'? The answer appears to be yes in principle so long as the customers are genuinely 'potential'. 'Potential customer' must be a term of art in restraint of trade law; it cannot, for example, include the thousands of persons to whom a circular letter has been sent by the plaintiff in the hope that they might do business with him. To take the argument to its extreme it could be said that every person is a potential customer for an everyday product. However does the plaintiff have to demonstrate that a potential customer is a person who is more likely than not to place an order with him. It seems to us that this approach may go too far in the other direction. In principle the plaintiff must be able to show a real and not merely a speculative or fanciful connection with the person whom he describes as a potential customer. It is possible to debate the relevant definitions *ad nauseam* but in practice it is our view that the prudent covenantee will seek to limit the ambit of who constitutes a potential customer by reference to the connection which the covenantor has had with that person. For example, a clause in an employment contract in which the covenantor is a salesman could properly seek to restrict the salesman's activities after termination of employment in relation to potential customers by identifying them as having been persons 'with whom the employee has dealt with a view to obtaining business'.

5 Reasonableness: between the parties business secrets

5.1 Restricted activities

The cases dealing with reasonableness and business secrets follow the same principles as those on competition and canvassing. The employer must show that the three tests set out in *Coco v Clark (AN) (Engineers) Ltd* [1969] RPC 41 are met (see p 39) and must particularly show that he is not seeking to restrict an employee's use of his general skills, knowledge and experience. Two recent cases in this area bear some study. They indicate the modern approach taken by the courts. In *Commercial Plastics Ltd v Vincent* [1965] 1 QB 623 the plaintiffs claimed protection for their confidential information in the field of PVC calendered sheeting. The court found that the plaintiffs had 80 per cent of the UK market in this sheeting for use as adhesive tape; this was very difficult to produce and secret processes were involved which were kept in code to which only a few employees had access. The defendant was recruited to be responsible for research and development in the plaintiff company. His contract contained an express term which stated that because of the highly technical and confidential nature of his appointment he was not to seek employment with any of the company's competitors in the PVC calendered sheeting field for a period of one year after leaving. The court found that as there was no geographical limit the restriction must have been of worldwide effect, and that by referring to 'competitors' the restriction must have meant those who were competitors at the time when the defendant's employment ended. The court also found that:

(a) technical knowledge of PVC calendered sheeting had become part of the defendant himself and was therefore not protectable:

(b) although the defendant had access to secret mixing specifications and test reports he could not take them away in his head and there was no question of him having actually taken documents;

(c) the plaintiffs' schemes and business organisation methods were not confidential;

(d) however, there was some confidential information which was protectable: the defendant was not likely to remember minute details recorded in mixing specifications, but would be likely to remember in general terms the nature of problems and solutions, what experiments had been made and whether the results had been positive or not: he would be likely, when the need arose, to dredge up from his memory the particular secret which he had found appropriate to deal with the customers requirements.

Therefore, the plaintiffs had established an interest meriting protection. However, had the plaintiffs succeeded in preventing him from working for a competitor for a year so that he would not be tempted to breach confidence? The court said that the clause was not reasonable to protect the interest of the plaintiffs. It was too wide because:

(a) it would stop the defendant from entering the employment of a competitor anywhere in the world, and yet the plaintiffs only operated in the UK;

(b) it was not limited to those who competed in the field of PVC sheeting for adhesive tape but extended to anyone who competed in any part of the PVC calendered field, and yet the business secrets only attached to the former area of manufacture;

(c) it was not limited to working in some department or activity connected with the production of sheeting for adhesive tape.

Although this decision was criticised in *Littlewoods Organisation Ltd v Harris* [1978] 1 All ER 1026, it is an indication of how the courts may approach this area. In *Marshall (Thomas) (Exports) Ltd v Guinle* [1978] 3 WLR 116, the defendant was the managing director of the plaintiff company who bought and sold textiles especially from countries which had restricted exports. An express clause in his contract of employment said that he was not, during or after employment, to 'disclose' any confidential information re the affairs, customer or trade secrets of the plaintiff company. Megarry V-C decided that apart from the express term, the defendant had breached his implied duty of fidelity as an employee and his fiduciary duty as a director. He then went on to consider the business secrets clause. It was argued by the defendant that this only prevented 'disclosure' of any business secrets and did not prevent him 'using' the information himself. It was argued that as another clause used the phrase 'use or disclose' the draftsman had intentionally left 'use' out of the business secrets clause. Megarry V-C agreed. He said he could not imply 'use' in 'disclose' nor add it on. On the facts of this case this conclusion was obviously right; by showing that another clause did include 'use' the defendant convinced the judge that by the word 'disclose' alone the draftsman had meant to exclude the implied duty regarding business secrets which would extend to use as well as disclosure. However, the judge went on to say:

> I can conceive of methods of use which would amount to making a disclosure. If any employee were to use his secret knowledge in such a way as to make it plain to others what the secret process or information was that might well amount to a disclosure. The mode and circumstances of use may be so ostentatious that they plainly constitute a disclosure.

The moral of this case from the draftsman's point of view is: be consistent. In this case activities which should have been restricted were not covered by the business secrets clause and, but for other matters, the defendant would have been free to carry on damaging his former employer's business.

5.2 Geographical extent

It is generally true to say that much wider areas can be legitimately covered by business secrets clauses than by competition clauses and that objections to the need for pure area covenants are irrelevant. In *Caribonum Co Ltd v Le Couch* (1913) 109 LT 385 and 587 a restraint which was unrestricted as to time and area was upheld as was a restraint, in *Kerchiss v Colora Printing Inks Ltd* [1960] RPC 235 which covered 16 countries. Indeed, it may be that the extraordinary approach to construction of the majority in the *Littlewoods* case is excusable on the basis that they were considering a restraint of trade clause which was entirely based on business secrets rather than a pure restraint of trade clause. In practice, it is very difficult for an employee to argue that the geographical area attached to a business secrets clause is too wide; even the duty implied by law does not include geographical limits. It may, however, be possible to argue that use or disclosure of business secrets in a geographical area with which the employer has no and can have no reasonably foreseeable connection is not an effective breach of the restraint but query, all the same, whether it makes it unreasonable. Whether this argument will succeed will primarily depend on the business in question. Use of business secrets in Paraguay by an ex-employee may very well have an effect on an employer who has an aircraft engine business in the UK but not if the employer's business is manufacturing peanut butter. Of course, should the secret come to lose its quality of confidence then any restriction will be irrelevant.

5.3 Time

Unlike the subject of geographical area, the courts have more reason to question time periods relating to business secrets. Such secrets rarely remain confidential for ever and it would be unfortunate if former employees were the only people prevented from using the information. It is submitted that the relevant matters are:

(a) the position of the employee: the higher up he or she is the more likely a longer term will be reasonable: see *Attwood v Lamont* [1920] 3 KB 571; and

(b) the type of industry involved: it may well be that in the more technologically advanced industries, the reasonable period of protection may be surprisingly short. For example, computer software is an area in which the state of the art is anything but static. The greater the susceptibility of the industry to change, the greater likelihood of the need to restrict time factors in business secrets clauses.

In *Commercial Plastics Ltd v Vincent* the plaintiffs had sensibly limited a restraint of trade clause based on business secrets to one year for the reason that the industry was growing and changing so fast that this was thought to be a sufficient period. In *Under Water Welders and Repairers Ltd v Street and Longthorne* [1968] RPC 498 the plaintiffs were licensees using a novel process and were the only company using it in the UK. Longthorne was prevented from competing or helping others to compete with the plaintiffs for three years insofar as such competition used 'any invention, principle or idea' practised by them. This was upheld.

In *Littlewoods Organisation Ltd v Harris* [1978] 1 All ER 1026 the plaintiffs had sensibly limited a restraint of trade clause which was designed to protect business secrets to a period of 12 months. As the secrets related to seasonal catalogues in the mail order business, any longer period might well have made the clause unreasonable.

6 Miscellaneous points on reasonableness

6.1 Professional restraints

In *Scorer v Seymour-Johns* [1966] 1 WLR 1419 Sellers LJ suggested that the existence of a professional restraint may be relevant to the question of reasonableness. Although the need for a covenant may be diminished by the existence of a professional rule of conduct, it really depends on whether the professional body in question has any effective sanction with which to enforce its rules of conduct and how quickly it can do so. The courts can act much more quickly to provide relief that any professional disciplinary body and in most cases speed is essential from the employer's point of view. In *Oswald Hickson Collier and Co v Carter-Ruck* [1984] AC 720, the most recent case in which the existence of a professional restraint was referred to, the court did not deal with the point at all.

6.2 Trade usage

If it can be shown by a defendant that a particular restriction is unusual within a certain trade then this may have some bearing on the question of reasonbleness, and, more fundamentally, it may be relevant to whether the restraint of trade doctrine applies at all. In *Page One Records Ltd v Britton*

[1968] 1 WLR 157 Stamp J was impressed by the fact that there was no evidence from the trade that any of the agreements were unusual or unfair. However, in *Schroeder (A) Music Publishing Co Ltd v Macaulay* [1974] 1 WLR 1308, the fact that an agreement was in standard form did not help the appellant company. As Lord Diplock said, standard form contracts were of two types. The first were those which set out the terms upon which mercantile transactions of common occurrence were to be carried out. The second type (an example of which was found in this case), was that resulting from superior bargaining power. The main difficulties with the trade usage argument are:

(a) actually getting evidence of what is common in the trade; and
(b) demonstrating that this particular employer has a business which is of a standard nature for the trade.

Obviously, even if there is evidence of trade usage it is still open to a plaintiff to argue that his business is so different from others that the standard approach is irrelevant. However, that argument was not possible in *Leng (Sir WC) and Co Ltd v Andrews* [1909] 1 Ch 763 and one of the reasons given by the court for finding the restriction unreasonable was the fact that it was unusual in the relevant trade.

6.3 Provisions which permit consent

In some employment contracts there is a provision which states that a restriction will not apply if the employer consents, which consent will not be unreasonably withheld. In *Kerchiss v Colora Printing Inks Ltd* [1960] RPC 235 Dankwerts J said that such a provision was relevant to reasonableness. In answer to defence submissions that a restrictive covenant was unreasonable he said:

> I have come to the conclusion that having regard to two things, first . . . the way in which the restriction is cut down by the provision for consent which cannot be unreasonably withheld and having regard also to another consideration, that the plaintiff is to be paid a substantial salary if he is not allowed to take up employment during the period in question and during which the restriction exists, there is something to be said for the view that this covenant . . . does not go too far . . . .

It may well be that it was the second point which was decisive. We think it unlikely that consent alone would have been enough for it is difficult for an employee to show that his former employer is acting unreasonably in withholding consent; obviously, if there is a financial penalty for so doing the employer will think twice before refusing permission. In our experiences such salary provisions are rare and will only be applicable in special situations. As in *Kerchiss*, they will probably only be found where the employee is a director or is very senior. Therefore, despite *Kerchiss*, it is our view that most courts will treat a 'consent' proviso as irrelevant in most cases. In *Chafer Ltd v Lilley* (1947) 176 LT 22 such a provision was described as a 'device'. They are frequently cosmetic and meaningless. If a clause is clearly unreasonable a consent proviso cannot redeem it and the fact of its inclusion may lead the judge to question whether the parties ever regarded the clause as reasonable. If the clause is reasonable anyway, the consent proviso is irrelevant. Moreover, in *Perls v Saalfeld* [1892] 2 Ch 149 a consent provision militated against the narrower construction of the clause for which the plaintiffs argued and in *Technograph Printed Circuits Ltd v Chalwyn Ltd* [1967] RPC 339 it did not help the plaintiffs defeat a defence of unreasonableness. However, in a small minority of cases it may tip the balance in favour of reasonableness but usually only because of the existence of a sanction such as in *Kerchiss*.

7 Suing third parties

Most successful restraint of trade actions against employees suffer from a major deficiency: they control the former employee's activities for a short time in the future but they fail to deal with the party which has probably gained most from the defendant's breach of contract, ie the new employer. For tactical and commercial reasons it may be undesirable to start an action against the new employer. However, if it is decided that he should be sued there are two causes of action which will be most commonly used: breach of confidence and inducing a breach of contract.

7.1 Breach of confidence

The position of third parties is discussed above at p 56.

7.2 Inducing a breach of contract

This tort is variously described as procuring, inducing or simply 'facilitating' a breach of contract. The ingredients are:

  (a) that a contract exists between X and Y;
  (b) that Z is aware of that contract;
  (c) that Z procures, induces or facilitates Y's breach of that contract.

Element (a) needs no further discussion. However, element (b) is more complex. In restraint of trade cases Z's knowledge of the existence of the contract may come from being told by Y. However X will usually not be able to prove that. What X will normally do is write to Z (having gathered that Y is joining or has joined Z as an employee) and give him notice of the relevant clause. It is clear that if Z employs Y innocently and without knowledge of the contract term (or of any breach) and then receives notice of its existence (and is warned about the breach) but continues to employ Y then he is liable for facilitating that breach: see *De Francesco v Barnum* (1890) 63 LT 514 in which the defendant who continued to employ the plaintiff's servants—five ballet girls—after notice of a prior contract of service was liable for damages. In *Jones Brothers (Hunstanton) Ltd v Stevens* [1954] 3 All ER 677, in principle a hotel proprietor would have been liable for continuing to employ a chef after having been told of his engagement by the plaintiff as a fish frier, despite the defendant's genuine mistaken belief that he was entitled to employ the chef. In fact the plaintiff failed to establish damage because the fact that the chef was content to earn lower wages at the hotel apparently showed that the chef had no intention of going back to his fish frying job anyway.

To be liable Z need not know of the precise terms of the contract; he need only have sufficient knowledge, including knowledge of the existence of the contract, to know or be deemed to know that he is facilitating a breach (*Stratford v Lindley* [1964] 3 All ER 102 CA), and a defendant who deliberately shuts his eyes to the fact will be fixed with constructive knowledge (*Emerald Construction v Lothian* [1966] 1 All ER 1013 CA). Contrast the defendant who suspects a breach but acts *bona fide*, if mistakenly, to allay those suspicions, as in *British Industrial Plastics v Ferguson* [1940] 1 All ER 479 HL. This case was distinguished in *Jones Bros v Stevens* where the defendant did know of the breach itself and was only ignorant of its consequences. Likewise see *Hivac v Park Royal Scientific Instruments* [1946] 1 All ER 350 CA, where an injunction was granted against a defendant who secretly employed the plaintiff's employees on Sundays during their spare time and realised, if not that it was legally wrong, at any rate that to do so was morally reprehensible.

There is no requirement that the defendant acts maliciously over and above his acting knowingly (*Jones Bros v Stevens*), and there is no need for there to exist a desire to injure the plaintiff (*Thompson v Deakin* [1952] 2 All ER 361 CA); motive is, broadly speaking, irrelevant.

The situation gets a little more complicated when one comes across the distinction between direct and indirect interference with contractual rights, as in *Thompson v Deakin* where the defendants during an industrial dispute persuaded employees of B to refuse to deliver paper to the plaintiffs, with whom the defendants were in dispute, with the result that B were unable to perform their contract with the plaintiffs. The Court held that here there was no direct invasion of the plaintiffs' rights under the contract—the breach directly procured, if any, was the breach by B's employees of their contract with B. Liability in such cases of indirect interference (which is unlikely to be relevant to restraint of trade cases) was clearly viewed as an extension of the scope of the tort, and the Court set out the following requirements in order for liability to be established:

(a) actual knowledge of the existence of the contract with the plaintiff;
(b) an intention to bring about the breach of that contract;
(c) unequivocal persuasion, inducement or procurement with that intent;
(d) that the breach ensued as a necessary consequence.

These requirements only apply to what is sometimes called 'interference with contractual rights by blacking', and not to direct interference with the contract with the plaintiff.

The inducement/procurement/facilitation

Inducement or procurement in the strict sense will be impossible to prove in most restraint of trade cases. However the existence of the concept of 'facilitation' does enable X to sue Z in a large number of restraint of trade cases. That facilitation is sufficiently established by a number of cases.

In *British Motor Trade Association v Salvadori* [1949] 1 All ER 208, the defendants, who were barred from being sold new cars by the plaintiffs, bought the cars instead from third parties they had put up to buy the cars from the plaintiffs, knowing that the third parties were thereby in breach of a covenant with the plaintiffs. The defendants claimed that to buy from a willing seller was not to induce a breach of contract by the seller. It was held by Roxburgh J that:

> Lord MacNaghten (in *Quinn v Leathem* [1901] AC 495) preferred the word 'interference' for his statement of the doctrine, and this seems to me to predicate active association of some kind with the breach, but, in my judgment, any active step taken by a defendant, having knowledge of that covenant, by which he facilitates a breach of that covenant is enough . . .

and that the defendant in that case took such active steps by agreeing to buy, paying for, and taking delivery of a motor car known by him to be offered in breach of convenant.

BMTA v Salvadori, and in particular the passage quoted above, has recently been approved in *Rickless v United Artists Corp* [1988] QB 40 CA, where Bingham LJ said it was an authority which had never to his knowledge been doubted.

If a defendant can only be said to have facilitated a breach it may be that he can escape liability by means of the argument that the breach would have happened anyway, so that no damage has been caused (see eg *Jones Bros v Stevens* above).

However, there have been some recent copyright cases in which facilitation was *not sufficient* and the Court required there also to be a common design between the defendant and the party in breach (see *Paterson Zochonis v Merfarken Packaging* [1986] 3 All ER 522 CA, *CBS v Amstrad* [1988] 1 AC 1013 HL). Clerk and Lindsell suggest that this requirement also applies to the tort of interference with contract, and it is true that, for example, in *CBS* the Court appears to have based its decision (that there was no liability) on a distinction not between copyright and contract but between 'facilitating' and 'procuring'. Furthermore, although it does not appear to be an express part of the judgments in *BMTA v Salvadori*, in that case too the defendants and the parties in breach did have a common design, ie to get round the bar against the defendants buying new cars.

However, we do not think that this would necessarily limit the application of the tort in restraint of trade cases, since arguably the scope of the common design required should be limited to what the breacher should do, rather than, say, a common design specifically that the contract be breached. This would be enough to allow for the copyright situation, where the defence being accepted by the courts is that it is up to the buyers of the goods (eg, in the *CBS* case, buyers of Amstrad's two-deck tape recorders) to decide what to do with them, and any number of goods can be used both lawfully and unlawfully. Such an approach would also be in line with the extent of knowledge required of the defendant in the contractual cases.

8 Public policy

This is the final ingredient of reasonableness, but it is rarely expressed as an independent basis for assessing its existence in employment contracts nowadays. If the clause is reasonable between the parties, then it is usually assumed that it is reasonable from the public point of view. Of course, public policy does underlie the tradition of bias towards the employee especially if there is a chance that he might be unable to work at his trade because of a restriction. It is also the foundation of the distinction between the employer's protectable interests and the employee's freedom to use his acquired skill and knowledge. Evidentially, public policy can be important because its very existence may allow the judge to raise points which had not been litigated by the parties (per eg *White (Marion) Ltd v Francis* [1972] 1 WLR 1423) although Lord Diplock said it should not: see *Petrofina (Great Britain) Ltd v Martin* [1966] Ch 146.

In *Oswald Hickson Collier and Co v Carter-Ruck* [1984] 2 All ER 15 it was accepted by Lord Denning MR that since the relationship between a solicitor and his client is a fiduciary one it is contrary to public policy for a solicitor to be persuaded from acting for a client when that client wants him to act, especially in pending litigation. A clause in a partnership deed preventing one of the partners from acting for a client in the future was accordingly contrary to public policy because there is a fiduciary relationship between them and the client ought reasonably to be entitled to the services of such solicitor as he wishes. However, in *Deacons v Bridge* [1984] 2 All ER 19; [1984] AC 705 the Privy Council declined to accept that proposition and in *Kerr v Morris* [1986] 3 All ER 217 the Court of Appeal, in a case concerning a partnership of general medical practitioners who were doing national health service work, did likewise. As was pointed out above (pp 16–17) it seems that public policy may well be coming back into fashion as an important factor in some cases although in others public policy arguments are frequently the refuge of the desperate.

8.1 Fiduciaries

Fiduciaries need not be employees but they frequently are. A director or a highly placed employee (*Canadian Aero Service Ltd v O'Malley* (1973) 40 DLR (3d) 371) will usually be a fiduciary. The consequence of being a fiduciary is that as well as the general duty of fidelity (which will be enforced rigorously) the director must never put himself in a position in which his interest and duty conflict. Even if his employer refuses to take an advantage available to him or is unable to do so, he may have to disgorge his gains (see *Industrial Development Consultants Ltd v Cooley* [1972] 2 All ER 162). The basis of the remedy against him is not his employer's loss but his unjust enrichment. See also *Normalec Ltd v Britton* [1983] FSR 318 which concerned an agent properly so called; *cf Roberts v Elwells Engineers Ltd* [1972] 2 All ER 890.

8.2 Statutory and EEC provisions

For a brief resumé of the relevant law see Appendices II and III. However an employment contract is unlikely to be registrable under the RTPA 1976 as it is unusual for 'restrictions' to be accepted by 'two or more parties' as the employee is typically the sole party restricted by a restraint of trade clause.

Article 85 of the EEC Treaty will not apply as an individual employee is not an 'undertaking' as required by Art 85(1): see *Sugar* (Case 40/73) [1975] ECR 1663. Article 86 by its very terms is of doubtful application.

Chapter 9

Drafting Restrictions in Employment Contracts

1 Introduction

We set out below typical clauses in the areas of competition/canvassing and business secrets which can form the bases for restrictive covenants in employment contracts. The precise contents of each clause will depend on the industry type, the responsibilities of the employee and the aims which the employer wishes to achieve in the light of his particular business. Before those clauses are read, however, there are two important points which must be covered. The first is the obvious need for express clauses rather than relying on duties which the courts will imply.

We have dealt with the duties implied by law in employment contracts because they complete the analysis and also because they are still frequently relied on in many situations. However, we hope that whilst what has been written about implied duties is of help to those involved in problems arising from current employment contracts, those who are concerned with drafting new agreements will include express terms. Although there are some disadvantages to these, eg the impossibility of anticipating what may happen, such a disadvantage also attaches to implied duties for, as explained earlier, the courts look at the reasonableness of all types of duty at the time at which the contract is entered into. Moreover, changes and amendments to the ambit of the restraint can be made effective by incorporating a clause which permits such changes etc to be made. The first advantage of an express clause is certainty. Although implied duties do cover some but not all areas protectable by express covenants, the problems which arise have an uncanny knack of falling outside the apparent scope of the implied duties thus necessitating an expensive trip to court. Moreover, from the employer's point of view, damage may have already been incurred in that the employee, unaware of the consequences of a certain course of conduct, may have done something which breaches the implied duties in the belief that the absence of express duties meant that no duty existed at all; even a swift remedy, such as an *ex parte* interlocutory injunction might well be of little practical value even were it to be granted.

In *Sanders v Parry* [1967] 1 WLR 753 Havers J made a useful comment when he said 'It may well be that the absence of a restrictive covenant gave some false confidence . . . to the defendant and encouraged him to do . . . what is alleged, in the belief that no proceedings could be taken against him by the plaintiff.

In *Printers and Finishers Ltd v Holloway* [1964] 3 All ER 731 Cross J said:

> Although the law will not enforce a covenant directed against competition by an ex-employee it will enforce a covenant reasonably necessary to protect trade secrets. . . . If the managing director is right in thinking that there are features in the plaintiff's process which can fairly be regarded as trade secrets and which their employees will inevitably carry away with them in their heads, then the proper way for the plaintiffs to protect themselves would be by exacting covenants from their employees restricting their field of activity after they have left their employment not by asking the court to extend the general equitable doctrine to prevent breaking confidence beyond all reasonable bounds.

In the area of business secrets an express covenant removes the need to prove the employee's subjective consciousness of the fact that certain information is secret. The difficulty of relying on the implied duty of confidence was highlighted in *Balston Ltd v Headline Filters Ltd* [1987] FSR 330 at pp 351–2. Scott J decided that the application for an injunction before him was another example of an attempt by an employer to use the doctrine of confidential information to place fetters on the ability of ex-employees to compete. He said that employers who want to impose fetters of this sort on their employees ought to be expected to do so by express covenant. The reasonableness of the covenant could then be subjected to the rigorous attention to which all employee covenants in restraint of trade are subject. In the absence of an express covenant, the ability of an ex-employee to compete could be restricted by means of an implied term against use or disclosure of trade secrets. But the case must be a clear one.

> An employee does not have the chance to reject an implied term. It is formulated and imposed on him subsequent to his initial entry into employment. To fetter his freedom to compete by means of an implied term can only be justified, in my view, by a very clear case.

Express covenants are, of course, especially important post employment in the field of restraint of trade. Without an express covenant the employee is free to compete with his former employer at the moment his employment ends. He can canvass customers, accept business from them and can set up a competing business across the street. So long as he is not using business secrets to do so he is entirely free to compete.

However, it may happen that a draftsman is inept. He may not include in an express term all that the law would have implied. In such a situation it is quite clear that, in the absence of manifest contrary intention, the law will still imply those terms. However, he must be very careful as was shown in the *Guinle* case in which the court refused to read 'disclose' as meaning 'use or disclose'; the law would have implied 'use' but it was decided that the contract as a whole manifested a contrary intention. What if a draftsman is so zealous in his efforts to express protection for the employer that the clause is struck down as being unreasonable: can the employer still rely on the terms implied by them? The answer appears to be yes, provided that there is no manifest contrary intention in the contract. (See *Wessex Dairies Ltd v Smith* [1935] 2 KB 80 and *Triplex Safety Glass Co Ltd v Scorah* [1938] Ch 211.)

It is important to realise the need for both restraint of trade and business secrets clauses in employment contracts. As Dankwerts J said in *Scorer v Seymour-Johns* [1966] 1 WLR 1419: 'It is difficult to protect . . . confidential knowledge without in some way imposing a restriction on competition' and as Lord Denning MR said in *Littlewoods Organisation Ltd v Harris* [1978] 1 All ER 1026:

> . . . experience has shown that it is not satisfactory to have simply a covenant against disclosing confidential information. The reason is because it is so difficult to draw the line between information which is confidential and information which is not; and it is very difficult to prove a breach when the information is of such a character that a servant can carry it away in his head. The difficulties are such that the only practicable solution is to take a covenant from the servant by which he is not to go to work for a rival in trade.

This approach was clearly accepted in *Lansing Linde Ltd v Kerr* [1991] 1 All ER 418, CA.

Those judgments point out that there is frequently an overlap between the areas of business secrets and restraint of trade. Restraints on competition are frequently an effective means of securing protection for business secrets.

A common problem in practice is the case of the employer who has neglected to include any restraint of trade or confidential information clause in the contract with the employee but who now wishes to do so. This is usually dealt with by inserting the relevant clauses in consideration for the payment of a higher salary. However it does happen that the employee refuses to accept any addition to his contract. This is unsatisfactory from the employer's point of view. An answer is found in *RS Components Ltd v Irwin* [1974] 1 All ER 41.

During the course of two years the appellants had received complaints from its sales force of loss of orders due to the activities of ex-employees. Apparently, on a number of occasions a salesman has left the appellants' employment after learning from experience the names and addresses of the appellants' customers within his territory, and the schedule in accordance with which calls were made on them. The salesman has then set up in business on his own account within the same territory and solicited orders from the appellants' customers. As a result of knowledge of the appellants' call schedules, the ex-employee has been able to visit a customer just before the customer was due to receive a visit from the appellants' salesman. This competition, founded on inside knowledge of the identity of the appellants' customers and call schedules, seriously prejudiced the appellants' salesman who succeeded to that particular territory and led to a loss of commission as well as reducing the appellants' profits. The appellants took advice and decided that an appropriate remedy would be to place their current sales force under a reasonable restrictive covenant. On 1 February 1973 Mr Turner, the appellants' sales director, wrote a circular letter to the respondent and to the other salesmen, enclosing a new service agreement which, it was said, would come into force on 1 March. The respondent was asked to study the new agreement carefully and to return it signed by 23 February. Although the letter asked for the views of the salesman, it was stated that the new terms were the only terms on which the appellants were prepared to employ any representative. It was not open to the appellants unilaterally to change the terms of the contract on which the respondent was employed. What the appellants could do at common law was to invite the respondent to sign a new contract and, if he declined, to give him the requisite period of notice to determine the existing contract, or pay him wages in lieu of notice. Having regard to his length of service the respondent was entitled, under the Contracts of Employment Act 1972, to six weeks' notice. The proposed new agreement altered the pay structure of salesmen and also changed certain other conditions of their employment. It introduced for the first time a restrictive covenant in the following terms:

> If for any reason you leave our employ, you undertake that for 12 calendar months you will not solicit any firm, person or company who is or has been a customer of this Company in goods in which the Company deals within any territory covered by you as a representative for RS Components Ltd.

The introduction of this restrictive covenant was the only change in the terms and conditions of employment which had any materiality for the purposes of the present case.

On 21 February the respondent wrote to Mr Turner declining to sign the new agreement. The appellants answered the next day to the effect that if the agreement were not signed the appellants would regretfully have to give the respondent notice terminating his employment. On the following day the respondent repeated his refusal. On 27 February he called at the appellants' offices at the invitation of the chairman. The chairman discussed fully with the respondent all the variations incorporated in the new agreement and explained why the appellants considered them necessary. It was left that the respondent would think things over. In the outcome the respondent telephoned the appellants to confirm that he was not willing to accept the new agreement. At the beginning of March his employment was ended by the appellants and he was given certain financial compensation. Although the respondent was not given a period of notice determining his employment, it was accepted in court that a proper payment was made or provided for in lieu of notice.

Out of the total work force of 92 salesmen, 88 signed the new agreement. There were four dissentients of whom the respondent was one.

The respondent presented an application to an industrial tribunal. He won before the tribunal. On appeal he lost. In fact the tribunal had accepted that the covenant was fair and that the effect on the future interests of the appellants' business of the respondent's refusal to enter into the new terms of service was so substantial as to justify his dismissal. However, as a matter of construction of the phrase 'some other substantial reason' (see now s 57(1)(b) of the Employment Protection (Consolidation) Act 1978) they found for the respondent. The National Industrial Relations Court (Brightman J) reversed the decision.

The court also commented that there might arise a situation in which it might be essential for a company embarking on a new technical process to invite existing employees to agree to some reasonable restriction on their use of the knowledge they acquire of the new technique and where it would be essential for the company to terminate, by due notice, the services of an employee who was unwilling to accept such a restriction.

What is clear both from this example and from the facts of the case is that in order to defend a claim for unfair dismissal the employer must demonstrate an objective commercial reason for varying the contract.

2 Specimen clauses

2.1 Whole time and attention

The employee will during the term of his employment give his whole time and attention exclusively to promotion of the employer's business.

The main purpose of this type of clause is to clarify the duty of the employee with regard to his spare time although it clearly strengthens the employee's obligations during his hours of employment. It is usually coupled with a clause such as is set out below governing competition during employment.

2.2 Duty of the employee not to compete during employment

The employee will not during the term of his employment engage or have an interest in any business in competition with that of the employer.

Whilst this clause will usually be justifiable because it covers the same ground as the employee's duty of fidelity, care should be taken if the employee is a part-time worker because it could then amount to a restraint of trade.

2.3 Quoted shares

Notwithstanding anything else contained in this agreement the employee shall be permitted to hold or otherwise have an interest in up to [2] per cent of the shares or securities of any company provided that they are publicly traded on a recognised stock exchange or securities market.

This provision is common in contracts for more senior grades of employee where other restrictions in the contract might restrict the employee's right to hold private investments.

2.4 Confidentiality during employment

The employee undertakes at all times during the term of his employment to keep secret except to the extent that disclosure is authorised by the employer and to use only for the purposes of the employer [and its subsidiaries and associated companies] all information which is of a confidential nature and of value to the employer including without limitation:

secrets of the design of the employer's products;
secret manufacturing processes of the employer;
secret business methods of the employer; and
confidential lists and particulars of the employer's suppliers and
customers;

whether or not, in the case of documents, they are marked as confidential.
Upon termination of his employment howsoever occurring the employee
will return all documents in his possession or control which contain
records of such information.

This clause could readily be adapted to include specific reference to business
secrets of particular importance to the employer.

2.5 Confidentiality after employment

The employee undertakes at all times after the term of his employment to
keep secret and not to use and/or disclose any information obtained by
the employee during the term of his employment which is of a confidential
nature and of value to the employer including without limitation:

secrets of the design of the employer's products;
secret manufacturing processes of the employer;
secret business methods of the employer; and
confidential lists and particulars of the employers suppliers and
customers;

whether or not, in the case of documents, they are or were marked as
confidential.

This clause could be amended to exclude from its ambit information which
has entered into the public domain. Such an amendment might, however, limit
the effectiveness of the clause to prevent use of information in the public
domain but learnt by the employee in his employment and used by him as a
'springboard' after employment.

2.6 Doing business with the (former) employer's clients

The employee undertakes to the employer that he will not for a period of
[   ] months/years after the end of his employment with the employer
[and within [area]] canvass or by any other means seek or solicit business
[similar to or in competition with [specify type of business]/[any type of
business of the employer in which the employee was engaged or in contact
in the course of his employment by the employer]] from any person who
during the term of the employee's employment with the employer was a
customer or prospective customer of the employer.

This clause will need to be carefully tailored to the particular circumstances in
the light of the considerations discussed at 4.2.
In general the formula set out in clause 2.7 below will be preferable in that it

limits the restriction to those clients of the former employer with whom the employee had actually had dealings.

2.7 Doing business with the (former) employer's clients with whom the employee had dealt

The employee undertakes to the employer that he will not for a period of [　] months/years after the end of his employment with the employer [and within [area]] canvass or by any other means seek or solicit business [similar to or in competition with [specify type of business]/[any type of business of the employer in which the employee was engaged or in contact in the course of his employment by the employer]] from any customer or prospective customer of the employer with whom the employee shall have had contact during [the last [　] months/years of] his employment by the employer.

The comments on the preceding clause are equally applicable to this clause.

Beware a variation on this clause which refers to clients during a certain period prior to employee's leaving employment. If a clause is drafted along the lines in *M & S Drapers* 'whose name shall have been inscribed upon the books of the firm as a customer during the three years immediately preceding such determination'. Morris LJ said this could refer to names actually *put* on books during three years or to those which have *remained* on books for that period.

2.8 Doing business with the (former) employer's subsidiaries' clients

The employee undertakes to the employer that he will not for a period of [　] months/years after the end of his employment with the employer [and within [area]] canvass or by any other means seek or solicit business [similar to or in competition with [specify type of business]/[any type of business of the employer's subsidiaries or associated companies in which the employee was engaged or in contact in the course of his employment by the employer]] from any person who during the term of the employee's employment with the employer was a customer or prospective customer of the employer's subsidiaries or associated companies.

This clause and the following clause follow the pattern of the preceding two clauses but they cover the interests of the subsidiaries and associated companies of the employer. It is probably advisable to include the provisions in a separate clause in case it is for any reason necessary to sever the clause.

In general it will also be advisable to define the subsidiaries and associated companies which the clause is to cover. See further pp 88–9.

2.9 Doing business with the (former) employer's subsidiaries clients with whom the employee had dealt

The employee undertakes to the employer that he will not for a period of [　] months/years after the end of his employment with the employer [and within [area]] canvass or by any other means seek or solicit business [similar to or in competition with [specify type of business]/[any type of business of the employer's subsidiaries or associated companies in which the employee was engaged or in contact in the course of his employment by the employer]] from any customer or prospective customer of the employer's subsidiaries or associated companies with whom the employee shall have had contact during [the last [   ] months/years of] his employment by the employer.

The comments on the preceding clause are applicable to this clause. This clause will, however, generally be preferable because it is limited to customers with whom the employee has had dealings.

2.10 Restricted activites

The employee undertakes to the employer that he will not for a period of [   ] months/years after the end of his employment with the employer and within [area] carry on or invest or work in any business similar to or in competition with [specify type of business] or any type of business of the employer in which the employee was engaged or in contact in the course of his employment by the employer with which the employee shall have had contact during [the last [   ] months/years of] his employment by the employer.

This type of clause is, in general, harder to justify than the preceding clauses because it is not as directly referable to the protection of the employer's business secrets or trade connections.

Part IV

Business Sales

Chapter 10

Introduction

The sale of a business usually involves the purchase and sale of a number of tangible assets such as stock and intangible assets such as goodwill (ie the business reputation and trade connections). It is important to draw a distinction between the sale of a business and a mere sale of stock.

Only in the former case will a restriction on the vendor's power to compete with the purchaser be contemplated between the parties. Of course, there is never any guarantee that the purchaser will be able to profit from the goodwill; he may find that when he runs the business the trade connections which once existed go elsewhere and that the reputation disappears. However, once the assets of a business have been sold the law will imply a transfer of goodwill as well unless expressly excluded (*Jennings v Jennings* [1898] 1 Ch 378) and the purchaser will not want the vendor to be able to set up next door; even if he uses a different name he will attract many of his former customers. Nor will he want the vendor to solicit the customers of his former business or use the business secrets of that business as an alternative way of competing with it. In order to protect the purchaser and restrict the vendor it is usual to have express contractual terms which circumscribe the ability of the vendor to compete. Moreover, the courts have been astute in applying the restraint of trade doctrine and the law of business secrets to make sure that the outgoing vendor does not achieve some unjust advantage because of his former association with the goodwill of the business and thereby derogate from the value of that which he has sold. If there are no express contractual terms dealing with goodwill then the courts will prevent the vendor from competing with his old business and to this end there will be imposed on the vendor the duties not to:

(a) solicit old customers;
(b) use business secrets of the old business; and
(c) represent that he is carrying on the business of the old company.

Where express provision has been made in the sale contract then the courts will consider whether such provision is reasonable in all the circumstances.

1 Distinction between employment and business sales agreements

It is sometimes difficult to draw a line between what is in substance an agreement analagous to an employment contract and one which is much closer to a business sale agreement. This problem most commonly arises when considering partnerships, especially professional partnerships. *Hadsley v Dayer-Smith* [1914] AC 979 concerned an estate agent's partnership in which an article of the partnership agreement prevented competition by a former partner for a period of ten years after he ceased to be a partner. The case was dealt with by the court on the same basis as if it had been a business sale. In *Jenkins v Reid* [1948] 1 All ER 471, which concerned medical practitioners who were not partners, counsel for the defendant urged the court to treat the case as analagous to a sale of a business, whereas the plaintiff claimed that the matter should be treated as an employment case. Romer J took the latter course. In *Whitehill v Bradford* [1952] Ch 236 at first instance Dankwerts J considered a restraint of trade clause in a medical partnership agreement, neither on the basis of it being analagous to an employment contract nor a sale of business contract. He looked at the matter from a practical point of view which was that all the parties had been legally advised about the ambit of the agreement and were professional people. In the Court of Appeal, Evershed MR rejected the employment approach for the reason that this was a case where the outgoing partner had sold his interest to the remaining partners.

More recently, in *Bridge v Deacons* [1984] AC 705 the Privy Council had to deal with a restrictive covenant which applied to a solicitors' partnership. Counsel for the appellants was so conscious of the special approach adopted in employment cases that, on behalf of the partner who had resigned and was claiming that the restrictive covenant was illegal, he urged the court to follow the US practice and view a partnership problem in the same way as an employee case. Counsel for the respondents urged the court to adopt an approach analagous to that of a business sale case. The court declined both suggestions and decided the matter on the basis of what constituted the legitimate interests of the respondents which they were entitled to protect. Their approach seems to be very close to that of Dankwerts J in *Whitehill v Bradford*.

The reason for the enthusiasm to categorise an agreement as falling within/without a specific contract type is based on the realisation that the courts do not look at restraints associated with the business sale in the same way as in employment cases. Whereas a special rule in employment cases was borne of judicial perception of inequality of bargaining power, the opposite is generally true in sale of business cases. It is assumed that the parties are of equal bargaining power and that the covenantee, the vendor, is getting an enhanced price of his business by selling its goodwill: see *North Western Salt Co Ltd v Electrolytic Alkali Co Ltd* [1914] AC 461 per Viscount Haldane LC:

> . . . when the controversy is as to the validity of an agreement, say for service, by which someone who has little opportunity of choice has precluded himself from earning his living by the exercise of his calling after the period of service is over, the law looks jealously at the bargain; but when the question is one of the validity of a commercial agreement for regulating their trade relations, entered into between two firms or companies, the law adopts a somewhat different attitude—it still looks carefully to the interest of the public, but it regards the parties as the best judges of what is reasonable as between themselves.

And see *Blake v Blake* (1967) 111 SJ 715 and *Silverman (George) Ltd v Silverman* (1969) 113 SJ 563: a sale of shares and an associated service agreement containing a restraint was treated as analogous to a business sale.

There is a second distinction drawn between employment and business sales agreements which, it is submitted, is a heresy. It is contained in many judgments including that of Lord Denning MR in *Office Overload Ltd v Gunn* [1977] FSR 39: 'In master-and-servant cases, the court will not restrain a servant from competing; but in a vendor-and-purchaser case, it will restrain the vendor from competing'. This notion, also taken up by Sellers LJ in *Gledhow Autoparts Ltd v Delaney* [1965] 3 All ER 288 seems to be based on Lord Parker's words in *Morris (Herbert) Ltd v Saxelby* [1916] 1 AC 688 and the judgment in *Attwood v Lamont* [1920] 3 KB 571 of Younger LJ. These *can* support the idea that a purchaser of a business can restrain competition *per se* by a vendor. However, such a pronouncement cannot be taken literally as the concept of reasonableness plays a part in business sales cases—possibly not such a great part as in employment contracts—but still a significant one, and in any case Lord Parker went on to say that a restriction must be confined to an area within which competition will in all probability inure to the injury of the purchaser (ie there must exist an interest which merits protection from injury).

A recent decision of Millett J has reaffirmed that the approach of the courts to restraint of trade clauses in business sale agreements is different from the approach when considering employment contracts. The case is also of wider interest. In *Allied Dunbar (Frank Weisinger) Ltd v Frank Weisinger* [1988] IRLR 60 the facts were that Weisinger had for many years been a self-employed 'sales associate' of Allied Dunbar Assurance plc. His income was derived from a commission based on the value of insurance policies and investments sold by him. These products included life assurance contracts, unit trusts and bonds, personal retirement policies and executive pension schemes.

He was very successful. In 1985 he earned about £194,000. He had approximately 600 clients based mainly in South Wales and the Home Counties. Almost all his business was based on personal and social connections and personal recommendation. He did almost no cold calling. New clients were obtained by recommendation from existing clients or from solicitors or accountants which, or clients of which, were among Weisinger's satisfied clients. He came to know most of his substantial clients personally and socially.

A disadvantage of being a sales associate was that it was difficult for such a person to realise any goodwill for his business connections when he retired. In order to remedy this Allied Dunbar conceived the idea of practice buyouts. In November 1985 Weisinger, then aged 50, entered into an agreement with an Allied Dunbar company (which later became the plaintiffs). Clause 8 of the agreement stated:

> The vendor hereby undertakes that he, his servants or agents will not without the consent of the purchaser approach, canvass, solicit, entice or otherwise contact, whether directly or indirectly, any person who is at the time a client or customer of the practice for the purpose of selling or issuing life assurance or pension or annuity policies or contracts for the provision of any other financial service or commodity which competes in

any way with any of the business which Allied Dunbar carries out either directly or through any of its subsidiaries, or with its sales associates or contracted independent intermediaries.

Clause 9 stated:

The vendor hereby undertakes with the purchaser that he will not without the consent of the purchaser during the period commencing on the date hereof and ending two years after he ceases to be a consultant to the purchaser pursuant to clause 15 below, either directly or indirectly engage in or be concerned with or interested in (whether on his own account in partnership or as a director or employee, consultant, shareholder or otherwise howsoever) in any business which involves the selling (whether as principal, agent or intermediary) or issuing of life assurance or pension or annuity policies or contracts for the provision of any other financial services or commodity which competes in any way with any of the businesses which Allied Dunbar carries out either directly or through any of its subsidiaries or with the purchaser's financial management consultants or contracted independent intermediaries. This clause shall not prohibit the holding (directly or through nominees) of investments listed on the stock exchange as long as not more than 10 per cent of the issued shares or stock of any class of any one company shall be so held without the written consent of the purchaser.

Millett J pointed out that clause 8, a non-solicitation clause, was of a kind which the court would have implied in any event. The price paid to Weisinger was for both the benefit of the restraints contained in clauses 8 and 9 and for the goodwill of his business. That goodwill comprised:

(a) his personal connections with clients including the commissions and business that could be expected to be derived from those clients in the future; and

(b) potential commission and business that could be expected to be derived in the future from other persons recommended to the plaintiffs by satisfied clients of Weisinger.

After the sale of his business Weisinger acted as a sales training consultant to Allied Dunbar. However, this arrangement proved unsuccessful and his consultancy was terminated by mutual consent after 16 months. Weisinger then wanted to work for another financial service group which mainly dealt with pensions business. His prospective employer agreed that clause 8 was valid but wished to obtain Weisinger's release from it. This was refused. It was claimed that clause 9 was unreasonable. The plaintiffs moved for an injunction. It appears that during the hearing, Weisinger, in order to persuade the plaintiffs not to rely on clause 9 or to persuade the judge that it provided unneccessary protection for them, offered to account to Allied Dunbar for any commission earned by him during the two year period after the end of his consultancy even if clients had approached him themselves. This was giving the plaintiffs more than they were entitled to under clause 8. The plaintiffs refused this offer. They stated that adequate protection against the risk of those clients following

Weisinger after the end of the two year period could only be achieved by imposing a period of discontinuity to service them. Weisinger then made a further offer: he would refuse to have any dealings with or give any advice to former clients during the two year period and, if so required, to refer such clients to plaintiffs. The plaintiffs refused this offer as it did not prevent Weisinger from dealing with new clients recommended to him by former clients of the practice or by accountants or solicitors. Weisinger then made a further offer: that he would refer to plaintiffs all such new clients who approached him during the two year period. The plaintiffs refused this further offer and insisted on enforcing the strict term of clause 9. This did not merely prevent Weisinger from dealing with former clients of the practice who approached him, or with new clients introduced by them, or by professional firms but from being involved in any capacity in a business which competed with that of the plaintiffs or their parent company, Allied Dunbar. In effect, this meant in the greater part of the entire financial services sector in the UK.

The judge in stating his general approach said:

> It is well settled that, in considering the validity of covenants in restraint of trade, very different principles apply where the covenant is taken for the protection of the goodwill of a business sold by the covenator to the covenantee from those that apply where it is taken by an employer from an employee. In the former case (though not in the latter) it may be legitimate to protect the covenantee from any competition by the covenantor, and the courts adopt a much less stringent approach to the covenant, recognising that the parties who negotiated it are the best judges of what is reasonable between them. The inclusion of such a covenant may be necessary to enable the covenantor to realise a proper price for the goodwill of his business and, by upholding the validity of the covenant, the courts may well facilitate trade rather than fetter it.

He decided that the correct approach was that applied in vendor and purchaser cases; the fact that the two year period of restraint was not to begin until the termination of the consultancy agreement gave it the superfluous but deceptive appearances being a covenant between employer and employee. The judge held clause 9 to be reasonable. It was argued that a clause which did not include a geographical restraint but which was restricted to non-dealing with existing clients or new clients introduced by them or by professional firms would have been sufficient. The judge rejected this by saying:

> The fact is that a non-dealing covenant, particularly one extending to new clients, is difficult to police and enforce, and depends to an unacceptable degree on the honest co-operation of the covenantor. It was conceded that such a covenant was not ideal, but it was submitted that there was no reason to doubt the defendant's honesty, and for once, in a case of this kind, I am disposed to agree. The defendant has conducted himself with unusual candour and fairness. He has been open about his intentions and generous in his offers. But in my judgment that is beside the point. The purchaser of a business who is paying £386,000 for the goodwill is entitled to protect his investment by a suitably worded covenant which does not

depend for its effectiveness on the vendor's honesty and co-operation. At the very least, if he obtains the vendor's agreement to the inclusion of a covenant which avoids these dangers, it hardly lies in the vendor's mouth to argue that he should have been content with less.

In *Prontaprint plc v Landon Litho Ltd* [1987] FSR 315, L was a former franchisee of P who, after the expiry of the ten year term of a franchise agreement, had continued in business in the same premises operating the same type of service but under a new name. P sought an injunction for breach of a clause which read:

> The licensee agrees that he shall not at any time within three years of the determination of this agreement engage in or be concerned or interested directly or indirectly in the provision of the service or anything similar thereto within a radius of half a mile of the premises or within a radius of three miles from any premises in the United Kingdom at which the service or anything similar thereto is carried on by any other licensee of the licensor or by the licensor itself.

It was argued by P that although this case was neither analogous to a business sale case nor an employer/employee case, L had enjoyed the goodwill of the Prontaprint name for ten years. Whitford J said that although this case did not concern the sale of a piece of property, the circumstances were closer to a business sale than to an employment agreement. P wanted to be able to grant franchises to interested parties and therefore wanted to ensure that he was in a position to prevent competition against franchisees whom they might appoint by persons who had been franchisees but were no longer. He granted an injunction.

In *Systems Reliability Holdings plc v Smith* [1990] IRLR 377 Harman J had to consider a claim by the plaintiff company against Smith who had been employed by them for a number of years and had then purchased shares totalling 1.6 per cent in the company. Subsequently, however, he was dismissed on grounds of misconduct and received nearly £250,000 for his holding. The share sale agreement contained a clause which stated that for a period of 17 months he was not directly or indirectly to 'carry on or be engaged or interested . . . in any business which competes with any business carried on at the date of this agreement . . . by the company or any of its subsidiaries'. A further clause provided that:

> . . . none of the vendors at any time after the date of this agreement shall disclose or use for his own benefit or that of any other person any confidential information which he now possesses concerning the business or affairs or products of or services supplied by the company or any of the subsidiaries or of any person having dealings with the company or any of its subsidiaries.

A short time after his dismissal and of the sale of his shares in the company, S set up his own business competing with the company. Harman J, after a full trial, declined to apply the tests as to reasonableness set out in the employer/employee cases. He stated that where a purchaser buys the whole of a business from a number of vendors, some of whom have only small stakes in the goodwill and business which is being sold but who are paid a price for their shares no different from that paid to other vendors and who thereby receive a substantial sum of money, the court should apply the tests as set out in the vendor/purchaser cases. The courts will decline to apply that test solely in relation to those who were either controlling shareholders or who had major interests. Applying that test to the evidence presented to him, he granted an injunction for the remainder of the 17 month period. As the business was demonstrated to be of an international nature it was reasonable that the restriction should be worldwide. He went on to hold that the clause in the share sale agreement restricting the defendant from using or disclosing confidential information was reasonable in the interests of the parties and would be enforced. He stated that in determining the reasonableness of an express convenant deliberately imposed between a vendor and a purchaser of business, guidance could not be drawn from the limitations on implied covenants restricting the disclosure of confidential information by an ex-employee as set out by the Court of Appeal in *Faccenda Chicken Ltd v Fowler*. Where there is a covenant between a vendor and a purchaser which is plainly intended to protect the information which the purchaser hoped to get the benefit of by his purchase of the company and its know-how the reasonableness of that covenant should be judged by the tests appropriate between persons selling such a business which has the information. It is in that capacity that the vendors make the covenants, not as employees or servants of the business. On the evidence presented to him he found that it was reasonable to restrict the defendant from using or disclosing the confidential knowledge which he had in his head concerning the business or services supplied by the company but as he found that the value to the plaintiffs of that information was gradually decreasing it would be unreasonable to extend the protection of the covenant beyond the date when the competition covenants ceased to have effect (ie the remainder of the 17 month period).

Chapter 11

Vendor's Ability to Compete with the Purchaser in the Absence of Express Covenants

In *Trego v Hunt* [1896] AC 7, Lord Herschell said 'I think it must be treated as settled that whenever the goodwill of a business is sold the vendor does not, by reason only of that sale, come under restriction not to carry on any competing business'. However, it is the extent to which the vendor is free to carry on trade and yet directly compete with the purchaser for the very goodwill which he has just sold which is circumscribed by the law even in the absence of express covenant. If there are no express provisions made in the contract of sale then the courts will, assuming no contrary intention is manifested by the parties, imply the following three terms or any of them.

1 The vendor must not solicit/canvass the customers of his old business

(See *Labouchere v Dawson* (1872) LR 13 Eq 322; *Ginesi v Cooper & Co* (1880) 14 Ch D 596 and *Leggott v Barrett* (1880) 15 Ch D 306.)

The matter was further considered by the House of Lords, in *Trego v Hunt*. That case concerned a partnership between Trego and Hunt in which Trego owned all the goodwill of the partnership business. It was found that Hunt had employed a clerk to copy for him the names, addresses and business of all of the firm's customers and he admitted that the list had been made so as to acquire information which could enable him, when the partnership expired, to canvass those people and to endeavour to obtain their custom for himself. Trego brought an action against Hunt and sought an injunction to restrain him from making any copy of or extract from the partnership books for any purpose other than for partnership business. This case did not directly deal with the sale of goodwill but the members of the House of Lords treated it as being equivalent to such a sale. All members of the court gave judgments in favour of implying a term that the vendor must not solicit/canvass the customers of his old business. Lord Herschell said:

> If a person who has previously been a partner of a firm sets up in business

on his own account and appeals generally for custom, he only does that which any member of the public may do, and which those carrying on the same trade are already doing. It is true that those who were former customers of the firm to which he belonged may of their own accord transfer their custom to him; but this incidental advantage is unavoidable, and does not result from any act of his. He only conducts his business in precisely the same way as he would if he had never been a member of the firm to which he previously belonged. But when he specifically and directly appeals to those who were customers of the previous firm, he seeks to take advantage of the connection previously formed by his old firm, and of the knowledge of that connection which he has previously acquired, to take that which constitutes the goodwill away from the persons to whom it had been sold and to restore it to himself. It is said, indeed, that he may not represent himself as a successor of the old firm, or as carrying on a continuation of their business, but this in many cases appears to me of little importance, and of small practical advantage, if canvassing the customers of the old firm were allowed without restraint.

He went on to say that possible bases for the decision of the court were either that a man cannot derogate from his own grant or that there is an implied term in the contract of sale that prevents the same happening.

A more recent application of *Trego v Hunt* is found in *Boorne v Wickeer* [1927] 1 Ch 667. In this case, a deed of partnership provided that on the death of a partner the surviving partner should acquire the deceased partner's share of the capital, property and assets of the partnership business, or alternatively, that the surviving partner might elect to have the whole of the assets of the partnership realised and divided. The defendant was a former employee of the partnership who had joined competitors of the partnership business and commenced to solicit the customers of that business. He had entered no covenant restraining him from soliciting the customers of the business in his capacity as an employee, but he was an executor of the dead partner and bound to give effect to the testator's contract. The plaintiff alleged that as an executor he was bound not to do anything to depreciate the goodwill of the partnership which he was selling. Tomlin J held that the principles laid down in *Trego v Hunt* extended to the vendor's executors carrying out a contract for the sale of the goodwill of a business and ordered that the executor be restrained from soliciting customers of that business. He said that the vendor's executor:

> may or may not have actual knowledge of who the customers of the firm are, though he certainly has every opportunity of ascertaining them, but whether or not he has actual knowledge of them, it seems to me to be against common honesty that he should be free at one and the same time to complete his testator's contract and to snatch away from the purchaser the property which he is affecting to convey to him.

The rule in *Trego v Hunt* does not apply, however, to a person whose property is being sold compulsorily by the operation of the law, as in the case of a man who has been made bankrupt and whose trustee has sold his property. See *Walker v Mottram* (1881) 19 Ch D 355, where it was held that the bankrupt could not be prevented from soliciting customers from his former business which had been sold by his trustee in bankruptcy. The reason for this appears to be because the trustee in bankruptcy sells without the consent of the bankrupt and therefore the bankrupt cannot be described as the vendor. See also *Farey v Cooper* [1927] 2 KB 384 in which it was held that a debtor who had assigned his business and goodwill to a trustee for the benefit of creditors was not precluded, in the absence of express restriction, from soliciting customers of the old business even though the deed assigning that business contained a covenant by him in which he undertook to aid the trustee to realise the property assigned and the distribution of proceeds among the creditors. See further *Green and Sons (Northampton) Ltd v Morris* [1914] 1 Ch 562.

There are two further comments to be made about the ruling in *Trego v Hunt*. The first is whether the prohibition is confined to soliciting/canvassing actual customers of the old business or whether it extends to potential customers. In our view, in the absence of any authority on the point, by applying the principle that the courts are determined to protect the goodwill of the business which has been purchased, and as potential customers must surely be included within the phrase 'goodwill', they cannot be solicited by the vendor. The phrase 'potential customers' means those who have made at least some contact with the business, eg by enquiring about products and prices but its meaning does not extend beyond that.

Secondly, it has been suggested that the restriction on canvassing/ solicitation may also extend so as to preevent a vendor from dealing with customers of his former business even if they approach him. It seems that in *Ginesi v Cooper* (1880) 14 Ch D 596 Jessel MR, albeit *obiter*, expressed a view that the rule did extend that far. The basis for his decision seems to have been that if such dealings were not prevented by the courts, it would undermine the goodwill of the business sold as much as active solicitation. However, in *Leggott v Barrett* (1890) 15 Ch D 306, the Court of Appeal disagreed with this view on the basis that there was no implied duty on the vendor to shut his door against a customer of his former business who came to the new business of his own free will. In *Trego v Hunt* [1896] AC 7, Lord MacNaghten specifically rejected Jessell MR's view, as did Lord Davey. It is submitted, that their view is to be preferred. Whatever test one uses as a basis for implying the duty that the vendor should not solicit or canvass the customers of his old business, whether it is the fact that a man may not derogate from his own grant, or is based on commercial morality, or common honesty, it is quite clearly not in the public interest in the absence of express covenant that the voluntary customer should be rejected by the vendor.

1.1 The scope of the injunction

An injunction to prevent a vendor soliciting and/or canvassing customers of the old business can be framed simply viz:

> That the defendant, his servants or agents be restrained from personally and/or directly canvassing and/or soliciting in any way all who, on the [day of sale], were customers of the business of the defendant formerly carried on as X at Y street in Z town and which was sold to the plaintiff on A day of B until the trial of this action or further order.

An illustration of an injunction which clearly went too far was given by Lord Davey in *Trego v Hunt*, when he referred to the earlier case of *Ginesi v Cooper*, in which case the injunction restrained the defendant from in any way endeavouring to obtain 'the custom of such of the customers of the plaintiff as were customers of the old firm, or from attempting to take away any portion of the business bought by the plaintiff'. It is quite clear that this form of order would prevent the defendant from issuing public advertisements, or generally carrying on business in competition with the plaintiff, whereas in fact the rule in *Trego v Hunt* quite clearly does not prevent him doing those things.

2 The use of business secrets by the vendor

The second example of a term which will be implied by law on the sale of a business prevents the vendor from using in his new business any business secrets which were attached to the former business and which were not specifically excluded from the sale of that business.

3 Representations by the vendor that he is carrying on the business sold

This duty was referred to in *Trego v Hunt*. Lord Davey said that the vendor 'may advertise himself as having been a partner in or the founder or manager of the business which he has sold, provided he does not represent the business which he is carrying on is the same business as or identical with that which he has sold'.

In *David and Matthews, Re* [1899] 1 Ch 378, Romer J held that the name of a partnership constituted part of the goodwill and that a vendor, whilst able to carry on a similar or rival business could not carry on that business so as to lead others to the belief that he was carrying on the partnership business; the reason for this seems to have been that by doing so the vendor would be wrongly appropriating to himself part of the goodwill which he had just sold, and that he would be acting fraudulently towards his customers.

What if the vendor has the same name as that of the business he has sold? This occurred in *May v May* (1914) 31 RPC 325. There is was said, *obiter*, that if the defendant had carried on a rival business with the same name without any attempt to pretend that the new business was the old one or in any way associated with it then no injunction would have issued. However, there was clear evidence that the defendant had intended to confuse customers by the fraudulent device of claiming an association with the old business which he had made over to his creditors. Coleridge J said '*Prima facie* every person has a right to trade in his own name, but what he has not a right to do is to pretend that he is connected with another business, and to utilise the name of that other business to palm off his own goods as the goods of that other business'.

4 Conclusion

It is possible to sum up the implied duties of a vendor who has sold his business as follows:

(a) he can advertise generally that he has set up a new business and can compete with the old business;

(b) he can serve former customers who come to him but he cannot solicit or canvass them;

(c) he can say that he was a partner etc of the old business but he cannot represent that he is now carrying on the same business as the old one or in any way pretend that the new business is associated with the old one;

(d) he cannot use any of the business secrets of the old business which formed part of the goodwill which was sold.

Chapter 12

Express Covenants

It is usual to find that a business sale agreement contains express terms which govern the position of the parties post sale regarding restraint of trade and business secrets. Moreover, frequently there will be an agreement protecting business secrets during the negotiations for sale in the event of a failure to finalise the sale. These are fully considered at pp 192–3.

The problems associated with implied terms so far as the purchaser is concerned are that they permit the vendor to act in ways which, although they do not directly allow him to derogate from his grant, may indirectly produce such a result. For example, although the vendor cannot directly solicit in person or canvass customers of the old business, he can set up a rival business and advertise its presence to everyone including his old customers. What the purchaser can achieve via express terms is considerable. He can prevent not only solicitation but any dealings with previous customers. He can prevent the vendor announcing that he was a partner or founder of the old business and most importantly, he can prevent the vendor setting up a rival business in certain limited circumstances. Therefore, express terms are vital to protect further the purchaser's position. These terms are subject, so far as restraint of trade is concerned, to the test of reasonableness. The reason why the courts will enquire as to the reasonableness of any express terms which may restrain the vendor's trade, is because of the public interest that a man who has sold his business should not be prevented from working in that area in which he is most skilled. The courts examine the goodwill of the business in question in order to decide whether a restraint is reasonable. The extent of the goodwill inevitably will circumscribe the ambit of what is reasonable. Having given value for goodwill, the purchaser will expect to be allowed to claim that any restraint attached to goodwill or reasonably referable to it is protectable. In this context, that means that it is necessary to examine whether the purchaser has an interest meriting protection and further whether the restraint is reasonable in the public interest. It is generally assumed that the restraint is reasonable as between the parties. So far as business secrets are concerned, the express terms seek to improve on the implied duty by identifying what is secret. The remainder of this section is concerned solely with examination of restraint of trade problems as the general law of business secrets applies in this area.

1 An interest meriting protection

As in all other areas of restraint of trade law, one cannot have a covenant not to compete *per se*; it must be attached to an interest meriting protection. Apart from business secrets the interest which a purchaser has which merits protection is goodwill. In *Vancouver Malt and Sake Brewing Co Ltd v Vancouver Breweries Ltd* [1934] AC 181, the appellants had a licence to brew a number of liquors but had only ever brewed sake. The respondents only brewed beer. There was a sale agreement between the parties in which the appellants sold to the respondents the goodwill in their brewing licence except insofar as it related to the manufacture of sake. There was a restrictive covenant in the contract by which the appellants agreed not to brew beer. The court concluded that the sale was a sham. The appellants had no goodwill to sell regarding the manufacture of beer and it was that which was purportedly restrained. The covenant was therefore a simple agreement not to compete—a covenant in gross. Lord MacMillan said: 'The receipt of a sum of money can generally be shown to be advantageous to a businessman, but his liberty to trade is not an asset which the law will permit him to barter for money except in special circumstances and within well recognised limitations'.

However, protectable goodwill would appear to be only that which attaches to the business which the vendor has sold. If the purchaser attempts to protect some other goodwill (eg of another current business or a future one) then the clause may fail for want of a proper interest meriting protection. See *British Reinforced Concrete Engineering Co Ltd v Schelff* [1921] 2 Ch 563. This case largely concerned the question whether, in an agreement for the sale of a business, the reasonableness of a vendor's restrictive covenant was to be judged by the extent of the circumstances of the business sold or by the extent and range of any business of the purchaser of which after transfer to him it was to form part. After reviewing the authorities, Younger LJ concluded that a covenant which was exacted for the protection of a business with which the covenantor has never had any connection, is no better than a covenant in gross. He concluded that the covenant was too wide as instead of pursuing the legitimate purpose of the protection of the business sold, it attempted to protect other businesses of the purchaser. Particular support for the views set out in this case are found in *Leetham (Henry) & Sons Ltd v Johnstone-White* [1907] 1 Ch 322, though there is a contrary decision in *Smedley's Ltd v Smedley* [1921] 2 Ch 580. In that case, the argument by the defendant that the court ought not to consider what was reasonably necessary for the protection of the three businesses already carried on by the purchasers at the time of the sale, but to confine its attention only to the business actually sold and consider whether the covenant was reasonably necessary for the protection of the goodwill of that particular business was rejected as 'an entirely novel argument' by Sargant J. Until recently it has been accepted that the *Leetham* case governed. However, it is important to examine this proposition in the light of the decision of the Privy Council in *Stenhoue Australia Ltd v Phillips* [1974] AC 391. There, Lord Wilberforce analysed the *Leetham* case and said that it was quite clearly a case where the agreement, as interpreted by the Court of Appeal, was with one company of a group, which company had a limited business whereas the restraint was expressed in far wider terms, extending to the area covered by the operations of the group as a whole. However, the evidence in the instant case showed that the business of the Stenhouse Group was controlled and co-ordinated by Stenhouse Australia Ltd and all funds generated by each of the companies were received by the plaintiffs. The subsidiary companies were merely agencies or instrumentalities through which the plaintiff company directed its integrated business. Not only did the plaintiff company have a real interest in protecting the businesses of the subsidiaries, but the real interest in so doing was that of the plaintiff company. Lord Wilberforce went on to say that it was not necessary to resort to a concept of a group enterprise to support this conclusion. The case was, simply, that of the plaintiff's business being to some extent handled for it by subsidiary companies. It would therefore seem that it is possible for there to be a valid interest meriting protection for the benefit of a group of companies, even though the restraint of trade clause is contained in a contract with one of those companies so long as there is proof of an identity of interest between the contracting company and the rest of the group. It is submitted that the view expressed by Lord Wilberforce in *Stenhouse* takes account of the realities of modern commercial law.

2 Reasonableness

2.1 The ambit of the activities restricted

In *Goldsoll v Goldman* [1915] 1 Ch 292, the Court of Appeal had to consider a restraint of trade clause which restricted the vendor from trading as a dealer in 'real or imitation jewellery'. It was found as a fact that the business sold by him dealt substantially in imitation jewellery. It was admitted that the business of the dealer in real jewellery is not the same as that of a dealer in imitation jewellery and therefore the court concluded that the provision was too wide for it was not limited to what was reasonably necessary for the protection of the covenantee's business. In the *British Reinforced Concrete* case, a covenant prevented the defendant from 'acting as a servant of any person concerned or interested in the business or manufacture or sale of road reinforcements in any part of the United Kingdom'. This covenant was struck down for two reasons. The first was that it prevented the defendant from manufacturing road reinforcements, something which the company which he had sold to the plaintiffs had never done. Secondly, it was said to be too wide as it would prevent the defendant from working for a trust company which held shares in another road reinforcement company. Whilst the second ground may appear somewhat fanciful, especially in the light of the authorities which deprecate such an *in terrorem* approach to construction, there can be no doubt that the first ground would still be valid today. In *Connors Brothers Ltd v Connors* [1940] 4 All ER 179, the Privy Council had to construe a restrictive covenant which prevented the respondent from 'directly or indirectly engaging in any other sardine business'. The court said that if the respondent held a small number of shares in such a competing company he might not be in breach of that clause, but if he held the controlling interest then he might. In *Ronbar Enterprises Ltd v Green*

[1954] 2 All ER 266, the Court of Appeal had to construe the following covenant: '. . . the partner whose share is purchased shall not for five years from such date (ie the time of purchase) directly or indirectly carry on or be engaged or interested in any business similar to or competing with the business of the partnership'. It was argued on behalf of the defendant that there had been no breach of that provision because on its true construction it did not extend to the rendering of services for a salary or wages as distinct from being engaged in business on one's own account. The Court of Appeal disagreed with this view. Jenkins LJ said that the words were apt, particularly in view of the word 'engaged', to include a case where the party, subject to the restriction, takes employment in a business of either of the kinds mentioned at a salary or wages, as well as a case in which he embarks on such a business on his own account, or in partnership. It had also been argued that if the clause did extend to prevent the defendant working as a salaried employee, then it was on that account too wide. The court also rejected this approach.

2.2 Geographical limits

The broad principles of how a court should approach the question of geographical limits in business sale cases, were set out in *Connors Brothers Ltd v Connors* by Viscount Maugham. He pointed out that since the question of reasonableness was a matter of law for the court, in relation to the trade of a large manufacturer or merchant, it was not necessary to prove to the satisfaction of the court that the business which the covenant was designed to protect had been carried on in every part of the area mentioned in the covenant. He said:

> In the cases in which the area has been the whole of England, or a substantial part of it, such as 100 miles or 150 miles from a named town, it has never been held that the covenantee was under an obligation to prove that the business has been carried on within all the towns and villages within the area. In *Nordenfelt v Maxim Nordenfelt Guns and Ammunition Co* [1894] AC 535, no attempt was made to prove that all the governments of the world, or even of the civilised world, had ordered goods from the company, though the greater number no doubt had done so. A great deal no doubt depends on the nature of the business and the area in question.

As to the fundamental question of whether the geographical limitations set out in the restraint of trade clause are necessary to further the purchaser's legitimate business interests, the courts have given different answers depending on the different facts of each case. In *Nordenfelt v Maxim Nordenfelt Guns and Ammunition Co Ltd* [1894] AC 535, a worldwide limitation was upheld because of the nature of the business and the limited number of customers which it served. It was essentially a worldwide business selling armaments and guns to governments.

On the other hand, in *Goldsoll v Goldman* it was held that a restrictive covenant was unnecessarily large insofar as it was intended to cover not merely the United Kingdom and the Isle of Man, but also a number of foreign countries as well. There was no evidence that any business has ever been done outside the United Kingdom or the Isle of Man. In *Vancouver Malt and Sake Brewing Co Ltd v Vancouver Breweries Ltd* [1934] AC 181, a worldwide restriction was struck down as the extent of the business sold was confined to British Columbia. Finally, in *Ronbar Enterprises Ltd v Green*, the court concluded that the phrase 'shall not . . . directly or indirectly carry on or be engaged or interested in any business similar to or competing with the business of the partnership' because of the words 'similar to or' meant literally that if the defendant were to carry on a business similar to the business of the partnership in any part of the world, then he would be in breach of the covenant. However, the court still found for the plaintiffs as the offending words were severed.

2.3 Time

In *Connors Brothers Ltd v Connors*, it was said that if a restriction as to space is considered to be reasonable, it is seldom in a case where the sale of goodwill is concerned that the restriction can be held to be unreasonable because there is no limit as to time. It is submitted that this is an old fashioned view and that the issues of time and geographical scope are not always inextricably linked. In *Pellow v Ivey* (1933) 49 TLR 422 a lifetime restriction on a vendor from setting up a business similar to one sold by him was held to be unreasonable because the agreement afforded the plaintiffs more than adequate protection. The position might have been different if the sale had involved business secrets as well as goodwill.

Recently in Scotland in *Rander v Pattar* [1985] SLT 270 it was doubted at the interlocutory stage whether five years was necessarily required in a covenant against competing on the sale of a hotel.

2.4 Statutory and EEC provisions

The Restrictive Trade Practices Act 1976 is discussed in general terms in Appendix II. Upon a sale of a business it is common for the vendor to restrict himself so as to ensure that the purchaser can take the value of his purchase. It is not unusual for managers of the business being sold who are not going to continue working for the purchaser also to enter into restrictive covenants. Accordingly there may often be two parties who accept restrictions, even in cases where the purchaser does not. As is mentioned in Appendix II in many cases the Agreement will be exempt under the Restrictive Practices (Sale and Purchase Agreements) (Goods) Order 1989 (and the corresponding Order for services), and in others it will generally be possible to obtain a direction from the Secretary of State under s 21(2) of the Act dispensing with the need for a court hearing. It is nevertheless vital that the agreement be registered for otherwise the restrictions (including those which would be implied) will be void. The relevant EEC provisions are dealt with in Appendix III. However, there have been some decisions concerning business sales. A mere business sale in the absence of contrary evidence does not give rise to any restriction on competition and therefore the agreement is not caught by Art 85(1) (see *Mecaniver* [1985] 3 CMLR 359). In that case the Commission also said that where a company sells subsidiaries to another company as a going concern the commitment by the vendor not to compete with the purchaser for three years in the areas of activity of the transferred subsidiaries is a legitimate means of ensuring the vendor's obligation to transfer the full commercial value of the business which necessarily includes not only the sale of physical assets but also commercial know-how and clients. See also *Reuter (Gottfried) v BASF AG* [1976] 2 CMLR D44; *Nutricia* [1984] 2 CMLR 165 and *Nutricia* 42/84 in which the Court said that the fact that non-competition clauses are included in an agreement for the sale of a business is not of itself sufficient to remove the clauses from the ambit of Art 85(1). However, it was necessary to examine what would be the state of competition if those clauses did not exist. There might then be a possibility that the vendor could force the purchaser out of the business and the court recognised that a non-competition clause did have the merit of ensuring that the transfer of the business had the intended effect. By that fact such clauses could contribute to the promotion of competition because they lead to an increase in the number of undertakings in the market. However, it seems that to have such a beneficial effect the clauses must be necessary and their scope and duration must be limited.

On 14 August 1990 the EC Commission published a notice 'regarding restrictions ancillary to concentrations' (OJ 90/C/203/05). This notice is an aid to the interpretation to Council Regulation 4064/89 which deals with the control of mergers between companies. The 25th recital to the Regulation states that its application is not excluded where the undertakings concerned accept restrictions which are directly related and necessary to the implementation of the merger; such restrictions are called 'ancillary restrictions'. Under Pt III of the notice, guidelines are set out in relation to non-competition clauses on the transfer of a business, ie usually a business sale. The notice recognises that in order to take over fully the value of the assets transferred the acquirer must be able to benefit from some protection against competitive acts of the vendor in order to gain the loyalty of customers and to assimilate and exploit any know-how transferred. However it comments that such protection cannot generally be considered necessary when the transfer is limited to physical assets (such as land, buildings or machinery) or to exclusive industrial and commercial property rights (the holders of which could immediately take action against infringements by the transfer of such rights). The notice goes on to set out guildelines as to what are usually reasonable prohibitions on competition where such a prohibition is *prima facie* necessary to protect the purchaser.

Duration

In most cases which involve the sale of both goodwill and know-how, a maximum period of five years is likely to be acceptable. However, where there is a sale only of goodwill a period of up to two years only will usually be reasonable. The point is made that in particular cases the periods can be longer: for example, if it can be demonstrated that customer loyalty to the vendor will persist for more than two years or that the economic life cycle of the products concerned is longer than five years, this should be taken into account.

Geographical area

The geographical scope of the clause must be limited to the area where the vendor had established the products or services before the sale.

Restricted activities

The non-competition clause must be limited to products and services which form the economic activity of the business which has been sold.

The notice also comments that the vendor may bind himself, his subsidiaries and commercial agents. However, an obligation to impose similar restrictions on others would not qualify as an 'ancillary restriction'. In particular, clauses which would restrict the scope for resellers or users to import or export would not be reasonable.

Part V

Partnerships and Joint Ventures

Chapter 13

Partnerships

1 Introduction

The term partnership is used in this chapter to denote partnerships of individuals. Partnerships of companies which in general give rise to few problems of restraint of trade are briefly discussed in the following section under the general description of joint ventures. Partnerships of individuals have attributes which give rise to particular difficulties in both the law of business secrets and of restraint of trade. In practice, many disputes concerning restraints on partners will turn upon the ownership of the goodwill of the partnership. This is an issue of partnership property and a discussion of the rules governing partnership property is outside the scope of this book (for an example of the problem see *Miles v Clarke* [1953] 1 All ER 779). However, once the questions of partnership property have been resolved the rules of restraint of trade must be applied. As will be seen below, retiring partners may in restraint of trade cases be treated more like sellers of businesses than employees for on retirement they relinquish their share of the partnership property. Similarly, in business secrets cases they may be treated as having contributed to the partnership property the secret information and in appropriate cases be restrained from using it on their own account (see *Morrison v Moat* (1851) 9 Hare 241).

2 Implied provisions during the currency of the partnership

2.1 Business secrets of the partnership

The scope of the implied obligations of the partners during the currency of their partnership will depend upon the nature and purpose of the partnership. In all partnerships there is an implied obligation on each partner to act in the utmost good faith with regard to the partnership: *Green v Howell* [1910] 1 Ch 495. This is substantially the same as the duty of fidelity owed by an employee to his employer and it will clearly place a like obligation on each partner to respect the confidence of partnership business secrets. It will also impose upon each partner an obligation to disclose to the partnership all information which he receives which is relevant to the partnership.

The Partnership Act 1890 (PA 1890) provides certain rights and duties that are to be implied into every agreement of partnership in the absence of any agreement to the contrary. Of particular relevance are the provisions of ss 28, 29 and 30.

Section 28 requires partners to render true accounts and full information of all things affecting the partnership to any partner and his legal representatives. This section would, therefore, appear to place upon each partner a duty to disclose to his partners any information which he receives which may be of value to the partnership. Nevertheless, there will be some circumstances in which a partner may be justified in withholding information from his partners where it is in the interests of the partnership for him to do so. An example of this is found in *Rakusen v Ellis, Munday and Clarke* [1912] 1 Ch 831. One partner in a firm of solicitors had acted for one party to an action. The other party subsequently instructed another partner who was ignorant of his partner's former involvement in the case. On an action brought to restrain him from acting the court held that, as it could rely upon the defendant not to discuss the case with his partner, there was no reason to restrain him from acting. It is clear that neither partner could have successfully brought an action against the other to require disclosure.

Section 29 of PA 1890 provides that every partner must account to the firm for any benefit derived by him from any transaction concerning the partnership, or from any use by him of the partnership property, name or business connection. This is perhaps just a restatement of one aspect of the duty of good faith. But it would seem to be directly applicable where one partner misuses confidential information which rightly belongs to the partnership.

By s 30 of PA 1890, it is provided that if a partner, without the consent of the other partners, carries on any business of the same nature as and competing with that of the firm, he must account for and pay over to the firm all profits made by him in that business.

3 Express provisions during the currency of the partnership

3.1 Business secrets of the partnership

Whilst the implied obligation of good faith will impose a high obligation on the partners to maintain the confidence of partnership secrets, it may well be valuable to include in the partnership agreement an express provision requiring the partners during the existence of the partnership to keep confidential the business secrets of the partnership and to use them only for the purposes of the partnership. Where particular secrets are regarded of great value, express provisions requiring formal approval or the like before any disclosure, even in the course of the partnership's business may prove useful, so long as this does not hamper the ability to do legitimate business.

3.2 Restrictions on engaging in other business

The implied obligation to act in good faith and the obligations imposed by PA 1890 will, as has been seen, prevent a partner from engaging in any business competitive with that of the partnership. However these implied obligations do not cover clearly the rights of partners to undertake other business not competitive with that of the partnership. The position should be covered by any well-drafted partnership deed.

The application of the restraint of trade doctrine to obligations not to engage in other businesses during the subsistence of the partnership has not been the subject of any decision of the courts. However it has been suggested, *obiter*, that the doctrine does not apply to obligations between partners during the subsistence of the partnership: see Lord Pearce in *Esso Petroleum Co Ltd v Harper's Garage (Stourport) Ltd* [1968] AC 269. However, the exemption from the doctrine was limited to restrictions which were incidental and normal to the positive commercial arrangements at which the partnership deed aims.

It would, therefore, appear that a similar rule to that applicable to contracts of employment will apply. Lord Greene MR said in *Hivac Ltd v Park Royal Scientific Instruments Ltd* [1946] Ch 169: 'It would be most unfortunate if anything we said, or any other court said, should place an undue restriction on the right of a workman, particularly a manual workman, to make use of his leisure for his profit'. He was, of course, speaking in the context of the obligations to be implied into a contract of employment. But his words do seem to indicate that in a proper case the courts might intervene to prevent the enforcement of an excessive restraint. The obvious tool to use would be the doctrine of restraint of trade.

If the courts were to apply the doctrine to such a case it would be necessary for the restraint to be reasonable in the interests of the parties and in the interests of the public. The court would first assess the legitimate interests that the partners were seeking to protect. It is submitted that the courts would without doubt regard the devotion by the partners of all their efforts towards the partnership business as a legitimate aim which could reasonably be protected by a covenant restraining the partners from participating in any other business. However, where such a restraint is imposed upon a partner for some reasons not connected with the objects of the partnership, but say to protect another business in which one partner has a personal interest, then it is far less probable that the restraint will be upheld. Until an example comes before the courts the position will remain uncertain, even in the light of the principles laid down in *Stenhouse Australia Ltd v Phillips* [1974] AC 391.

4 Implied restrictions after partnership

In the absence of any contrary agreement between the members of a partnership, the only means by which a partner may retire from a partnership is upon its dissolution. In the case of a partnership at will, this may be brought about at any time by any partner giving notice of his intention so to do to all the other partners: s 26 of PA 1890. Sections 32 to 35 deal with other means by which the dissolution of a partnership may be brought about.

Upon the dissolution of a partnership, the assets of the partnership are to be applied as set out in s 44 of PA 1890. Basically, this provides that after discharging the debts of the partnership the remaining assets are distributed in the shares in which profits were distributed. The question of what restraints are imposed upon the partners upon dissolution ultimately comes down, therefore, to a question of what rights attach to the assets of the partnership which fall to be disposed of in the winding up of the partnership.

Of particular importance, are the rights which attach to the goodwill of the partnership upon its winding up. It has been held that where the goodwill is sold following a dissolution, no restriction is thereby imposed on the partners preventing them from carrying on the trade in which they were formerly engaged: see the discussion of the earlier cases in *Trego v Hunt* [1896] AC 7. Several difficult issues are left unresolved by this case.

The first problem is the right to use the name of the old firm. This presumably is one of the assets of the firm which may be got in and, if necessary, sold upon dissolution. However, the extent of the ancillary rights which may be sold with it is more doubtful. Presumably a purchaser cannot acquire a sufficient element of the reputation in the name to enable him to bring an action for passing off against a former partner carrying on business in his own name.

Secondly, it is not clear what becomes of business secrets upon a dissolution. It is certainly arguable that all the partners should be free to use them, for to hold otherwise might prevent the partners from continuing in the trade in which the partnership was formerly engaged. This would seem to be the consequence of *Trego v Hunt*. But if the partnership has developed a valuable and secret process through the expenditure of substantial sums, it may be that this should more properly be regarded as an asset which should be sold for the benefit of all the partners. That these problems remain unresolved indicates that most persons embarking upon significant partnerships must adopt the sensible course of regulating their relationship with a written agreement.

It should not, however, be assumed that the same meaning will be given to the word goodwill where an express agreement has been made between the partners governing the ownership of the goodwill of the partnership, in the event of a retirement or dissolution. The courts will take notice of the fact that the meaning given to the word goodwill in cases where it is being sold in the winding up of a partnership due to the absence of any agreement between the partners, is not perhaps the commonly understood meaning of the word. Thus in *Trego v Hunt* and in *Leggott v Barrett* (1880) 15 Ch D 306, where it was expressly provided that one partner should have the goodwill, the term was construed in the same sense as it would have been in a contract for the sale of a business. Accordingly, there was an implied term that the former partner who did not keep ownership of the goodwill could be restrained by injunction from canvassing the former customers of the business, or holding himself out as carrying on business in succession to the business of the partnership. However, he would not be restrained from advertising generally even though these advertisements might reach the ears of former customers.

5 Express provisions after partnership

That the restraint of trade doctrine is applicable to restraints imposed on former partners is beyond doubt. Agreements between partners have some of the characteristics of employment agreements but because the partners are the owners of their business, their agreements also have some of the characteristics of agreements for the sale of businesses, at least as far as retirement and dissolution is concerned. In applying the restraint of trade doctrine it is therefore tempting to seek the closest analogous case from the field of employment or business sales and to try to apply it to the restraint in question. Indeed such an approach has been adopted in many cases: see for example *Trego v Hunt* and *Ronbar Enterprises Ltd v Green* [1954] 1 WLR 815. The Privy Council has recently indicated that this approach should not be adopted. In *Bridge v Deacons* they held that the proper approach is that adopted by Lord Reid in *Esso Petroleum Co Ltd v Harper's Garage (Stourport) Ltd* [1968] AC 269, where he said: 'I think it better to ascertain what were the legitimate interests of the appellants which they were entitled to protect and then to see whether these restraints were more than adequate for that purpose'. The interests of the covenantees (usually the remaining partners) can in general be divided into two parts: there will be the protection of their business secrets and the preservation of their goodwill.

As regards the protection of business secrets, it is likely that a similar distinction between business secrets and personal skills to that drawn in employment cases will be made. For it cannot reasonably be said that a partnership has a legitimate interest in the individual skills of the partners which would justify the imposition of a restriction on a departing partner.

A partnership will, however, have an interest in its confidential information which it may legitimately protect. Since the interest of a partnership in those secrets is similar to that of an employer as regards his employees, it is probable that a partnership may protect itself in like manner to a former employer.

It is in the protection of goodwill, that the difference in approach to partnership and employment contracts becomes apparent. For each of the members of a partnership has a share in the value of the goodwill of a partnership and participates by way of a share of profits in the benefits which that goodwill brings to the firm. Restraints imposed in partnership agreements have a dual function. They both protect a partner whilst he is a member of the partnership and they restrain him if he retires. In addition, they provide a means whereby an older partner may dispose of the share in the business which the partners have built up to younger men. This may be in the interests both of the public in that it ensures continuity of trade and of the parties in that it may enable the more senior partner to sell his share of goodwill to the more junior partners (either by means of a cash sum or by means of a higher share of profit during the last few years of partnership). These then are the elements of protectable interest which comprise a partnership goodwill. All these elements were taken into account by the Privy Council in *Bridge v Deacons* [1984] AC 705.

In *Kerr v Morris* [1986] 3 All ER 217 the Court of Appeal considered a restraint of trade clause in a partnership deed between general medical practitioners who worked as national health service contractors. As s 54(1) of the National Health Service Act 1977 makes it unlawful to see the goodwill of a national health service medical practice, it was argued that there was no goodwill to which any restraint could legitimately attach. Therefore, it was said the restraint was unreasonable as there did not exist an interest which merited protection. This argument was rejected. Dillon LJ said: '. . . goodwill, in the sense of the tendency of patients whom the doctors have treated to continue to refer to the firm for further treatment, must remain one of the most valuable assets, albeit not a saleable asset, of the partnership on which the partners' livelihood as doctors substantially depends'. This seems a sensible approach as NHS doctors are rewarded by the number of patients on their list.

The nature of the legitimate interest which may be protected by the three most common types of covenants can conveniently be considered separately. The first example is a covenant against acting for or canvassing the clients of the old firm. In the case of a sale of goodwill simpliciter if all that will be implied is an obligation on the seller not to canvass the customers of the business, such an obligation is in many cases inadequate. For example, in the case of solicitors canvassing for business it is in general prohibited (see Rule 1 of the Solicitors' Practice Rules). Therefore, it may be impossible to protect goodwill, except by prohibiting the outgoing partner from acting for clients of the firm. The validity of such a restraint was the subject of the Privy Council's decision in *Bridge v Deacons*. That concerned a provision placed on all retiring partners which prohibited them from acting as a solicitor in Hong Kong for a period of five years for any person who had been a client of the firm during the period of three years prior to the departure of the partner. The provision sensibly contained exceptions which permitted employment in industry or government.

The restriction was held to be reasonable. The interest of the firm which could legitimately be protected was the goodwill of the firm as a whole and they could reasonably guard against the appropriation by the retiring partner of any part of it.

The importance of this decision is that it shows that, unlike employment cases, it is not necessary to show that the retiring partner dealt with all the clients encompassed by the restriction (which happened in this case to be all clients of the firm) before his retirement or that he even knew who they were. If the partner held a share in the goodwill of the firm as a whole, then on relinquishing that share, he could be restrained from acting for any former client for these comprised that goodwill.

It will, of course, be important to ensure that the restraint is properly for the protection of the business of the firm. Thus, if the restraint as drafted covers other businesses it will be unenforceable, unless severable: *British Reinforced Concrete Engineering Co Ltd v Schelff* [1921] 2 Ch 563. For example, a restraint against practising as a medical practitioner will be unenforceable if what is sought to be protected is a general practice for it would prevent the covenantor from acting as a consultant: see *Routh v Jones* [1947] 1 All ER 758 and *Lyne-Pirkis v Jones* [1969] 1 WLR 1293; *cf Clarke v Newland* [1991] 1 All ER 397, CA where a covenant not to practice [sic] following the termination of a general practitioner partnership agreement was construed to be a restriction on practising as a general medical practitioner.

It is likely that the restriction in *Bridge v Deacons* would have been invalid had the exceptions for practice in industry and government not been included for this could not be regarded as affecting the goodwill of the business.

The second example is a covenant against trading within a defined geographical area. It has long been accepted that a restriction on trading within a defined geographical area for a specific period, may be justified as necessary for the protection of goodwill. Such a restraint has an obvious advantage over a restraint on seeing customers of the old firm: it is far easier to police. The covenantees need only detect that the covenantor is carrying on business in the defined area and he can take action, if the covenant is valid. He need not prove the identity of the clients of the covenantor.

However, it must be shown that the covenant is still for the protection of goodwill. Therefore, the area must be framed carefully with regard to the nature of the business to be protected. It will be necessary to show that the protection of the goodwill of the old business reasonably required the exclusion of the covenantor from the defined area. This will require a careful examination of the scope of the business to be protected. Whilst the reasonableness of the restriction must be judged as at the date it is entered into, the parties may take into account the contemplated expansion of the business in framing the extent of the restriction: see *Putsman v Taylor* [1927] 1 KB 637.

Not all businesses will lend themselves to the use of area covenants to protect goodwill. If the business ranges over a wide area but has only a small share of the market in the area in which it operates, it is submitted that an area covenant would be inappropriate. Such a covenant would, whilst protecting the covenantee, deprive the covenantor of many customers who may never even have heard of the covenantee. For an example of this difficulty arising in the context of employer and employee, see *Gledhow Auto Parts Ltd v Delaney* [1965] 3 All ER 288. It is only in rare circumstances that a wide-ranging area covenant would be enforceable. Where vital business secrets are to be protected (see for example *Littlewoods v Harris* [1977] 1 WLR 1472 and *Standex International Ltd v CB Blades* [1976] FSR 114) or the covenantee has a business which is pre-eminent in the market throughout a large area (such as in *Nordenfelt v Maxim* [1894] AC 535), an area covenant may be reasonable.

On a smaller scale, area covenants entered into by medical practitioners prohibiting practice within a small radius (ten miles) have been held enforceable. In the case of solicitors, a five mile radius was thought, at the interlocutory stage, not to be excessive: *Edwards v Worboys* [1984] AC 724.

It is, however, to be recommended that, where possible, area covenants should not be relied on as the primary means of restraint for they are blunt instruments. It is preferable to tie the restraint to the clients of the business as in *Bridge v Deacons* for this is more closely linked to the goodwill to be protected. In addition, changes in the scale of the business are automatically taken into account.

The third example is a covenant not to engage in any competing business. As has been seen earlier, an employer has no right to protect himself against competition from his former employees; he may only impose such restraints as are necessary for the protection of his customer connection and business secrets. The position of partners is different. For they are usually participants in the goodwill of their business. This goodwill includes not just its customer connection but also its reputation generally. It is therefore reasonable for the protection of that goodwill to apply a restraint upon departing members of the partnership restricting them from engaging in any competing business. The leading case on this type of provision is *Ronbar Enterprises Ltd v Green* [1954] 1 WLR 815. The plaintiff and the defendant had entered into a partnership agreement for the purpose of publishing a weekly newspaper covering the sporting and entertainment business. The agreement provided that either party could terminate in the event of a breach by the other and thereupon purchase that other's share of the partnership at a valuation. In the event of such a purchase it was provided that the selling partner should not for five years from the date of dissolution of the partnership 'directly or indirectly carry on or be engaged or interested in any business similar to or competing with the business of the partnership'. Following a breach by the defendant, the termination and purchase provisions were applied. Soon after the defendant became involved in writing for a paper which competed with the partnership business. The covenant was attacked as being too wide to be enforceable. After finding that the words 'similar to' were severable, the Court of Appeal rejected this submission. The absence of any limitation as to area was not fatal for, as Harman J pointed out, the interest which the purchaser was entitled to be protected against in a vendor and purchaser case is competition. By contrast, in the Australian decision *Geraghty v Minter* (1979) 26 ALR 141 a covenant against involvement in a 'similar business' was upheld. Nevertheless, it is submitted that covenants against managing in any 'similar business' should be treated with caution.

Whether *Ronbar Enterprises v Green* can be regarded as authority for the proposition that in any partnership agreement which leaves the remaining partners with the goodwill a restriction of competition by outgoing partners will be enforceable, is not clear, for in this case there was a clear sale by the defendant of his share of the goodwill. In the case of agreements, such as that in *Bridge v Deacons* where no payment is made for goodwill, it is not clear whether a general restraint on competition can be justified.

It must of course be remembered that for a restriction against competition to be enforceable the goodwill which is sought to be protected must actually exist: *Vancouver Malt and Sake Brewing Co Ltd v Vancouver Breweries Ltd* [1934] AC 181.

The position of salaried partners, that is to say persons held out to the world as partners but in fact having no share in the profits of the firm, should be distinguished. Their position will be analysed by the court as if they were employees, for the reality of the position is that they hold no stake in the goodwill of the firm (see *Briggs v Oates* [1991] 1 All ER 407).

5.1 Common aspects of reasonableness

As far as reasonableness between the parties is concerned the courts take account of the element of mutuality usually present in partnership agreements. In *Bridge v Deacons*, the fact that the parties were solicitors who would presumably have cast their minds upon the issue of reasonableness also tended to show that the restraint was reasonable. Where the parties have taken professional advice this will be evidence as to reasonableness: *Whitehill v Bradford* [1952] Ch 236.

The circumstances in which the restraint may come to apply may be material to considerations of reasonableness. Thus if a restraint may apply to a partner who is expelled from a partnership for no good reason and who receives no compensation, it may for that reason be held unreasonable as between the parties: see *Hensman v Trail* (1980) 124 SJ 776 but contrast the approach in *Geraghty v Minter* where the Australian court thought this issue was irrelevant to the validity of the restraint but relevant to whether a remedy would be available in equity.

The courts generally seem to have great difficulty in assessing the reasonableness of the periods for which restraints may apply. They are most reluctant to interfere with restraints on this ground. In *Bridge v Deacons*, their Lordships considered that the justification of particular periods were hardly susceptible of proof by specific evidence. In that case, both the five year period of the restraint, and the three year period by reference to which the clients who the retiring partner could not act for, were defined and were held reasonable. In *Whitehill v Bradford*, a 21 year restraint on a doctor from acting within a ten mile radius was held valid.

It should be remembered that reasonableness is to be judged at the time that the restraint is entered into (but see p 21). Thus, in *Bridge v Deacons* the fact that a retiring partner received no payment for goodwill had to be considered together with the fact that on entering into the partnership he did not have to make any payment for it. This was a convenient and practical arrangement.

It will, in general, be difficult to show that a restraint is contrary to the public interest as opposed to showing that it goes further than is reasonably necessary for the protection of the legitimate interest of the covenantee. The public interest in the individual's liberty to trade will have been satisfied by showing that the restraint is necessary to protect the interests of the covenantee. In *Oswald Hickson Collier and Co v Carter-Ruck* [1984] AC 720, it was suggested by the Court of Appeal that it might be contrary to public policy for a solicitor to bar himself from acting for any person who required his services. This was rejected by the Privy Council in *Bridge v Deacons* as being without authority and directly contrary to a considerable volume of authority including the decision of the House of Lords in *Fitch v Dewes* [1921] 2 AC 158. In *Hensman v Trail*, it was held by Bristow J that a restriction on a doctor's right to practise in a partnership agreement, which might lead to a doctor being prevented from giving to patients the care which he is obliged to give them by the provisions of the National Health Service Act 1977, was contrary to public policy as mirrored by that Act. He accordingly held it unenforceable. However this decision has now been overruled by the Court of Appeal in *Kerr v Morris* [1986] 3 WLR 217 where it was held that since a doctor was free to leave the area in which he practised at any time, there could be no rule of public policy which bound him not to contract to leave. The ordinary rules of restraint of trade applied and, not withstanding the bar on sale of goodwill in a National Health partnership, the remaining partners still had an interest to protect.

It should be remembered that in many cases statutes will not be regarded as mirroring the public policy adopted by the courts in applying the restraint of trade doctrine. In *United Shoe Machinery Co of Canada v Brunet* [1909] AC 330, the Privy Council declined to adopt the policy of holding ties invalid evidenced by the patents legislation. Similarly, in *Regent Oil Co Ltd v Leavesley (JT) (Lichfield) Ltd* [1966] 1 WLR 1210, the court declined to find that there was anything void or illegal at common law about an agreement containing resale price maintenance provisions in spite of the subsequent enactment of legislation prohibiting it.

When considering the question of reasonableness in relation to professional partnerships, it is useful to find out from the governing professional organisation whether it provides any guidelines to its members relating to what is generally considered reasonable in the profession. For example, the Royal College of Veterinary Surgeons in its *Guide to Professional Conduct* makes it clear that competition with a former partner or employer is not a matter for disciplinary action but for negotiation and contract. In respect of partners it recommends a maximum period of five years and points out that where a retiring partner has been paid for his goodwill, there is a much stronger case for upholding longer periods of restraint than in the case of a retiring partner who has received nothing more than undrawn profits and his share of the capital. It recommends that a restraint of trade clause between a principal and an assistant 'should not in any circumstances exceed two years, the minimum might be one year . . .'.

6 Drafting considerations

As has been seen, where no express covenants govern the obligations of partners on retirement or dissolution of the partnership, the position can become most unclear. It is, therefore, of the utmost importance that the rights of the parties are clearly specified in an express agreement. Whilst detailed drafting considerations are outside the scope of this work the following points should be covered:

(a) The partners rights to engage in private business outside the partnership during its term should be clearly stated.

(b) The ownership of goodwill in the event of retirement death and other dissolution of the partnership should be provided for and particular attention should be paid to rights in business secrets and to the use of the name of the firm.

(c) If retiring partners are to be subject to restrictive covenants the choice of a restriction on soliciting or dealing with clients of the firm, on carrying on business within a defined area or on carrying on a competing business must be made carefully in the light of the known or anticipated nature of the business of the partnership. It will also be important to consider the interaction of the restraints with the provisions as to ownership of goodwill.

(d) Salaried partners should be considered as employees for restraint of trade purposes and particular care should be taken in dealing with the consequences of retirement or termination of the partnership, especially in small partnerships (see eg *Briggs v Oates*).

7 Statutory and EEC limitations

The Restrictive Trade Practices Act 1976 is considered in Appendix II. Partnerships of individuals will rarely be caught by the Act because they are considered to constitute a single person for this purpose.

For EEC provisions see Apendix III.

It is unlikely that the very existence of a partnership will contravene Art 85(1). Moreover, so long as post-partnership restraints on competition are reasonable and necessary, then it is unlikely that they will infringe Art 85(1). (*Gottfried Renter v BASF AG* [1976] 2 CMLR D44.) In any event, professional partnerships in the UK will, in general, not infringe Art 85(1) since the effect on trade between member states will be minimal.

Chapter 14

Joint Ventures

1 General applicability of the doctrine

The application of the restraint of trade doctrine to joint ventures constituted by means other than partnerships does not seem to have come before the courts directly. However, as the doctrine is not dependent upon precise formal considerations there would seem to be no good reason why restrictions accepted by parties to joint ventures should not be just as susceptible to scrutiny as restrictions accepted by partners.

2 Statutory and EEC limitations

The provisions of the Restrictive Trade Practices Act 1976 contain no exemption for partnerships between companies similar to that available to partnerships of individuals. The provisions of the Act are considered in Appendix II.

Joint ventures must always be examined carefully with regard to EEC competition law, particularly where they are between competitors or potential competitors, for there is a risk that the co-operation between the parties will restrict competition. The EEC Commission has made a block exemption for joint ventures for research and development which may be of use in certain cases. It has however not been able to develop a block exemption for joint ventures in manufacture or distribution. Such joint ventures require individual examination. The Commission has, however, published draft guidelines which indicate the approach which it will take although these are informal in nature and are somewhat out-of-date. It should be noted that a limited class of joint ventures, so-called concentrative joint ventures, fall within Council Regulation 4064/89 and the Commission has published a notice clarifying the meaning of the term 'concentrative joint venture'.

Part VI

Commercial Contracts

.

Chapter 15

Introduction

1 Relevance of the restraint of trade doctrine

This Part is primarily concerned with the application of the restraint of trade doctrine to commercial contracts. Later it deals with express confidentiality agreements.

As has been seen earlier, contracts of employment and contracts for the sale of business are not the only ones to which the doctrine of restraint of trade can apply. The doctrine is potentially unlimited in its application for, being founded on public policy, the courts are clearly capable of bringing within its scope the contracts which have hitherto escaped its scrutiny. The extent of the doctrine, put at its widest, is concisely expressed by Lord Diplock in *Petrofina (Great Britain) Ltd v Martin* [1966] Ch 146 as follows: 'A contract in restraint of trade is one in which a party (the convenantor) agrees with any other party (the convenantee) to restrict his liberty in the future to carry on trade with other persons not parties to the contract in such manner as he chooses.' However, it is clear that not all contracts which fall within this definition are in restraint of trade. For example, a contract of employment under which the employee undertakes to supply his services exclusively to his employer for the duration of the contract would not usually be said to be in restraint of trade. The difficulties of developing a test which will determine which contracts are in restraint of trade and consequently must be justified and those which are not are examined at the beginning of this book. In this Part, the treatment given by the courts to a number of the more commonly used forms of commercial contracts is examined with a view not so much to deveoping any general statement of principle (because we believe this impossible) but to show the approach of the courts and where possible to highlight some of the provisions which the courts have found particularly objectionable so that practitioners may avoid them. For this reason emphasis is placed upon more recent decisions for these reflect the current application of public policy.

2 Attitude of the courts

The history of the development of the doctrine of restraint of trade has been marked by a contest between two conflicting aspects of public policy. Firstly, contracts between businessmen should be upheld. Secondly, the courts should not sanction interference in liberty to trade. It is this conflict which makes the application of the restraint of trade doctrine so difficult in practice. It is not always obvious which aspect should prevail in any given case. To these two aspects of policy a third can be added, which may help to explain some of the more obscure distinctions in the field. This is the convenient administration of justice.

It would seem at first glance that no difficulties would arise if all contracts were subject to the doctrine of restraint of trade. However, the consequence of this would be that a party seeking to escape from any restrictive provision of an agreement could, however unmeritorious his case, put his opponent to proof of the reasonbleness of the provision. The courts are clearly concerned that this could unnecessarily delay proceedings and add to their expense. The courts have available two weapons to deal with this difficulty. In the case of certain types of contract (for example, ties contained in leases) they may be prepared to say that the restraint of trade doctrine has no application. Alternatively, where the court, as Lord Pearce put it in *Esso Petroleum Co Ltd v Harper's Garage (Stourport) Ltd* [1968] AC 269, 'sees its way clearly' no question of onus arises. Thus the court can dispense with the need for the plaintiff to prove the reasonableness of the provision if there is no possibility of the provision being unreasonable.

In assessing the likely reaction of the courts to a contract in restraint of trade, it is important to remember that the courts do not regard themselves as the administrators of any general economic policy. This is especially true in the consideration of the public interest as opposed to the interests of the parties. Therefore, the courts will listen attentively to the commercial justification of a particular period of restraint in a solus agreement. They will take account of such factors as the supplier's convenient administration of contracts with his distributors and his need for a stable distribution system for his production facilities. They will not, however, be unduly impressed by general economic evidence as to the effect of the solus agreement system on competition. What is of concern is the liberty to trade. A good example of this approach is provided by *Texaco Ltd v Mulberry Filling Station Ltd* [1972] 1 All ER 513 where Ungoed-Thomas J said:

> For my part, I prefer to decide that the restraints relied on in this case are reasonable in the interests of the public, not on balance of existing or possible economic advantages and disadvantages to the public, but because there is, in conditions as they are, no unreasonable limitation of liberty to trade. It seems to me to follow that much of the evidence in our case directed to general considerations of economic policy was irrelevant.

There is much to be said in favour of this robust approach to economic evidence. At any time there are usually a number of different economic theories which are adhered to by different experts. To expect a court to have to decide, amongst other things, which theory to adopt in determining whether a particular provision should be enforced would cause delay in proceedings which in most cases have to be pursued quickly to be of any value to the parties to the action. In addition what is an already difficult area of law would be made almost incomprehensible.

Amoco Australia Pty Ltd v Rocca Bross [1975] AC 561 is another example of the suspicion with which the common law courts will treat economic or financial evidence: the High Court of Australia concluded that a calculation of the profitability of a filling station based on conservative estimates of the likely gallonage could not be regarded as a justification for a 15 year tie.

3 Vertical and horizontal agreements

Whilst agreements between parties at different stages within the distribution process (eg between a wholesaler and a retailer) are commonly called 'vertical agreements', those between different parties at the same stage (eg between two wholesalers) are termed 'horizontal agreements'.

In this chapter this convention is adopted, more for convenience than for any other reason. The common law courts have not, in practice, adopted any markedly different test for the two types of agreement. This similarity differs from the approach of the legislature which has, on the whole, regarded horizontal agreements with greater suspicion than vertical agreements. For example, the Restrictive Trade Practices Act 1976, which is discussed in Appendix II, contains specific (albeit narrow) exemptions for the more common types of vertical agreements. This difference in approach is perhaps explained by the courts' emphasis on individual liberty to trade rather than the achievement of broad economic objectives. The court's only concern, in restraint of trade cases, when considering a horizontal agreement is to ensure that the individual party's freedom to trade is not excessively restricted. The court is not concerned with the consequences of the agreement on third parties (see for example *Mogul Steamship Co Ltd v McGregor, Gow & Co* (1889) 23 QBD 598). By contrast, third parties adversely affected by arrangements rendered void by the Restrictive Trade Practices Act 1976, are given specific rights to proceed against the parties to the offending arrangements.

Chapter 16

Solus and Other Exclusive Purchasing Agreements

1 Introduction

Exclusive purchasing agreements are agreements under which one party to a contract agrees to purchase all his requirements for goods of a certain type from the other party alone. Two of the more common examples of this type of contract are petrol station agreements and public house ties. These have each been the subject of many decisions of the courts. Most cases of the former have been heard in the last 20 years, whilst the significant decisions concerning public houses date from the last century. However, the recent extensive development of franchise operations, in the restaurant business and in other fields, may prove to be a fertile field for restraint of trade arguments. The European Court has already had the occasion to consider franchise agreements under the competition provisions of the Treaty of Rome in *Pronuptia de Paris GmbH v Pronuptia de Paris Irmgard Schillgallis* (Case 161/ 84) [1986] 1 CMLR 414 and the European Commission has issued a block exemption for franchise agreements: Commission Regulation No 4087/88.

Solus agreements, public house ties and franchise agreements have a number of common characteristics which are of relevance to the application of the restraint of trade doctrine. There is often a substantial difference in the size of the supplier compared to the purchaser. For example, in the case of solus agreements the supplier is often an oil company whereas the garage operator may be a small family company. However, the disparity of size need not necessarily lead to the supplier having an unfair advantage in negotiating the terms of the agreement. In the *Esso* case the evidence was that the extensive competition between rival oil companies to establish solus systems after the abolition of petrol rationing gave garage proprietors the power to negotiate with the suppliers on equal terms in many cases. Often the purchaser will be required to make a significant capital investment in making his premises conform to the suppliers' house style. The supplier may frequently assist the purchaser in making this investment by providing finance on advantageous terms. These and other factors must all be taken into account in assessing whether any agreement will, if it is in restraint of trade, satisfy the requirement of reasonableness.

2 Common restrictive provisions

The essential element of solus agreements and public house ties is an obligation placed upon the purchaser to buy its requirements for goods of a specified type, usually for sale from defined premises, only from the supplier with whom he is contracting. Franchise agreements will often include such a provision although they will also include important restrictions relating to use of the franchisor's trademark.

The obligation on the purchaser to buy its requirements of goods of a specified type only from the supplier can be, and in practice often is, divided into two separate obligations: an obligation to purchase specified goods only from the supplier and an obligation not to sell other goods. Where the supplier is able to fulfil the purchaser's demands for all types of goods, the distinction is not of great significance. However, where the range of goods which is available from the supplier is less extensive than that which the purchaser wishes to obtain, a heavier burden of justification is likely to be placed upon the supplier.

Certain ancillary obligations often found in agreements may vary the practical effect of these basic obligations. The purchaser will often be obliged to keep his premises open for a minimum period in each week. The price at which he is obliged to purchase the goods from the supplier will often be set by the supplier. Where the supplier has entered into similar agreements with the purchaser's competitors it may, as will be seen below, be prudent to include a provision against discrimination by the supplier in favour of competitors. Consideration must also be given as to whether to allow the purchaser to seek supplies elsewhere or to terminate the agreement if the supplier's prices do not remain competitive.

3 Restraints falling outside the restraint of trade doctrine

As has been seen already, the precise limits to the doctrine of restraint of trade are unclear. The House of Lords in *Esso Petroleum v Harper's Garage* has given some guidance but unfortunately, due to the multiplicity of reasons given by their Lordships, no clear rule has emerged.

In *Esso*, the House of Lords were faced with the argument, which had already been rejected by the Court of Appeal only a short while before in *Petrofina v Martin*, that the doctrine of restraint of trade had no application to restrictions relating only to the use to which a certain piece of land could be put. The argument was based less on any express authority but more on the fact that in many early cases relating to restrictions on particular pieces of land (including several public house ties), the issue of restraint of trade had not been considered. The House of Lords had no difficulty in rejecting this argument. They did not find it easy to explain those cases. Lord Reid was prepared to say that ordinary negative covenants preventing the use of a particular site for trading of all kinds, or of a particular kind, were not within the scope of the doctrine of restraint of trade. But, he thought, there was some difficulty if a restraint in a lease not merely prevents the doing of certain things, but also obliges the person who takes possession of the land to act in a particular way. Lord Pearce likewise accepted that covenants restraining the use of land imposed as a condition of a sale or lease were not subject to the doctrine of restraint of trade at all. But, he said, when a man fetters with a restraint land which he already occupies or owns, the fetter may come within the scrutiny of the court. Lord Morris expressed a similar view saying 'In such a situation [that is, that of voluntarily taking a lease of land with a restrictive covenant] it would not seem sensible to regard the restraint of trade doctrine as having application'. Lord Morris thought the same principle would apply to a sale of land.

It is difficult to know what weight to attach to these dicta for they were not strictly speaking necessary for the disposal of the case; all that was required was that the argument that restrictions on the use to be made on a particular piece of land should be held not to be automatically outside the restraint of trade doctrine. In addition, neither Lord Hodson nor Lord Wilberforce were prepared to accept that restrictions imposed on the sale or leasing of land were automatically outside the doctrine. Indeed, Lord Hodson reiterated his view that it was impossible to segregate any particular class of case so as to exclude it from the ambit of the doctrine: see *Dickson v Pharmaceutical Society of Great Britain* [1970] AC 403 (although he accepted that there are many cases where it is futile to raise it). A further difficulty is caused by the fact that their Lordships limited the exemption to restrictive covenants. Therefore a common provision such as an obligation to keep premises open at reasonable hours, which imposes a positive obligation regarding the trade to be conducted on the premises, would not be exempt.

The only reported example of the direct application of the dicta of Lords Reid, Morris and Pearce is found in *Cleveland Petroleum Ltd v Dartstone* [1969] 1 WLR 116. There the provision in question was contained in an underlease and was in the following terms: 'At all times to carry on the business of the petrol filling station at the premises and not to store handle sell or distribute on or from the premises any motor fuels other than those supplied by the lessors'. Lord Denning, after referring to the speeches of Lords Reid, Morris and Pearce in *Esso*, held that when a person takes possession of premises under a lease, not having been in possession previously, and on taking possession, he enters into a restrictive covenant tying him to take all his supplies from the lessor, *prima facie* the tie is valid. It is not an unreasonable restraint of trade.

It seem clear that Lord Denning was aware of the difficulty created by the positive covenant to carry on the business of a petrol filling station, otherwise he would not have needed to state that the provision was not an unreasonable restraint of trade for the question of restraint of trade would have had no application at all.

In spite of the uncertainty created by the diversity of the judgments in *Esso Petroleum v Harpers*, there appears recently to have been an increasing acceptance by the courts that the restraint of trade doctrine does not apply to restrictions in leases and the like where the lessee gives up no prior freedom. In *Gloucester City Council v Williams and Others* (1990) *The Independent*, 9 May the Court of Appeal held that the doctrine had no application to restrictions on the nature of goods which could be sold by a market stallholder imposed by the city council because at the date of the licence the stallholder had no previous right to occupy the stall or trade there. In the New Zealand Court of Appeal decision *Robinson and Another v Golden Chips (Wholesale) Ltd* [1971] NZLR 257 a covenant given by a purchaser of premises to the vendor to sell from those premises only chips supplied by the vendor was held, following *Cleveland v Dartstone* and *Esso v Harpers*, to fall outside the doctrine. Likewise, in the Australian High Court decision *Quadramain Pty Ltd v Sevastopol Investments Pty Ltd and Another* (1976) 8 ALR 555, the majority held that a covenant given by a purchaser or lessee of land on the acquisition of its interest in the land was not within the restraint of trade doctrine.

However, even where the provisions of a solus or like agreement are to be contained in a lease, it may be necessary to have regard to the restraint of trade doctrine in drafting the terms.

It is essential, if the exemption from the restraint of trade doctrine for disposals of interests in land is to be available, that the covenantor must not have any prior right to trade on the land in question before the transaction in question. Thus, if the owner of a site leases or sells the site to the supplier and takes a lease-back containing a tie, the fact that the tie is in a lease will not free it from the restraint of trade doctrine. This was clearly shown by the recent Court of Appeal decision in *Lobb (Alec) (Garages) Ltd v Total Oil (Great Britain) Ltd* [1985] 1 All ER 303. In that case the plaintiff, the owner of a freehold site on which it carried on business as a garage proprietor, had got into financial difficulties. In order to solve these difficulties the first plaintiff (Alec Lobb (Garages) Ltd) granted a long lease to the defendant in return for a premium which represented the full value of the long lease. The defendant then granted a lease for a shorter term to Mr and Mrs Lobb (the second and third plaintiffs). Mr and Mrs Lobb were the proprietors of the first plaintiff. The court held first that the choice of Mr and Mrs Lobb as lessees instead of the first plaintiff was a 'palpable device' in an endeavour to evade the doctrine of restraint of trade. The court held that accordingly the second and third plaintiffs were to be identified with the first plaintiff for the purposes of applying the doctrine. The court further held that the lease and lease-back were to be treated as two essential parts of one transaction. Accordingly, the agreement constituted by the lease and lease-back was in restraint of trade. In the Australian case *Amoco Australia Pty Ltd v Rocca Bros Motor Engineering* [1975] AC 561, the same conclusion was reached on a similar lease and lease-back transaction.

It is clear from this case that the courts will not allow technical devices to thwart the application of the doctrine of restraint of trade founded as it is upon public policy.

As was seen earlier (pp 6–10), various other tests were suggested in *Esso* which could take an agreement outside the restraint of trade doctrine. Of particular relevance is Lord Wilberforce's first test. In *Esso Petroleum Co Ltd v Harper's Garage (Stourport) Ltd* [1968] AC 269, Lord Wilberforce was unable to accept that restraints imposed upon the disposal or leasing of land were automatically outside the doctrine. He preferred an altogether different approach. He said:

the judges have been able to dispense with the necessity of justification under a public policy test of reasonableness in such contracts or provisions of contracts as, under contemporary conditions, may be found to have passed into the accepted and normal currency of commercial or contractual or conveyancing relations.

Lord Wilberforce was able to explain the brewery tie cases and, more generally, the cases where restraints imposed on the disposal of land had been upheld, in terms of this test. However, he indicated that the test was to be applied flexibly so that a restraint which in former times might have been acceptable could in the light of modern trading conditions become subject to scrutiny. In particular, he pointed out that if one finds a deviation from the accepted standards or some artificial use of an accepted legal technique, it is right that this should be examined in the light of public policy.

The judgment of Lord Denning in *Petrofina v Martin* [1966] Ch 146 contains some interesting observations on the development of the law on brewery ties. He pointed out that at the time when the leading case of *Catt v Tourle* (1869) 4 Ch App 654 was decided, the accepted view on restraint of trade was that partial restraints (the category of restraints not covering the whole country) were good if the consideration was adequate and the restraint reasonable. The consideration was adequate because the innkeeper got his lease at a lower rent or the loan of money which he needed at a lower rate. The restraint was reasonable so long as the brewer was ready to supply good beer at a reasonable price during the continuance of the security or the loan. For this reason, Lord Denning thought, no one ever doubted the validity of the ties. This explanation whilst on all fours with that of Lord Wilberforce is at variance with the view of the majority in *Esso*. It cannot be said with absolute certainty whether a simple tie in a lease or mortgage is within the doctrine of restraint of trade.

It will be apparent from the discussion above that even in the case of brewery ties contained in leases one cannot be certain that the doctrine of restraint of trade will not apply. It is many decades since these ties were fully examined by the courts in the light of public policy. The conditions of trade have changed much and such factors as the increase in concentration in the brewery industry may justify a re-examination. In addition, the terms of such ties may have changed. For a recent discussion of the current market see the Monopolies and Mergers Commission Report CM 651 entitled *The Supply of Beer—a report on the supply of beer for retail sale in the United Kingdom*, which lead to the making of two orders concerning brewery ties under the Fair Trading Act 1973 (see section 6 below).

4 Reasonableness

Once it has been determined that the doctrine of restraint of trade applies, the restraints must be justified.

Lord Reid in *Esso* broke the test to be applied into three elements. Firstly, it is necessary to consider whether the restraint goes further than to afford adequate protection to the party in whose favour it was granted; secondly, whether it can be justified in the interests of the party restrained, and thirdly, whether it must be held contrary to the public interest.

It is clear that as regards the second element the courts will not be quick to find that in a commercial contract a restraint is not in the interests of the party restrained. This would require the court to say that it knows the party's interest better than the party itself. An early example of this approach can be seen in *Badische Anilin und Soda Fabrik v Schott Segner & Co* [1892] 3 Ch 447 where Chitty J said 'Although not conclusive on the subject, the opinion of mercantile men, manifested by their acts, is not to be disregarded on the question of reasonableness'. The court will be willing to interfere on this ground in cases where there is an unconscionable conduct (see for instance *Schroeder (A) Music Publishing Co Ltd v Macaulay* [1974] 1 WLR 1308).

Where there is no unconscionable conduct, the courts will nevertheless require proof that the restraint satisfies the first element. Generally, the third element must be raised by the defendant.

4.1 The interest to be protected

The courts have not given any clear guidance as to the principles to be applied in ascertaining what is a legitimate interest which may be protected. The doctrine of restraint of trade has its origins in cases concerned with two types of restraint: those imposed by masters upon their servants and those imposed upon the sales of businesses. Outside these two categories the doctrine had until recent times received little consideration. Indeed, it is clear from the 19th century brewery tie cases that by the time the doctrine was sufficiently well formulated to be applied to brewery ties, there had been so many decisions upholding such ties without reference to the doctrine that the court felt that they could not then subject the ties to scrutiny. This is shown by the following passage from Selwyn LJ in *Catt v Tourle*, quoted by Lord Wilberforce in *Esso*:

> Every court of justice has had occasion to consider these brewers' covenants, and must be taken to be cognisant of the distinction between what are called free houses and brewers' public houses which are subject to this very covenant. We should be introducing a very great uncertainty into a very large and important trade if we were now to suggest any doubt as to the validity of a covenant so extremely common as this is.

The modern authorities on the nature of the interest to be protected begin with *Petrofina v Martin*. In that case Lord Denning MR said he thought that the early solus agreements, ie those entered into before most of the outlets for petrol were tied, might well have been in restraint of trade because the company which introduced them was 'really seeking to protect itself from competition and nothing else'. However, by the time that the agreement in that case was entered into most outlets were already subject to ties. Therefore it was important for the supplier to be able to protect his outlets from being swallowed up by his rivals. The protection by a supplier of his outlets, at least where there is a possibility that the outlets will be hard to replace, is an interest which merits protection. In the context of public houses, the existence of the tied house system and the difficulties of obtaining planning consent and appropriate liquor licences are significant barriers to entry and would seem to indicate that the preservation by a supplier of a particular public house as an outlet for his products would be an interest meriting protection. Similarly, the shortage of prime high street sites would indicate that a fast food franchisor would have good grounds for arguing that he had an interest which required protection.

Before passing on from *Petrofina*, it should be noted that whilst the court said that Petrofina might legitimately protect their outlet for petrol, they also thought that Petrofina could not impose the same degree of protection in relation to motor oils. This is somewhat curious. The reason behind the distinction was that motorists might be under the impression that it was unsatisfactory to mix Petrofina oil with their preferred brand of oil. Accordingly, motorists who wanted oil as well as petrol might pass by a garage which advertised Petrofina only. However, it is hard to understand why Petrofina should not have the same interest in securing exclusive outlets for their oil as for their petrol. One would not expect a provision in a public house tie that required the publican to purchase soft drinks and mixers as well as beer from his supplier to be unacceptable. Nevertheless, it must be of some concern in the light of *Petrofina*. Lord Reid in *Esso* doubted the reasoning in *Petrofina*; it may have been this point that he had in mind. (See also the Supply of Beer (Tied Estate) Order 1989 discussed at section 6 below.)

In *Esso*, the concept of the supplier's interest was interpreted more widely. Lord Reid accepted that the supplier might be concerned not only with maintaining individual outlets but also with maintaining and managing his distribution system as a whole. Their Lordships held it was legitimate to take account of, not just the likely period it would take the supplier to replace the outlet following expiry of the tie, but also the number of outlets that the supplier had to manage. Esso had some 6,600 outlets and the need to avoid an excessive number of ties expiring in any year was a legitimate interest. The fact that Esso had expended large sums on the construction of refineries and accordingly needed secure outlets for the distribution of the product of those refineries, was another interest which required protection. So too the economies of distribution to be made from supplying to solus outlets were relevant interests and more generally the economies of overall planning were to be taken into account.

It is important to note that Lord Reid, at least, did not appear to think that a mortgage in respect of which the right of repayment had been deferred was an interest meriting protection. For he said 'But as [the respondents] have tendered repayment, I do not think that the existence of the loan and the mortgage puts the appellants in any stronger position than if the original agreements had permitted repayment at an earlier date'. This approach is entirely logical. The supplier who provides finance to the purchaser at advantageous rates can legitimately expect to reap the corresponding advantage of a tie for so long as the purchaser takes advantage of that finance. However, once the purchaser has offered to repay that finance the supplier cannot say that his security will suffer if the tie falls away for he will no longer have any need for security.

Whilst the mortgage remains in force, however, the supplier may well have an interest to protect. He may, therefore, be able to justify the tie for so long as the loan remains outstanding provided that he does not prohibit early repayment.

Although this principle must, following *Esso*, be regarded as clearly established, it should be noted that a number of cases on the permissibility of mortgages coupled with ties in which the right of redemption has been deferred have been decided in favour of the mortgagee with no reference to the restraint of trade doctrine (see *Biggs v Hoddinott* [1898] 2 Ch 307 and *Hill v Regent Oil Co Ltd* (1962) EGD 452). If the view expressed by Lord Diplock in *Petrofina* that the court cannot raise the issue of restraint of trade of its own motion is correct, one cannot be certain that the doctrine would not have been applied in these cases had it been raised.

The approach in *Esso* should, however, be contrasted with that in *Queensland Co-operative Millies Association Ltd v Pameg Pty Ltd* (1973) 1 ALR 47 D. The High Court of Australia held that a commitment by a baker to use only a particular supplier's flour which lasted so long as any sums lent to the baker by the supplier were outstanding and which prohibited complete repayment before seven years, was a reasonable covenant. The issue which had to be decided was whether a seven year tie could be justified, leaving to one side the loan, by reference to the legitimate interests of the supplier in securing his outlets.

In *Texaco Ltd v Mulberry Filling Station Ltd* [1972] 1 All ER 513 it was suggested that the price stability provided by the solus system was relevant. However, as mentioned earlier, the judge preferred not to rely on the economic evidence and so it is difficult to determine whether he thought that price stability was a relevant interest.

Once the interest to be protected has been ascertained the court will then assess whether the restriction goes further than is necessary to protect that interest.

In the case of solus agreements and similar ties, the court will not look at the individual provisions of the agreement in isolation. Thus the reasonableness of a tie will depend not just upon its length but also upon the extent to which the purchaser is obliged to keep his premises open and whether the purchaser is given any protection as to the price which the supplier will charge. Whether the provisions are contained in a lease will no doubt also be extremely significant. Although, in principle, the courts will not weigh the adequacy of the consideration provided by the covenantee to the covenantor, the Australian Court, at least, has held that the quantum of the consideration may be examined as part of the circumstances of the case against which the question of reasonableness is to be decided (see *Amoco v Rocca Bros*).

4.2 Time and other factors

The term of the tie is clearly of vital importance. In *Esso* a tie of just under five years in a petrol station solus agreement was held to be reasonable whereas a ties of 21 years was not. As was mentioned above the court took notice of the fact that Esso wished to ensure that on average no more than 20 per cent of its ties came up for renewal every year in holding the shorter tie to be reasonable. However, the court took the view that it was impossible to foresee trading conditions 20 years hence, and in the absence of any evidence to justify the tie being longer than five years were not prepared to find it reasonable.

It was, however, a material factor that Esso had not assured to Harpers Garage a supply of petrol at a reasonable price come what may. If they had done so then a longer period of restraint may have been justifiable.

In addition, their Lordships took the fact that the purchaser was obliged to carry on trading to be a restrictive element of the agreement: this could compel the purchaser to trade at a loss. This was also a factor in the decision to uphold a 15 year tie in *Amoco v Rocca Bros*.

Following *Esso Petroleum Co Ltd v Harper's Garage (Stourport) Ltd* [1968] AC 269 only in two reported English cases has there been any serious consideration of the reasonableness of solus ties. Although in the first of these cases, *Texaco v Mulberry*, the judge discussed at length the economic evidence relating to the agreement in question, he did not when deciding the question of reasonableness give any real explanation as to how he reached his decision (beyond saying that he did not think that the evidence directed to general considerations of economic policy was relevant). In addition, he did not discuss the first two elements of Lord Reid's test of reasonableness separately. Accordingly, it is difficult to draw any conclusion from the judgment.

The second decision, *Lobb (Alec) (Garages) Ltd v Total Oil (Great Britain) Ltd* [1985] 1 All ER 303, concerned a rescue operation mounted, reluctantly, by the supplier to save an ailing garage business. The garage owner granted a 51 year lease at a premium and a peppercorn rent to the supplier. The supplier granted a lease-back to the proprietors of the owner. (As was seen above, the different identity of the garage owner and its proprietors was not considered relevant by the court.) The lease-back was for 21 years and contained a tie for the whole of that period. The lease-back gave the tenants a right to break after seven and 14 years. The court held the tie reasonable. Amongst the factors that they took into account was the fact that it was unlikely for planning reasons that during the 21 year term the property would be used for any purpose except a filling station. The court found that it made no significant difference to the public at large whether the station sold one brand of petrol or another. Of particular importance was the right to break after seven years. Bearing in mind that the station was already subject to a tie for three to four years the court saw no real significance in the difference between a tie for five years and the term of seven years until the first break. The court did not think that the fact that upon exercising the right to break the proprietors would have to leave the site was unreasonable, for value had already been given in the premium under the lease to the supplier.

In *Amoco v Rocca Bros*, a case which like *Alec Lobb v Total* involved a sale and lease-back (although it was not a rescue operation), the Australian High Court, following *Esso v Harpers*, held a 15 year tie unreasonable. Of particular importance to the finding of unreasonableness was the obligation to purchase a specified minimum gallonage of petrol and, perhaps more importantly, the obligation to carry on the business of a petrol station throughout the term. These provisions could, if business declined, have imposed an unreasonable burden on Rocca and the long period of the lease rendered them unduly harsh.

How far reasonableness might be affected by unforeseen or unlikely circumstances which might result in the tie causing hardship to the purchaser came before the Court of Appeal in *Shell UK Ltd v Lostock Garage Ltd* [1977] 1 All ER 481. The defendant was subject to a tie to Shell. The tie was to last for five years and was valid in the light of the circumstances foreseeable at the time it was entered into. The agreement contained no express provision to the effect that Shell would not discriminate against Lostock in the prices it would charge to its neighbours. During a spell of intense petrol price competition Shell made a support scheme available to neighbouring garages but not to Lostock. As a result Lostock had to trade at a loss. Lostock thus sought cheaper supplies elsewhere. Lord Denning, relying on some rather tenuous dicta from *Esso*, held that the principle that the reasonableness of a restraint of trade was to be assessed only in the light of the circumstances at the time the contract was entered into was fallacious. Since the effect of holding a covenant to be in unreasonable restraint of trade was merely to render it unenforceable if the court finds that a covenant has operated unfairly or unreasonably it will not enforce it. Thus Lord Denning was able to hold that for the period while Shell was supporting Lostock's competitors the restraint was unenforceable. Whether this principle will be followed by future courts remains to be seen. Bridge LJ and Ormrod LJ found themselves unable to agree with Lord Denning's reasoning although Bridge LJ felt able to come to the same decision as the Master of the Rolls by holding that there was an implied term in the agreement to the effect that Shell would not discriminate unfairly against Lostock.

The cases so far referred to have concerned situations where prior to the restraint being imposed the covenantor already had a right to trade on the land in question. *Cleveland Petroleum Co v Dartstone Ltd* [1969] 1 WLR 116 concerned a 25 year lease of a petrol station where the original lessee had no right to trade on the land in question prior to the grant of the lease. The lease contained a tie for its entire period. The defendants took an assignment of the lease and covenanted to abide by the terms of the assignment. The defendants then told the plaintiffs that they considered the tie void. The plaintiffs applied for an injunction to restrain the defendants from breaking the agreement by storing, handling or distributing on or from Country Oak service station any motor fuels other than the plaintiffs'. The Court of Appeal held that the covenant was not an unreasoanble restraint of trade and that the injunction should be granted. The principal basis for the decision was, as has been mentioned before, that such a tie is *prima facie* valid where it is contained in a lease granted to a person not previously in possession of the land. However, if Lord Denning had been satisfied that this was sufficient to dispense with the case it is hard to explain why he categorised the tie as not being in unreasonable restraint of trade. It is possible that he thought that the existence of the positive obligation in the lease to carry on the business of a filling station could taint the simple restriction on stocking other motor fuels so as to expose it to a test of reasonableness. But it may be that this is reading too much into his words.

Another interesting point which was touched upon in *Cleveland v Dartstone* was whether the validity of a restraint in a lease as against an assignee of the lease depends upon whether the covenant would have been valid against the original lessee. In *Cleveland*, it was assumed that the original lessee did not at the time that the lease was granted have a right to trade on the premises. If this had not been the case and the restraint had accordingly been unenforceable against the original lessee the position is unclear. The answer may depend upon the circumstances of the assignment. If the incoming lessee enters into a direct covenant with the lessor to comply with the terms of the lease, it is submitted that this should cure any defects in the original lease for the new lessee has no prior right to trade on the site. But if the new lessee enters into no such covenant then, by virtue of privity of estate, the new lessee will be bound by the original covenants. If one of these covenantts is void as in restraint of trade it is hard to see how it can revive upon an assignment.

If the term of a tie is reasonable it will be reasonable to provide that the purchaser will not dispose of the business without procuring that the person to whom he disposes of it covenants with the supplier to abide by the terms of the tie. For as Lord Reid explained in *Esso*, this is the only means by which the supplier can maintain his outlet for the duration of the tie. Such a provision must, in any event, be more reasonable than requiring the purchaser to remain in occupation for the duration of the tie.

Whilst the conclusions to be drawn from the case mentioned above are directly applicable to solus agreements they can be applied with caution to brewery ties and other forms of franchising. Clearly, where the person entering into the tie is entering into a lease of premises on which he had no prior right to trade, the same rule must apply. But it would be dangerous to conclude that five years would automatically be a reasonable period for a tie. One would suspect that in the case of tied houses ties are frequently of much longer periods. This may be reasonable. The development of a profitable trade for a new brand of beer at a particular public house may well take longer than five years, particularly in a local community and for this reason the supplier may require a longer tie.

Similarly in a franchising operation the capital investment in equipment provided by the supplier may not be recouped in five years and this may justify a longer tie.

It is not uncommon, in franchising agreements, to find some form of restriction applying after the expiry of the term of the franchise. *Prontaprint plc v Landon Litho Ltd* [1987] FSR 315 was an interlocutory decision on such a restriction. An injunction was granted in respect of a restriction on the former franchises from, *inter alia*, engaging in the franchised services within a radius of half a mile of the franchised premises for a period of three years.

4.3 Public policy

The first two of the three elements of Lord Reid's test of reasonableness have now been examined. That leaves only the question of whether the restraint is contrary to the public interest. However, Lord Reid, in the same judgment in which he discerned these three elements, said that he thought the reason why the court will not enforce a restraint which goes further than affording adequate protection to the legitimate interest of the party in whose favour it is granted, was because too wide a restraint is contrary to the public interest. The distinction between the first and third element lies perhaps in the onus of proof. The first element is part of what has been traditionally regarded as reasonableness in the interests of the parties. The onus of proof of this generally lies on the party seeking to enforce the restriction. The third element is what has traditionally been regarded as the reasonableness in the public interest. The onus is on the party asserting unreasonableness to prove it.

In the case of solus agreements, the third element has usually been dispensed with simply by saying that the public do not much care which brand of petrol is sold at a particular filling station. It is difficult to foresee a case arising in relation to tying agreements in which the public interest would require a covenant that went no further than protecting the supplier's interests to be held unenforceable. A possible example might arise if, as part of a brewery tie, the supplier required the publican to rent gaming machines only from approved suppliers with whom the suplier had a commission arrangement. Whilst the supplier might have a legitimate interest to protect (although this is not certain) it is arguable that the arrangement might be contrary to the public interest in preventing suppliers of gaming machines access to potential customers. As will be seen below, the gaming machine supplier would have no cause of action (except possibly for a declaration) in such circumstances.

5 Drafting

It is not sensible in a book of this nature to suggest particular forms of clause to be used as precedents in the drafting of solus and other tying agreements for each contract must be tailored to make it reasonable in the circumstances. However, the following may serve as a useful checklist of points to be remembered when drafting tying clauses.

5.1 Term

In petrol station solus agreements five years' fixed term is likely to be held reasonable (see *Esso v Harper's*). It has not been decided whether a five year rolling term (ie a tie terminable upon five years' notice) would be reasonable and a shorter term might be safer. Where the provisions are contained in a lease and the tenant has no prior right to occupy a tie for the duration of the lease should be reasonable but it might be wise to give the tenant a right to break, particularly where he has no guarantee as to competitive pricing (see *Alec Lobb, Shell v Lostock, Amoco v Rocca Bros* (High Court of Australia) and *Cleveland v Dartstone*). Avoid ties whose terms depend upon selling specific quantities for the less benefit the purchaser receives the longer the ties will last (see *Petrofina*).

Similar rules probably apply to brewery ties, but it may well be the case that longer ties are acceptable.

5.2 Price

It is important that the price or means of determining the price is specified, otherwise an undertaking to supply at a reasonable price may be implied (see *Foley v Classique Coaches Ltd* [1934] 2 KB 1). Some means of dealing with difficulties which might arise if price competition makes the purchasers' trade unprofitable should be included, particularly in longer ties (see *Shell v Lostock* and *Amoco v Rocca Bros*).

173

5.3 Obligations to trade

If a positive obligation is to be placed on the purchaser compelling him to trade, this has two consequences. Firstly, greater attention must be paid to pricing for the purchaser may be forced to trade at a loss (see *Esso*). Secondly, an agreement in a lease which might otherwise be outside the doctrine may be subjected to scrutiny.

5.4 Mortgages

Including a tie in a mortgage will not automatically exclude the restraint of trade doctrine. It may be permissible to continue a tie for so long as the mortgage remains on foot, but not if the only reason for retaining the tie is that the right to redeem the mortgage has been deferred unless the duration of the tie can be shown to be reasonable independently of the mortgage.

5.5 Ancillary restraints

Restraints which relate to items for which the supplier cannot independently justify a tie should, if possible, not be included in the tie. (See for example the difficulties caused by including motor oil in *Petrofina v Martin* [1966] Ch 146— NB motor oil is perhaps not a good example for it has not subsequently caused difficulty.)

5.6 Assignment

It should be permissible to require the purchaser to sell his business only to someone who undertakes to perform the tie. (See *Esso and Amoco v Rocca*.)

6 Statutory and EEC limitations

Following the report of the Monopolies and Mergers Commission on its enquiry into the supply of beer, two orders were made by the Secretary of State under the Fair Trading Act 1973 which are of direct relevance to beer ties. These were the Supply of Beer (Loan Ties, Licensed Premises and Wholesale Prices) Order 1989 (SI No 2258) and the Supply of Beer (Tied Estate) Order 1989 (SI No 2390). Article 2 of the Supply of Beer (Loan Ties, Licensed Premises and Wholesale Prices) Order 1989 provides that it is unlawful to make or carry out an agreement under, or in relation to, which a brewer, or a member of a brewery group, makes a loan or gives any other term of financial assistance to another person if it precludes 'relevant purchases'. Relevant purchases are defined as purchases of beer or other drinks for retail sale on licensed premises of beer or any other drink *not* purchased from a party to the agreement. However, relevant purchases by the persons to whom the loan or financial assistance is given may be precluded provided that repayment may be made at any time on not more than three months' notice and the restrictions on relevant purchases cease on repayment. Article 2(3) of the Order gives a very limited power to increase interest rates where repayment is made during the first year of the agreement.

The Order also prohibits brewers or, with limited exceptions, members of a brewery group from imposing any prohibition on the use of premises which they are selling as licensed premises after the sale (see Art 3).

The main object of the Supply of Beer (Tied Estate) Order 1989 is to impose limits on the size of brewers' tied estate. However, it also provides, in Art 7, that in certain circumstances brewers must allow their tied houses to offer a guest beer and must not extend the tie to non-alcoholic drinks. Article 7 applies to any agreement to which a large brewer (essentially a brewer or brewery group with interests in more than 2,000 licensed premises) is a party which precludes or restricts 'relevant purchases' (defined as mentioned above). It provides that no party may make or carry out such an agreement to the extent that, in so far as it relates to beer, the person restricted from making relevant purchases from whomsoever he may choose is prevented from purchasing at least one brand of draught cask-conditioned beer selected by him (the so called 'guest beer') or to the extent that it restricts relevant purchases of low or non-alcoholic drinks. It should be noted that Art 7(3) of the Order provides that if the agreements subjects the publican to any disadvantage in consequence of his selection of the source of his guest beer he is deemed to be prevented from purchasing it from whomsoever he may choose.

The provisions of the Restrictive Trade Practices Act 1976 must be considered carefully in the drafting of any solus agreement or like tie. For a general discussion of the provisions of the Act see Appendix II. In general resale price maintenance is now prohibited by the Resale Prices Act 1976.

In addition, the provisions of EEC competition law must be considered (see Appendix III). The scope of this book does not extend to a full discussion of the application of EEC competition rules to solus agreements, brewery ties and franchise agreements but it should be borne in mind that if any such agreement is not of purely local effect and may have an effect upon trade between member states of the European Community, the rules may apply. Of particular relevance are the provisions of Commission Regulation 1984/83 which exempts certain forms of exclusive distribution agreements from the provisions of Art 85(1) of the Treaty of Rome. This regulation contains specific provisions concerning brewery ties and petrol solus agreements. Also relevant is Commission Regulation No 4087/88 concerning franchise agreements. In addition, the EEC Commission has published various notices in relation to such agreements.

Chapter 17

Exclusive Distribution and Agency Agreements

1 Introduction

Exclusive distribution and agency agreements are amongst the most common forms of distribution arrangements found in commerce. In each case, they are used by suppliers who wish to distribute their products in particular territories but do not wish to go to the expense of setting up their own distribution network in the territory. By appointing a distributor or agent in the territory the supplier can take advantage of the distribution and marketing skills of his agent or distributor. The distributor may have local knowledge not readily available to the supplier. Furthermore, the supplier is saved the significant expense of establishing for himself the distribution network.

The distinction in legal terms between a distribution agreement and an agency agreement is that under the former the supplier sells to a distributor who then resells on his own account. In the case of the latter the agent procures orders for the supplier. On each order which the supplier accepts he pays the agent a commission. For the purpose of the application of the doctrine of restraint of trade the key feature is not the distinction between distributor and agent but the exclusivity granted to the agent or distributor. Under an exclusive agreement, the supplier agrees not to give anyone else the right to sell or to procure orders from customers in the exclusive territory. Indeed, a further distinction is sometimes drawn between exclusive and sole arrangements. Under the former the supplier undertakes in addition that he will not himself sell to customers in the exclusive territory.

2 Typical restrictions

Three types of restriction are commonly found in exclusive agency and distribution agreements. There is the grant of exclusivity. This typically takes the form of an undertaking by the supplier not to sell the products the subject of the agreement to any other person for resale in the territory. In the case of an agency agreement, it may take the form of an undertaking not to appoint any other agent for the territory. Depending upon whether the arrangement is exclusive or sole, the supplier may himself be limited.

Next there are often undertakings by the agent or distributor not to sell, distribute or act as agent for any products which compete with the products the subject of the agency agreement. This restriction may last beyond the expiry of the agency or right to distribute for a period of one or two years.

Finally, there are resale price maintenance provisions. These do not arise in agency arrangements because the supplier contracts directly with the customers in the agent's territory so there is no element of resale. In distribution arrangements, the supplier may be anxious to maintain the market price of his goods and to avoid excessive discounting. As is noted later, resale price maintenance is in general prohibited by statute in England although there are some exceptions such as the net book agreement which regulates the resale prices of books. Generally, EEC competition law regards resale price maintenance with disfavour.

It is clear that most exclusive agency and distribution agreements will be enforceable notwithstanding the restraint of trade doctrine. Indeed, there have been very few cases in which the issue of restraint of trade has ever been raised. Earlier, the tests for determining whether an agreement is subject to the restraint of trade doctrine were discussed. There is no great degree of certainty as to whether the restraint of trade doctrine will apply to exclusive distribution or agency agreements so as to render it necessary to examine their reasonableness. Lord Hodson in *Esso*, seemed to think that the doctrine applied. However, he said that he did 'not anticipate a spate of litigation in which contracts of say 'sole agency' will be assailed'. Presumably he thought that it was most unlikely that the court would hold such a contract unreasonable. Lord Pearce was more robust. He said:

> The doctrine does not apply to ordinary commercial contracts for the regulation and promotion of trade during the existence of the contract, provided that any prevention of work outside the contract, viewed as a whole is directed towards absorption of the parties' services and not their sterilisation. Sole agencies are a normal and necessary incident of commerce and those who desire the benefits of a sole agency must deny themselves the opportunities of other agencies.

Lord Wilberforce also indicated that contracts of sole agency would fall within the class of contracts to which the restraint of trade doctrine need not be applied.

The dicta of their Lordships would tend to suggest that all contracts of sole agency of distribution would fall outside the restraint of trade doctrine. However, the decision of the Privy Council in *AG of the Commonwealth of Australia v Adelaide Steamship Co* [1913] AC 781 has cast some doubt on the point. The case concerned an exclusive distribution agreement between a group of colliery proprietors and a number of shipping companies. The essence of the agreement was that the colliery proprietors undertook to supply their coal exclusively to the shipping companies and that the shipping companies undertook to purchase their requirements only from the colliery proprietors. The agreement also contained maximum (but not minimum) resale price provisions. The court held that the agreement was without doubt a contract in restraint of trade. It was not necessary for the court to decide in that case whether the contract was reasonable in the interests of the parties, for the case concerned a statutory provision which made the entry into an agreement or combination to restrain trade to the detriment of the public an offence. The court held that the agreement was not to the detriment of the public. It is not clear from the decision exactly why the agreement was held to be in restraint of trade. It may have been held so, not simply because it imposed the restrictive provisions mentioned above but because it involved the combined action of a group of colliery proprietors and a group of shipping companies which had the effect as between the members of each group of eliminating competition. The case should not, it is submitted, be regarded as authority for the proposition that ordinary contracts of sole agency are to be regarded as subject to the restraint of trade doctrine.

An example of the usual approach may be found in *Elliman Sons and Co v Carrington & Son Ltd* [1901] 2 Ch 275. This case concerned not an exclusive arrangement but a resale price maintenance provision. The defendants were wholesalers. They agreed not to sell the plaintiffs' goods below specified prices and to bind retailers purchasing from them to do likewise. Kekewich J held that the plaintiffs were fully at liberty to sell their goods on the terms that they did and that the doctrine of restraint of trade had no application. More typically, in *British Oxygen Co Ltd v Liquid Air Ltd* [1925] Ch 383 and *Servais Bouchard v Princes Hall Restaurant Ltd* (1904) 20 TLR 574, the issue of restraint of trade was barely considered. In *Prudential Assurance Co v Rodiques* [1982] 2 NZLR 54, a clause providing that an insurance selling agent's entitlement to payment of commission terminated on termination of his agency (with the result that substantial repayments by the agent became due) was held not to constitute a restraint of trade.

It seems, therefore, that the parties need not, when entering into sole or exclusive agency contracts containing restrictions of the type described above and no other unusual restrictions or circumstances, be concerned with the restraint of trade doctrine. However, a note of caution must be sounded. There is a strong analogy between contracts of exclusive agency or distribution and contracts of employment. Thus, whilst restrictions placed on the agent or distributor during the term of the agreement may escape examination, restrictions applying after the end of the term are likely to require to be justified in accordance with the restraint of trade doctrine. Likewise a restriction which is not included for the purpose of directing the distributors' or agents' efforts towards the promotion of the supplier's products may require justification. Take for example, the case of a supplier requiring the distributor, as a condition of the grant of agency for one of its products to stop acting as agent for another supplier's products. If the other supplier's products are competitive with the products to be supplied under the agency, then all well and good. The doctrine will not apply for the restraint will be aimed at directing the agent to promoting the suppliers' products effectively. But if the products to be dropped compete with products of the supplier which are not being made available to the agent, the doctrine may still have to be applied, for it may not be possible to show that the restraint is aimed at the absorption of the agent's services but merely at preventing competition. The size of the agent's business may be relevant. If the agent has only resources to handle only a few products at a time, the restraint may be directed to the absorption of the agent's services. Much will depend on the facts.

3 Reasonableness

As has been seen above it will only infrequently be necessary to justify the reasonableness of a contract of sole agency or distribution. When it is necessary to do so, it will be because of some unusual restriction which has been imposed. It is, therefore, difficult to give any general guidance as to the factor which will be taken into account in determining the reasonableness of any provision. It will be necessary to examine the position in the light of the principles set out earlier and to draw upon any analogous contracts discussed elsewhere in this book.

Unusually, in *Badische Anilin und Soda Fabrik v Schott Segner and Co* [1892] 3 Ch 447, a restriction in an exclusive distribution agreement came before the court. The defendants had been appointed exclusive agents for the sale of the plaintiffs' products in the north of England. The agency was initially for four years but if not determined by notice it ran for successive two year periods. The defendants bound themselves after termination of the contract not to enter any like or similar business for three years. The restraint was held to be reasonable. The judge held that the restraint amounted in effect to a sale by the defendants of their interest in the goodwill of a large business built up by the capital, skill and industry of the contracting parties. The defendants had received a large remuneration and to hold the restriction void would tend to deprive persons in the position of the defendant of the advantage of making their own bargains for their remuneration. (See also *Prontaprint plc v London Litho Ltd* above p 172.)

4 Drafting

It has been seen that only in unusual cases will an exclusive distribution or agency agreement be held to be in restraint of trade. Accordingly, the only guidance which may be given is that if any unusual restraint is to be included, its validity should be considered in relation to the general principles discussed at the beginning of this book. In such a case it would also be advisable clearly to separate the unusual restraints from the rest so as to ensure that, if for any reason the unusual provision is held unenforceable, the remaining provisions are not also struck down.

5 Statutory and EEC limitations

The provisions of the Restrictive Trade Practices Act 1976 must be considered. A general discussion of the provisions of the Act is contained in Appendix II. Of particular importance in the case of exclusive agency and distribution agreements is the exemption set out in para 2 of Sched 3 to the Act. It should be noted that this exemption only applies to agreements between two persons.

Therefore the inclusion in the agreement of a third party to guarantee the obligations of the distributor may render registrable an otherwise exempt agreement.

In the case of self-employed commercial agents particular regard must be had to the EC Council Directive of 18 December 1986 on the coordination of the laws of member states relating to self-employed commercial agents. This directive must be implemented by the United Kingdom no later than 1 January 1994 and it will impose limits on the scope of post-termination restraints on agents and imposes certain requirements as to the calculation of commission. The Department of Trade and Industry has issued draft implementing regulations.

In addition, the provisions of EEC competition law must be considered (see Appendix III). The scope of this book does not extend to a full discussion of the application of EEC competition rules to exclusive agency and distribution agreements. If the agreement is not of purely local effect and may have an effect upon trade between member states of the European Community the rules may apply. Of particular relevance are the provisions of Commission Regulation 1983/84 which exempts the more common forms of exclusive distribution agreements from the provisions of Art 85(1) of the Treaty of Rome and of the Commission Notice on agency agreements which indicates that agency agreements where the agent does not have substantial independence of action as regards price and certain other matters, will not be regarded as falling within the EEC competition rules. (It is understood that the EC Commission is working on a revised draft of the notice on agency agreements.) There will, of course, be many cases where the arrangements will fall within the EEC Commission Notice on minor agreements.

Agreements for the distribution of cars and spare parts for cars have been singled out for special consideration both by the UK government and by the EEC Commission: Commission Regulation No 123/85 is a block exemption directed specifically at motor vehicle distribution and servicing agreements. The Restriction on Agreements (Manufacturers and Importers of Motor Cars) Order 1982 (SI No 1146) promulgated under the Fair Trading Act 1973 also prohibits the imposition of certain restrictions on the distribution of spare parts for motor vehicles.

Chapter 18

Licences and Tying Agreements

1 Introduction

Patent licences have for many years been a common means by which an inventor has been able to reap the fruits of his invention without the need to involve himself in its manufacture and distribution. In the field of high technology, licences of copyright or know-how are often used to similar effect. Likewise, the owner of a valuable trademark is able to extend the availability of his products by licensing third parties to manufacture and sell goods to his specification under the trademark. Although ties have commonly been included in licences, licences are not the only agreements which contain ties; that is to say covenants to purchase goods exacted by a seller as a condition of entering into another transaction. Such obligations may for example be imposed as a condition of the sale of other goods.

2 Common restrictions

The restrictions commonly imposed upon licensees can, broadly speaking, be divided into two categories. The first category contains provisions which are limits on the rights granted by the licensor. Before entering into the licence, the potential licensee could be restrained by the licensor from carrying on any of the activities prohibited by the first category of restriction through the exercise of his intellectual property rights.

The second category contains restrictions which restrain the licensee from doing things which he would otherwise have been free to do.

Restrictions falling into the first category include limits placed on the quantities of licensed products which the licensee may produce, limits on the territory in which the licensee may manufacture and sell the products, limits on the customers to whom the licensee may sell the products and limits on the field of application in which the licensee may use the licensed technology.

In the second category, one finds undertakings not to be concerned with the manufacture or sale of products which compete with the licensed products, undertakings to assign the benefit of any improvements to the licensed technology to the licensor, and obligations to buy products not covered by the licence from the licensor. These undertakings, apart from undertakings in relation to improvements, are often found in agreements other than licences.

3 The relevance of the restraint of trade doctrine

As regards the restrictions falling into the first category, the restraint of trade doctrine would appear to have little application for the restraint, if it can properly be said to be a restraint at all, arises not as a consequence of the contract between the parties, but because of the rights granted by Parliament to the owner of the relevant intellectual property right. For the court to hold that the licensor could not limit the rights he grants, would be to place the doctrine of restraint of trade above the express provisions of statute. It is of interest that in *British Leyland Motor Corporation Ltd v Armstrong Patents Co Ltd* [1986] 2 WLR 400, which concerned the use of copyright by a car manufacturer to prevent third parties from manufacturing spare parts for its cars, the House of Lords made no reference to the application of the doctrine of restraint of trade. If the doctrine were capable of being used to control the limits which a licensor could place upon a licensee, one might have expected it to have been applied in that case.

As regards restraints in the second category, there seems to be no reason in principle why the doctrine of restraint of trade should not apply. However, in practice the courts have been reluctant to apply the doctrine. In *Tool Metal Manufacturing Co Ltd v Tungsten Electric Co Ltd* [1955] 1 WLR 761, the licensee was authorised under a patent to manufacture the contract material subject to a quota. If the licensee exceeded the quota, compensation was payable to the licensor. The licensee's argument that the provision requiring payment was in restraint of trade was rejected.

A more significant example of the courts' reluctance to interfere in cases involving tying restrictions was shown in *United Shoe Machinery Co of Canada v Brunet* [1909] AC 330. The plaintiffs had supplied machinery for the manufacture of shoes to the defendants under leases. The leases contained tying provisions which prohibited the defendants from using the machines for manufacturing shoes if any other part of the manufacturing process was carried out by machines not supplied by the plaintiffs. The court rejected the defendants' arguments that the restriction was in restraint of trade. The reasoning of the Privy Council was, as Lord Reid remarked in *Esso Petroleum v Harper's Garage* [1968] AC 269, not very satisfactory. The Privy Council was able to dispose of any proper consideration of the reasonableness of the restraint by saying:

> Their Lordships do not think that the case of *Nordenfelt v Maxim Nordenfelt Guns and Ammunition Co* [1894] AC 535 or authorities of that class can have any application to this case. In each of them the person restrained from trading had granted, presumably for adequate consideration, some property, privilege or right to the person who desired to impose the restraint upon him and, in order that the latter might receive, without injury to the public, that for which he had paid, the contract imposing the restraint was held to be valid only where the restraint was in itself reasonable in reference to the interests both of the contracting parties and of the public.

It is submitted that this reasoning is indeed defective for it does not take account, for example, of the many cases in which restraints on employees had been held invalid.

However, whilst the reasoning, such as there was, may not have been very satisfactory, the decision itself would appear to be on all fours with the dicta of their Lordships in *Esso*. The restraint imposed by the leases related only to the use of the machines which were leased by the plaintiffs. The defendants had no prior right to use the machines before the grant of the leases and accordingly, in accepting the restraint, gave up no freedom which they would otherwise have had. Similar restraints, whilst perhaps not quite so extensive in nature, are often found in modern leasing agreements for high technology equipment. These will often provide that the equipment, which might for example be a computer, should not be used in conjunction with any other equipment not approved by the lessor. It would be surprising if such a provision could be challenged on the grounds of restraint of trade. If the logic for exempting such a restriction from the restraint of trade doctrine is indeed that the lessee gives up no freedom which he would otherwise have, then there should be no reason why a similar provision could not be imposed upon the sale of equipment. Suppose for example, a manufacturer of computers were to sell only upon terms that the purchaser should not interconnect his equipment to that of any other manufacturer. If the reasoning of the majority in *Esso* is correct, then a purchaser should be in the same position as a lessee and the doctrine should not apply. Likewise, if a car manufacturer were to sell his cars upon terms that no spare part might be used except that of his own manufacture, the doctrine should not apply. But this would be contrary to the entire spirit of the judgment in *British Leyland v Armstrong*, referred to above, and it therefore seems probable that the court would reformulate or distinguish *Esso* and apply the doctrine.

If the doctrine is to be applied, one has to consider whether the restriction is reasonable. The question of reasonableness as between the parties can, as has been seen above, be left to the parties in commercial contracts where there is no great inequality of bargaining power. As far as injury to the public is concerned, this will be hard to demonstrate. That leaves the question whether the restraint goes further than is necessary to protect the legitimate interests of the covenantee.

In the case of restriction in a licence against dealing in other products, the arguments discussed in relation to distribution and agency agreements will be relevant. The issue will be whether the restriction is directed towards concentrating the efforts of the licensee on the licensed products or has some other motive. As far as obligations to purchase other products from the licensor or supplier are concerned, it is arguable that these should not be held unreasonable. It is of the essence of liberty to trade that a supplier should be able to make the best use of his competitive advantages. If, therefore, he can persuade a customer to buy one product as a condition of the sale of another, so much the better. Due to the paucity of authority, it is difficult to predict the outcome of such a case.

Obligations accepted by licensees to assign the benefit of any improvements to the licensor's technology to the licensor have never been considered in relation to the restraint of trade doctrine. It is submitted that such provisions would be likely to be held valid. The poublic is not much concerned with the identity of the owner of a particular right and so objections on the grounds of the public interest are unlikely. As between the parties, the licensor is likely to regard an agreement under which he does not receive the benefit of improvements to the technology as closer in nature to a sale of the technology than a mere licence and would accordingly be likely to require a higher licence fee. It is thus in the interests of both licensor (for it protects his rights) and licensee (for it assures a lower licence fee) that such a provision be held valid. Similar logic was used by Chitty J in *Badische Anilin und Soda Fabrik v Schott Segner and Co* when he upheld a restraint on trading by an agent after termination of the agency when he said 'to hold the restriction void would tend to deprive persons in the position of the defendant of the advantage of making their own bargains for their remuneration'.

4 Drafting

Due to the lack of authority concerning licences and the restraint of trade doctrine, it is not possible to point to particular provisions which have been found objectionable. The advice given in relation to agency and distribution agreements may again be worth following: keep any unusual restraint separate from the more usual ones. Similarly, where provisions can be so drafted, a limitation on the extent of the licence granted is wiser than positive contractual obligations. (By all means include the same provisions as positive obligations as well.)

5 Statutory and EEC limitations

The provisions of the Restrictive Trade Practices Act 1976 must be considered. A general discussion of the provisions of the Act is contained in Appendix II. Of particular importance in the case of licence agreements are the exemptions set out in paras 3, 4 and 5 of Sched 3 to the Act.

In addition, the provisions of EEC competition law must be considered (see Appendix III). A licensing agreement, whether it relates to a patent, copyright or a trade mark can infringe Arts 85(1) and 86. In *Consten and Grundig v Commission* 56 and 58/64 [1966] ECR 299 the court drew its famous distinction between the 'existence' and 'exercise' of an intellectual property right. The exercise of such a right can affect competition. There is now a block exemption for patent licences: Reg 2349/84. Article 2(7) permits a non-disclosure clause regarding know-how and third parties. In this area regard must also be had to Arts 30–37 of the Treaty which cover the free movement of goods. Tying agreements may also offend Arts 85 and 86. They are most frequently found in clauses in distribution agreements or intellectual property licences. See also the block exemptions for know-how licencing agreements (Reg 556/89), research and development agreements (Reg 418/85) and specialisation agreements (Reg 417/85).

There will, of course be many cases where the arrangements will fall within the EEC Commission notice on minor agreements.

The provisions of s 44 of the Patents Act 1977 are of critical importance in relation to tying provisions in patent licences.

Chapter 19

Cartels, Trade Associations and Co-operatives

1 Introduction

This section is concerned with the application of the doctrine of restraint of trade to agreements constituting cartels, co-operatives and trade associations. The inclusion of cartels in the same section as trade associations and co-operatives is not intended to imply that the normal operation of co-operatives and trade associations involves anything sinister or anticompetitive. However, on the rare occasions when the restraint of trade doctrine is of relevance to co-operatives or trade associations, it is usually because they are being operated in the manner of a cartel.

2 Common provisions which give rise to difficulty

Three types of case can be distinguished where restraint of trade has been an issue. Firstly, there are cases where the rules of an association have been attacked as unreasonably restricting the freedom of the members or potential members to trade as they wish. Secondly, and these cases are perhaps a subset of the first, there are the cases where the members have undertaken to supply their produce exclusively to the association and wish to escape from that undertaking. Thirdly, there are those cases where third parties have sought to proceed against the members of an association or cartel in relation to injury caused to them by the operation of the assocation or cartel. The boundaries between these classes of case are vague, but as little turns on the classification, this is of no great concern.

It may reasonably be stated that as a general rule, the rules of any association, co-operative or cartel are open to scrutiny under the restraint of trade doctrine (see the judgment of Lord Upjohn in *Dickson v Pharmaceutical Society of Great Britain* [1970] AC 403). There is no rule like that put forward in the *Esso* case which might exempt them (although as will be seen, many of the normal consequences of a provision being in restraint of trade do not apply in relation to trade unions and employers' associations by reason of statute). The rules must therefore be shown to be reasonable both in the interests of the members and of the public.

186

3 Reasonableness

Restraints regulating the trading activities of members of an association must be justified as being in the interests of the members individually and as a whole and in the interests of the public. In practice, the distinction between the interests of the members and of the public may become blurred, particularly where the association is concerned with the regulation of a large profession. Thus it will be reasonable for a professional association to impose rules which require its members to meet the highest standards of ethical conduct for it is both in the interest of the profession and the public that the public should be able to place their trust in the members of the profession (see Lord Upjohn in *Dickson v Pharmaceutical Society*). But in other fields of endeavour, such as acting, a restriction preventing persons with criminal records from entering and becoming members will be in restraint of trade (see *Faramus v Film Artistes Association* [1964] AC 925, where such a provision was held to be in restraint of trade but was validated by statute). In such cases, the interest of the public in the integrity of the members is not such as to justify an arbitrariliy strict provision.

Where an association has acted capriciously by passing a resolution with the intent of specifically restricting the activities of a particular member, then it will prove very difficult to establish reasonableness: see *Lennon v Davenport* (1984) 56 ALR 409.

Even in cases where the association may claim to represent the interests of a profession, it will be necessary to produce evidence to justify any restraint imposed upon members. Thus in *Dickson v Pharmaceutical Society* when the Pharmaceutical Society passed a motion to amend the rules of professional conduct to provide that new pharmacies should only be situated in physically distinct premises and should be devoted only to a limited range of goods outside of pharmaceutical products. The respondent claimed that the motion was both *ultra vires* and in restraint of trade. The House of Lords found in favour of the respondent. It rejected the argument that, because the rules were not strictly speaking binding on the members except in honour, the doctrine could not apply. The Society declined to furnish evidence on the reasonableness of the restraint, preferring to rely on its argument that the matter was not justiciable (which, as has been noted, was unsuccessful). In the absence of evidence as to reasonableness, the House of Lords felt bound to decide in favour of the respondent for the motion was a manifest restraint.

The sporting world has been a field for the growth of the law of restraint of trade as applied to associations. The reason for this would seem to be that the bodies responsible for the government of the various sports cannot usually rely upon the statutory provisions which protect employers' associations and trade unions to exempt them from the consequences of the restraint of trade doctrine.

The principle which has emerged is that the bodies responsible for the management of each sport can legitimately have regard to the orderly management of the sport. Thus, in *Eastham v Newcastle United Football Club* [1964] Ch 413, the ability of a club to transfer a player for a fee and to use that fee to acquire another player was potentially of benefit to the sport and was possibly an interest which could be protected; as the transfer system was held to be in restraint of trade on account of its combination with other rules, however, no final decision on the adequacy of this interest was made. Similarly, in *Greig v Insole* [1978] 3 All ER 449, Slade J held that the International Cricket Conference as organisers of international cricket had a legitimate interest to protect for the purpose of the restraint of trade doctrine and the Test and County Cricket Board likewise had a requisite interest. The interest was the organisation and administration of the game.

The test of reasonableness, in the light of this definition of interest is easier to apply for if the rules contain restraints which are more than are reasonably necessary for the protection of that interest, they are bad.

Thus, in *Eastham v Newcastle United Football Club Ltd*, the rules of the Football League and the Football Association were called into question. The plaintiff was a professional footballer with Newcastle United. He wanted to be transferred to another club but Newcastle United refused to allow him to go. They placed him on the retained list. The effect of this was that even if Eastham left Newcastle no other professional football club would employ him for to do so would be a breach of the rules of the Football Association. Eastham applied for a declaration that the rules were in restraint of trade and void. Wilberforce J granted the declaration. The legitimate interests of the Association could not justify a restraint which effectively compelled a player to remain with one club all his playing life if the club so desired. Similar decisions have been reached in a number of Australian cases: see, eg, *Buckley v Tutty* (1971) 125 CLR 353; *Adamson v Wife* (1979) 27 ALR 475; *Barnard v Australia Soccer Federation* (1988) 81 ALR 81.

In *Greig v Insole*, the ICC and the TCCB imposed rules which effectively banned the plaintiff from first class cricket. The plaintiff had entered into an agreement with World Series Cricket to play in a number of matches. The ICC and the TCCB regarded World Series Cricket as a threat to the orderly management and finances of cricket. They accordingly responded by banning cricketers who entered into contracts with World Series Cricket from playing in test matches or first class cricket. The ban applied not only to players who entered into such contracts in the future, but also to those who had already done so. Slade J, after considering all the evidence, held that to deprive, by a form of retrospective legislation, a professional cricketer of the opportunity of making his living in a very important field of professional life was *prima facie* both a serious and unjust step to take. He accordingly held the rules *ultra vires* and in restraint of trade.

It should be noted that the courts will be slow to hold that parties whose right to work is affected by restraint of trade are not entitled to relief even if they are strictly not members of the restrictive association. Thus in *Eastham* Wilberforce granted a declaration, even though the plaintiff was in fact not a member of the Football Association himself. A declaration was granted in *Greig v Insole* (see also *Hughes v Western Australia Cricket Association (Inc) and Others* [1969] ALR 660 at p 700). Similarly, in *Nagle v Feilden* [1966] 2 QB 633, the Court of Appeal held that there was an arguable case that a woman who had been refused a trainer's licence by the Jockey Club on account of her sex had power to make a declaration that the Jockey Club's practice was contrary to public policy see also *McInnes v Onslow-Fane* [1978] 1 WLR 1520. The jurisdiction is however limited to situations where the decision of the body concerned places an unreasoanble restriction on the person's capacity to earn a living or he is in a direct contractual relationship with the body (see *Currie v Barton* (1988) *The Times*, 12 February, CA), although in *Hughes v WACA* it was held that the fact that the respondent had not made large sums was irrelevant if he was affected in a professional capacity (see also *Buckley v Tutty* (1971) 125 CLR 353 at 325). The jurisdiction should also be contrasted with the right to seek judicial review. The restraint of trade doctrine is directed at the effect of contracts or rules but does not bite directly upon the decisions of tribunals although the Australian and New Zealand courts have been willing to allow wider scope to the doctrine (see, eg, *Stintinato v Auckland Boxing Association (Inc) and Others* [1978] INZLR 1, and *Lennon v Davenport*, and *Forbes v NSW Trotling Club Ltd* (1979) 25 ALR 1. The scope of judicial review has itself been extended to cover bodies whose authority does not derive from statute, statutory instrument or prerogative (see *R v Panel on Takeovers Mergers, ex parte Datafin plc* [1987] QB 815 and *R v Code of Practice Committee of the British Pharmaceutical Industry, ex parte Professional Counselling Aids Ltd* (1990) *The Independent*, 1 November; (1990) *The Times*, 7 November). However, there remains a gap between the restraint of trade doctrine and judicial review through which cases may fall (see, eg, *R v Jockey Club, ex parte Messingberd Mundy* (1989) *The Independent*, 29 December; *R v Jockey Club, ex parte Ram Racecourses* (1990) *The Independent*, 19 April; and *R v Royal Life Saving Society, ex parte Howe* (1990) 15 May (unreported) (A)).

The cases just referred to all concerned actions by individuals challenging the validity of restraints on employment. The position is no different where the restraints are challenged by an employer. For example, in *Kores Manufacturing Co v Kolok Manufacturing Co* [1957] 3 All ER 163 the parties, both carbon paper manufacturers, had each undertaken not to employ persons employed by the other in the previous five years. The restraint was held to be unenforceable because it applied to all categories of employees and there was no evidence to suggest that any interest which the parties might have had to protect could justify such an indiscriminate restraint. No doubt a more limited restraint could have been justified if there had been confidential information or customer connection to protect (see *Hivac v Park Royal Scientific Instruments* [1946] Ch 169). A similar agreement between members of an employers' association was held unenforceable in *Mineral Water Bottle Exchange and Trade Protection Society v Booth* (1887) 36 Ch D 465.

It is not necessarily unreasonable for groups of traders to form associations and to supply all of their produce to such associations or to allocate business between them if the intention is to secure economies by improving distribution or by eliminating competition between them.

Thus in *Collins v Locke* (1879) 4 App Cas 674, the Privy Council held an agreement to parcel out between the various companies the business of stevedoring at a port was reasonable save in one regard: the agreement provided that in certain circumstances none of the parties was to act as stevedores. This was held to be unreasonable both in the interests of the parties (for none of them could take the benefit of this business) and in the interests of the public (for the company affected by the refusal could not get its stevedoring done). Therefore, in the absence of exceptional evidence it seems unlikely that a 'blacking' contract would be enforceable.

However, where members of a trade association agree to restrict output and to fix prices under rules which last for as long as the association remains in existence, this will be unreasonable in the interests of the parties (see *Evans (Joseph) and Co v Heathcote* [1918] 1 KB 418). Similar reasoning was adopted in *McEllistrim v Ballymacelligott Co-op Agricultural and Dairy Society* [1919] AC 548. The appellant was a member of the co-operative and was as a result of a change in the rules of the society compelled to supply all his milk to the society at a price fixed by the society's committee. There were no means by which he could unilaterally withdraw from the society. The House of Lords held that the restriction was designed to do no more than protect the co-operative from competition and that, accordingly, the restraint was invalid. The inability of the appellant to withdraw from the society was again an important factor in assessing reasonableness.

English Hop Growers Ltd v Dering [1928] 2 KB 174 was a case where an obligation undertaken by a member to supply all his hops to the plaintiff society was held to be enforceable. There the obligation was limited to a five year period. Scrutton LJ said:

> In view of the fluctuating character of the yearly supply of hops, I see nothing unreasonable in hop growers combining to secure a steady and profitable process by eliminating competition amongst themselves and putting the marketing in the hands of one agent with full power to fix prices and hold up supplies, the benefit and loss being divided amongst the members.

Finally, it should be mentioned that there is authority for the proposition that 'knockout agreements' between rival bidders at auctions are not in restraint of trade (see *Harrop v Thomson* [1975] 2 All ER 94). The position as regards dealers is regulated by statute: see the Auctions (Bidding Agreements) Act 1927.

4 Actions by third parties affected by cartels

Whilst there is, following *Nagle v Feilden*, the chance that an individual whose right to work is threatened by the activities of a body exercising the *de facto* right to control a particular trade or profession may seek redress, there seems to be no such comfort at common law for third party traders affected by combinations in restraint of trade. For, as has been mentioned earlier, an agreement in restraint of trade is not unlawful, it is merely unenforceable.

Mogul Steamship Co Ltd v McGregor, Gow and Co [1892] AC 25 is the classic example. The respondents, a number of shipping companies, entered into an agreement with the intent of securing as much of the Hankow and Shanghai tea-carrying trade as possible. As a result of this agreement the appellants, having sent their ships to Hankow, were unable to obtain a profitable cargo. An action ensured. The House of Lords held that the respondents had committed no wrongful act in giving effect to their agreement by joining to offer their ships at low rates. Accordingly, the appellants' claim failed. In *Brekkes Ltd v Cattel* [1972] 1 Ch 105, the plaintiffs were banned by the members of a market from using their own vehicles to ship fish to the market. The proceedings were based primarily on the Restrictive Trade Practices Ac 1976 for the judge held, citing only *Mogul* as authority, that even if the resolution imposing the ban was in restraint of trade it would not be unlawful so as to give the plaintiffs a cause of action.

As has been seen, whilst a remedy in damages or an injunction may not be available, the courts are on occasion prepared to grant a declaration where they think it might be beneficial.

5 Statutory and EEC limitations

The provisions of the Restrictive Trade Practices Act 1976 are discussed in Appendix II. When considering trade associations, particular attention should be paid to the provisions of s 8.

In addition the provisions of EEC competition law must be considered (see Appendix III). The main activity of a cartel-price fixing is clearly caught by Arts 85 and 86. Whether this takes place by way of a formal agreement or via informal collusion, it is difficult to envisage an exemption being granted by the Commission. The activities of trade associations are specifically referred to in Art 85(1).

When considering the application of the common law rules of restraint of trade to trade associations and trade unions, the provisions of ss 2(5) and 3(5) of the Trade Union and Labour Relations Act 1974 are important for they effectively exempt trade unions and trade associations from the restraint of trade doctrine for many purposes (for an example of their application see *Goring v British Actors Equity Assocation* [1987] IRLR 122). In the absence of such legislation the rules of a trade union would be subject to the restraint of trade doctrine: see *Clark v Printing and Kindred Industries Union* (1976) 15 ALR 71.

Chapter 20

Other Agreements

1 Negotiation and Evaluation Agreements

1.1 Introduction

It is common for parties in the course of negotiating agreements for the licensing of technology, the sale of complex equipment, the establishment of joint ventures and many other purposes, to disclose to their opposite numbers significant confidential information regarding the products and processes to be the subject of the ultimate agreement. Likewise, information may be disclosed to the other party to enable him to evaluate the product or technology before negotiations begin. As has been seen above, it is likely that an obligation of confidence will be implied in such circumstances. However, the exact scope of the information which will be subject to the obligation and the nature of the remedy which will be available in the event of a breach are uncertain. For, as Megarry V-C said in *Marshall (Thomas) (Exports) v Guinle* [1979] Ch 227, the obligation may not be so much not to use but rather not to use without paying.

Accordingly, any party contemplating such negotiations would be well advised to ensure that before negotiations begin, the other party signs a confidentiality agreement.

1.2 The terms of the agreement

Generally, a confidentiality agreement should contain four provisions. Firstly, the information and the purpose for which it is to be supplied must be clearly defined. The definition of the purpose will have to be drafted afresh in every case. The definition of the information is more difficult. The first question to resolve is whether all information relating to the purpose which is disclosed is to be regarded as confidential or merely that which is marked 'confidential'. Generally, this will be determined by the practicalities of the situation. The advantage of the former approach is that less care need be taken in the adminstration of the disclosures. The advantage of the latter is that proof of the confidential disclosure may be easier should it prove necessary. The second question is whether information entering into the public domain (except as a result of a breach by the other party) should be excepted from the definition. The reason for doing this is that it is thought that it might be an unreasonable restraint of trade to include a restriction without such a proviso. As there has been no case on the point it is difficult to give positive guidance. A compromise solution is to limit the agreement to 'confidential' information disclosed to the other party. The court would then have to decide whether the information had become sufficiently publicly known to bring the obligations under the agreement to an end.

The remaining provisions give rise to fewer difficulties. The other party should be obliged to keep the information confidential and to make it available only to such employees as is necessary for the purpose. This provision can vary in sophistication from a simple provision to this effect to a sophisticated procedure for approval of employees to have access and for physical access control. In many cases, it may be advisable to require him to obtain and produce undertakings from his employees to observe the obligations of confidence. He should be obliged to use the information only for the defined purpose. Lastly, he should be obliged to return on demand the information, and all copies which have been made of it. Care should be taken when negotiating the terms of the main agreement to ensure that the information disclosed under the evaluation or negotiation agreement is adequately protected.

2 Authors and performers

Contracts with authors and performers have received special treatment in a number of cases which have come before the courts. In these cases, the courts have had the sometimes difficult task of reconciling the interests of promoters and publishers in protecting their sometimes sizeable investment in promoting the author and performer, and the freedom of the individual. In considering these cases two factors must be borne in mind. Firstly, each case turns on its particular facts not all of which may be entirely apparent from the judgments. Secondly, the emphasis placed upon the solemnity of contract has somewhat declined during the course of this century.

The principal factor which differentiates contracts with authors and performers from other contracts of employment is the personal reputation of the individual concerned. This reputation is in some respects analogous to the goodwill of a business. Like the goodwill of a business, it can be developed through industry and investment; unlike goodwill, it cannot be detached from the individual and disposed of separately.

Two situations in which a performer or author may enter into a restrictive agreement can be readily discerned. Firstly, there are contracts for a short period during which the individual binds himself to work exclusively for a single promotor. Where the individual has no established reputation and the contract provides for a reasonable wage, then the contract is likely to be regarded by the court as a simple contract of employment and no unusual problems will arise (but if the restraint remains binding even if the employer gives no work to the employee and pays no wage then it will be in restraint of trade: *Young v Timmins* (1831) 1 Cr and J 331). Where the individual already has an established reputation, the court will in general grant an injunction to restrain a breach of the covenant and damages (see *Lumley v Wagner* (1852) 1 De GM and G 604 and *Gaumont-British Picture Corporation Ltd v Alexander* [1936]

2 All ER 1686). It should be noted that the courts will not enforce a positive obligation to provide services. Therefore, any restraint should be phrased negatively as an obligation not to provide services to others. The court will not however grant an injunction to enforce such a covenant which would prevent the defendant from working altogether but it will be prepared to enforce the covenant to the extent required to prevent the performer from performing in breach of the covenant: see *Warner Bros Pictures Inc v Nelson* [1937] 1 KB 209. The decision in *Warner Bros Pictures* where a three year injunction was granted, has been criticised in recent cases. In *Warren v Mendy* [1989] ICR 525, CA it was held that to grant an injunction to a manager preventing a rival manager from acting for a boxer in breach of a covenant in the boxer's management agreement would, in the circumstances, be tantamount to compelling the boxer to use the original manager on the subject of what constitutes compulsion the court said: 'compulsion is a question to be decided on the facts of each case with a realistic regard for the probable reaction of an injunction on the psychological and material, and sometimes the physical, need of the servant to maintain [his particular] skill or talent'. Thus the fact that the boxer could have obtained work as a security guard did not diminish the element of compulsion. (See also *Nichols Advanced Vehicle Systems v De Angelis* (1979) 21 December (unreported) and *Lotus Cars Ltd v Jaguar Car Ltd* (1982) 1 July (unreported).)

The second situation in which a performer or author may enter into a restrictive agreement is that of the young artist with no established reputation seeking to break into the business. Where he enters into a long-term commitment under which he binds himself to perform exclusively for one company or to sell his works exclusively to one agent, the courts are more ready to strike down the agreement.

The most striking examples of this approach concern music publishing contracts. In two separate cases contracts between agent/manager and songwriters in what was, it appears, a form common in the business, were struck down as being in restraint of trade (*Davis (Clifford) Management Ltd v WEA Records Ltd* [1974] 1 WLR 61 and *Schroeder (A) Music Publishing Co Ltd v Macaulay* [1974] 1 WLR 1308). In each case, the contracts were for a term of at least five years and provided for the automatic assignment of copyright of all of the artist's works to the manager. No corresponding obligation to promote the works was placed upon the management. The court held that the agreements were in restraint of trade and unenforceable. In the *Clifford Davis* case, the court set aside certain assignments of copyright which had already been made under the contract. Although the lack of bargaining power of the inexperienced artists was relevant in these cases it was not perhaps the most important factor. The principal objection was that the artist's ability to make his livelihood was placed for a long period entirely in the hands of the other party who was under no countervailing obligation to promote the artist. *Schroeder v Macaulay* was followed recently in *Zang Tumb Tuum Records Ltd and another v Holly Johnson* (1989) *The Independent,* 2 August, CA where a certain provisions recording contract said a publishing contract made by a sister recording and publishing company with young members of a group of little business experience were held to be one-sided and unfair. The provisions singled out were the potential term (up to nine years at the option of the company), the absolute assignment of copyright and the binding up of the group exclusively to the company. Factors which were relevant to the finding included the lack of an obligation on the company to release records, the companies freedom to terminate the agreement at 12–15 month intervals and the prohibition on the group members performing without consent. The companies arguments that the provisions were required to compensate for the group which proved unsuccessful and to reap the benefit from early recordings did not justify such a long and one-sided term. These cases can be contrasted with *Warner Bros v Nelson* where although the company was not bound to use the artist, they were bound to pay her an ever-increasing substantial salary. It should be noted that restraint of trade is not the only basis upon which songwriter agreements have been attached: in *O'Sullivan v Management Agency Ltd* a similar result to *Clifford Davis* was reached on the basis of undue influence.

An intriguing device was used by a company of film producers before the First World War to try to retain the benefit of their efforts to promote their artists. In *Hepworth Manufacturing Co Ltd v Ryott* [1920] 1 Ch 1 the company required the actor to work under a pseudonym and they provided in their agreement that the pseudonym would belong exclusively to them and could not be used by the actor after he left their employment. The court held the contract to be in unreasonable restraint of trade and that the actor was correspondingly free to use the pseudonym. The court was clearly swayed by two factors. Firstly, the pseudonym was of no use to the producers without the actor, therefore, there was no interest to protect. Secondly, the evidence was that the actor could command only half the salary if he could not use the pseudonym. The court, therefore, held that the contract was a device to ensure that they could retain their artists at unreasonably low wages.

Finally, even where restraint of trade considerations do not apply, the courts will only grant an injunction to enforce a covenant if the corresponding obligations of the plaintiff could be enforced by injunction. Thus in *Page One Records Ltd v Britton* [1968] 1 WLR 157 a manager could not enforce a covenant to prevent a pop group using other management because his obligation to manage the group was one of trust and confidence which could not be specifically enforced by the group. This was followed in the recent case *Warren v Mendy*.

Part VII

Interlocutory Relief

Chapter 21

Injunctions

Interlocutory relief usually plays a major part in cases concerning restraint of trade and business secrets. In the vast majority of cases the effect of the interlocutory hearing will be to decide the final outcome of the case. In those cases where the outcome is not determined by the result of interloctory proceedings they are still important as a means of providing temporary relief.

However, given that attempts at settlement have failed or are inappropriate, the plaintiff then has to consider three questions:

(a) which form of interlocutory relief is appropriate and what is the practice and procedure relevant to an application for that relief;

(b) in which court should he begin his action; and

(c) is it necessary to make an *ex parte* application for relief.

In this chapter, we endeavour to cover those areas of interlocutory relief which are most relevant to restraint of trade and business secrets cases. Therefore, we consider interlocutory prohibition injunctions, Anton Piller orders, orders under ord 29 RSC and orders for delivery up/destruction.

1 Prohibitory interlocutory injunctions

The power to grant an injunction both at the interlocutory and final stages is found in s 37(1) of the Supreme Court Act 1981:

The High Court may by order (whether interlocutory or final) grant an injunction or appoint a receiver in all cases in which it appears to the court to be just and convenient to do so.

See further s 38 of the County Courts Act 1984. RSC Ord 29, r 1 deals specifically with applications for interloctory injunctions.

2 General criteria for the grant of a prohibitory interlocutory injunction

The usual basis on which a court will approach the question of whether the plaintiff should be awarded an interlocutory prohibitory injunctions is by applying the tests set out by Lord Diplock in *American Cyanamid Co v Ethicon*

Ltd [1975] AC 396. This was a patent action in which an application for an interlocutory injunction reached the House of Lords. The hearing had taken up three days at first instance, eight days in the Court of Appeal and was estimated to last 12 days in the House of Lords. It was clearly a very complex case and the House of Lords were appalled by the fact that so much court time had been taken up by an interlocutory application. In their judgment in response to this they effectively revolutionised the law in this area. The court laid down the following criteria to test whether an interlocutory injunction should be awarded:

(1) Is there a serious question to be tried? This means that the plaintiff must demonstrate his claim is not frivolous or vexatious. Unless the material available to the court at the hearing of the application for an interlocutory injunction discloses that the plaintiff has no real prospect of succeeding in his claim for a permanent injunction at the trial, then the court should go on to consider whether the balance of convenience lies in favour of granting or refusing the interlocutory relief that is sought.

(2) Regarding the balance of convenience, the governing principle is that the court should first consider whether, if the plaintiff succeeds at trial, he would be adequately compensated by damages for any loss caused by the refusal to grant an interlocutory injunction. If damages would be an adequate remedy and the defendant would be in a financial position to pay them, no interlocutory injunction should normally be granted, however strong the plaintiff's claim appears to be at that stage. A comment made by Nourse LJ in *Warren v Mendy* [1989] 1 WLR 853 at 868; [1989] 1 RLR 210 at 216, may assist defendants in some cases. He pointed out that in most of the decided cases it is assumed that damages will not be an adequate alternative remedy in comparison with the grant of an injunction. That was especially true of those cases which would have been tried by a jury. However as damages are now invariably assessed by a judge or master it cannot be so readily assumed that they will not be an adequate remedy. He gave an example relating to the case: it would be open to the court to refuse injunctive relief at the interlocutory stage on an undertaking by the defendant to keep full and proper accounts of his receipts from acting in alleged breach of contract and to pay a specified proportion of them into court or into a joint account. Nourse LJ commented: 'An arrangement such as that would achieve the twin objective of going some way to quantify the plaintiff's damages and preserving funds to meet any award which might later be made'. In an appropriate case a defendant might make such an offer and escape an injunction being made against him. However, it is true to say that in the vast majority of restraint of trade and business secrets cases damages are genuinely very difficult to quantify and therefore they will never be an adequate remedy. On the effectiveness of the defendant paying sums into an account pending the outcome of the trial, see also *Brupat Ltd v Sandford Marine Products Ltd* [1983] RPC 61.

(3) If, on the other hand, damages would not be an adequate remedy for that plaintiff, the court should then consider whether, if the injunction were granted, the defendant would be adequately compensated under the plaintiff's undertaking to pay damages should his defence succeed at trial. If damages in the measure recoverable under such an undertaking would be an adequate

remedy and the plaintiff would be in a financial position to pay them, there would be no reason upon this ground to refuse an interlocutory injunction.

(4) It is where there is doubt as to the adequacy of the respective remedies in damages that the question of balance of convenience arises.

(5) Where other factors appear to be evenly balanced it is a counsel of prudence to take such measures as are calculated to preserve the status quo.

(6) The extent to which the disadvantages to each party would be incapable of being compensated in damages in the event of his succeeding at the trial is always a significant factor in assessing where the balance of convenience lies.

(7) If the extent of the uncompensatable disadvantage to each party would not differ widely, it may not be improper to take into account the relative strength of each party's case as revealed by the affidavit evidence adduced on the hearing of the application. This, however, should be done only where it is apparent on the facts disclosed by evidence as to which there is no credible dispute, that the strength of one party's case is disproportionate to that of the other party.

(8) In addition to the above, there may be many other special factors to be taken into consideration in the particular circumstances of individual cases.

The question whether the *American Cyanamid* approach applies in restraint of trade and business secrets cases has been much discussed. As is pointed out below, some judges have decided that the test which *American Cyanamid* appears to have supplanted (ie that in *Stratford (JT) and Son Ltd v Lindley* [1965] AC 269) is the proper test. That case said:

(1) That the plaintiff must demonstrate a strong *prima facie* case. This was interpreted in *Harman Pictures NV v Osborne* [1967] 1 SLR 723 as meaning that the plaintiff must show (a) a strong *prima facie* case for the existence of his right and that he is likely to succeed on this issue; and (b) as regards infringement of the right, a *prima facie* case which is capable of succeeding. This clearly casts upon him a higher duty than that under the *American Cyanamid* tests; it means that he has to demonstrate that he has a good chance of winning at trial.

(2) It is also necessary to examine the defendant's case to see whether he might have a reasonable answer to the plaintiff's claim (ie the court must look at the relative strength of each party's case). However, in the *American Cyanamid* case it was said you only do this as a last resort rather than making it a primary question for the court.

(3) Further, once the plaintiff has made out a *prima facie* case then the court should go on to consider the balance of convenience. In *Cayne v Global Natural Resources Plc* [1984] 1 All ER 225 the Court of Appeal commented that the balance of convenience in these circumstances does not mean the same as under *American Cyanamid*; it means avoiding injustice. In *Coco v Clark (AN) (Engineers) Ltd* [1969] RPC 41 a factor which militated against granting the injunction sought was the fact that Coco had not started to produce the product whereas the defendants had. See *Belfast Ropework Co Ltd v Pixdane Ltd* [1976] FSR 337 in which the Court of Appeal allowed an appeal on the basis that the balance of convenience was in the plaintiff's favour as the defendant would not be driven out of an established business but would

merely be delayed in starting it up. See also *Potters-Ballotini v Weston-Baker* (1976) 120 SJ 231.

3 The correct test in restraint of trade and business secrets cases

There is no doubt that the *American Cyanamid* case has some strange aspects about it. In particular, *Stratford (JT) & Son Ltd v Lindley* [1965] AC 307 was never referred to by counsel or by the court. The decision in *Stratford* was also a decision of the House of Lords and it was not specifically overruled in *American Cyanamid*. For that reason and because Lord Diplock said that there might be 'other special features to be taken into consideration in the particular circumstances of individual cases' which might warrant an approach different from that laid down generally in the *American Cyanamid* case, there has grown up a body of opinion which says that that approach is not appropriate in business secrets and restraint of trade cases and that the old test under *Stratford* or its recent restatement in *Cayne v Global Natural Resources plc* [1984] 1 All ER 225) is correct.

The first case in this area to question *American Cyanamid* was the Court of Appeal judgment in *Fellowes and Son v Fisher* [1976] 1 QB 123. That case concerned a restrictive covenant which prevented the defendant, a solicitor's clerk, for a period of five years after his employment had ceased from, *inter alia*, working in the legal profession within a certain area of Greater London. The plaintiffs alleged that he had breached that covenant and they applied for an interlocutory injunction. This was refused and the plaintiffs appealed. The defendants' counsel urged the Court of Appeal not to apply *American Cyanamid*. He said that that case was one of great complexity and the result of the decision was to refuse both to attempt to resolve conflicts of evidence on the basis of affidavits and to decide difficult questions of law. However, in a restraint of trade case like the present one the court was in a position to express an interlocutory view on the validity or otherwise of the restrictive covenant for the real argument was not one of fact but was a simple question of law viz: when the covenant was made was it valid or not? The court was at that time in a position to see with some degree of certainty what the outcome of the trial might be. In any event, the balance of convenience even under *American Cyanamid* favoured the defendant. Lord Denning MR said that the *American Cyanamid* judgment was in direct conflict with *Stratford v Lindley*. The only way to avoid the problem was to take into account what Lord Diplock had laid down about individual cases. Lord Denning said that such cases were those in which 'it is urgent and imperative to come to a decision'. Such cases were those which would almost certainly be disposed of at the interlocutory stage (ie in which there would be no trial because of the nature of the case). He cited confidential information and restraint of trade cases as falling within this category of special, individual cases. He decided that by applying the traditional approach the plaintiff had not made out a *prima facie* case and there was good reason to think that the clause was invalid. In the alternative he applied another remark made by Lord Diplock in *American Cyanamid*: '. . . if the extent of the uncompensatable disadvantage to each party would not differ widely, it may not be improper to take into account in tipping the balance the relative strength of each party's case . . .'. Lord Denning went on to decide this was such a case where damages on either side would not be an adequate remedy.

The two remaining members of the Court of Appeal reached the same result but by an entirely different route. They accepted that *American Cyanamid* governed their reasoning and working through Lord Diplock's principles, they decided the balance of convenience was against granting the injunction quite simply because the defendant might not get other work in a solicitor's office so long as the case was hanging over him. They did go on to say, however, that in any event they thought the defendant was more likely to succeed at trial and Pennycuick J went some way in support of Lord Denning's approach.

Soon after *Fellowes v Fisher* came the case of *Office Overload Ltd v Gunn* [1977] FSR 39 in which Lord Denning MR said that covenants in restraint of trade were a special category if they were *prima facie* valid and *prima facie* there was an infringement, the court would grant an injunction. They were very rarely fought out to the bitter end; they were invariably decided at the interlocutory stage.

Lawton LJ appears to have agreed with Denning MR, and Bridge LJ decided that *American Cyanamid* was inapplicable because it dealt with cases in which there is an unresolved dispute on the affidavit evidence before the court or a question of law to be decided. Neither of those matters arose in this case. He concluded:

> If it were not possible for the court to grant interlocutory relief to enforce a restrictive covenant of limited duration such as this, then, in cases like the present, such covenants would never be enforced by the courts and parties entitled to the benefit of them would always be left to their remedy in damages, which in such cases might frequently be an indeterminate remedy.

In *Dunford and Elliott Ltd v Johnson and Firth Brown Ltd* [1978] FSR 143, a case which concerned confidential information, Lord Denning MR again qualified the approach of *American Cyanamid*. He said that this case, which involved an application by the plaintiffs to prevent an imminent takeover bid by the defendants, was one of those special cases which had to be decided 'today' (ie a case in which, because of the facts, the decision could not practicably be delayed). Therefore, the court had to look at the strength of each party's arguments and make up its mind. Roskill LJ seemed to accept that if the hearing had been likely to dispose of the case he also would have felt obliged to examine the strength of each party's case, but he was not so convinced and in applying the *American Cyanamid* tests he found for the defendants on the balance of convenience. Lawton LJ decided the case on the basis of 'broad justice'. It is not clear what he meant by this.

In *Marshall (Thomas) (Exports) Ltd v Guinle* [1979] Ch 227 although purporting to follow *American Cyanamid* Megarry V-C, in a case which was clearly to be determined on the basis of a hearing on a motion which lasted for more than a week, appears to have applied the *Stratford* test in preference to *American Cyanamid*. In *NWL v Woods* [1979] 1 WLR 1294 the House of

Lords said that if the grant or refusal of an interlocutory injunction will have the practical effect of putting an end to the action because the harm that will have been already caused to the losing party by its grant or refusal is complete, then the court can legitimately take into account the plaintiff's chances of success at trial. However, in *Bullivant (Roger) Ltd v Ellis* [1987] ICR 464, the Court of Appeal appear to have applied *American Cyanamid* to a confidential information case.

The Court of Appeal has in two recent decisions (*Dairy Crest Ltd v Piggott* [1989] ICR 92 and *Lawrence David Ltd v Ashton* [1989] 1RLR 22; [1991] 1 All ER 385) rejected the argument that special rules apply in restraint of trade cases in which an interlocutory injunction is applied for. In *Dairy Crest Ltd v Piggott* the Court, when considering a two year non-solicitation/dealing with customers clause reaffirmed the *American Cyanamid* approach. Balcombe LJ considered *NWL Ltd v Woods* [1979] ICR 867 and *Cayne v Global Natural Resources plc* [1984] 1 All ER 225 and stated that in each case the grant or refusal of the injunction would have effectively disposed of the action leaving nothing to be dealt with at trial. However that was not correct in the instant case. There was clearly going to be a trial. *Lawrence David v Ashton* was an appeal from the refusal of Whitford J to grant the defendant's employers interlocutory injunctions (a) against the employee disclosing confidential information acquired during the course of employment, and (b) enforcing, pending trial, a two year contractual restriction against the employee entering into a trade similar to that carried on by the employers. The defendant was a sales director for one of the plaintiff's UK regions. The restraint of trade clause in his contract read:

> For a period of two years after the determination of this Agreement for any reason whatsoever Mr Ashton shall not without the written consent of the Board, either alone or in partnership undertake to carry on or be employed in any capacity or be interested directly or indirectly in the design and development, manufacture or supply of any sliding door vehicle body, tension or sliding curtain vehicle body or any other vehicle body for which a patent has been applied for or granted in the name of the Company or any part of the aforementioned vehicle bodies within the United Kingdom.

> The defendant was given notice on the basis that he had failed to achieve the expected improvement of sales performance in his area, but at court it was accepted by the plaintiff that the termination of his employment was in breach of contract since he had been given neither written nor one month's notice. Whitford J concluded that this was not a clear repudiatory breach and he doubted whether the clause quoted above would be held at trial to be a justifiable restraint.

> The Court of Appeal rejected the view that restraint of trade cases were a special category to which *American Cyanamid* did not apply. In doing so it rejected the approach of Lord Denning MR in *Fellowes v Fisher* and *Office Overload v Gunn*.

> Applying *American Cyanamid* to this case the Court agreed with Whitford J's refusal to grant an injunction to protect the alleged confidential information. A fundamental principle relating to the granting

of an injunction was that it should be capable of being framed with precision sufficient to enable the injuncted person to know when he might be in breach of the order of the court. However, here the plaintiff was unable to define with any degree of precision what amounted to confidential information. The court did however grant an injunction to prevent the clause quoted above being breached. Applying *American Cyanamid* it adopted the following approach to the facts:

(a) Is there a serious question to be tried? This divided into 2 questions:
   (i) Was there here a repudiatory breach of contract which had been accepted by the defendant. The court decided that there was a serious question to be tried on this point. There were unresolved issues of fact and law.
   (ii) What was the proper construction of the restraint clause? As it was 'quite impossible to say this covenant is obviously bad' there was a serious question to be tried on this issue.
(b) If the plaintiff is right it will not be adequately compensated in damages.
(c) If the defendant is right, then provided the period of the interlocutory injunction is kept reasonably short, he should be adequately compensated by the plaintiff's cross-undertaking in damages.

The court awarded the injunction for a period of about three and a half months anticipating that a trial would occur in that period.

Balcombe LJ also said that it is only if the action cannot be tried before the period of the restraint has expired or has run a large part of its course, that the grant of the interlocutory injunction will effectively dispose of the action, thus bringing the case within the exception to the basic rule in *American Cyanamid* such as was considered by the House of Lords in *NWL Ltd v Woods* [1979] 1RLR 478 and also by the Court of Appeal in *Cayne v Global Natural Resources plc* [1984] 1 All ER 225. It is then that the judge may properly go on to consider the prospects of the plaintiff's succeeding in the action. Another way of reaching the same conclusion is to say that the longer the period of the interlocutory injunction, the more likely it is that the defendant may suffer damage (if the injunction is wrongly granted) which is uncompensatable by the plaintiff's cross-undertaking, and therefore it becomes necessary to consider the relative strength of each party's case as revealed by the affidavit evidence.

The dictum of Balcombe LJ has recently been applied in *Lansing Linde Ltd v Kerr* [1991] 1 All ER 418, CA. In that case the defendant was employed by the plaintiff, the English subsidiary of an international company which manufactured forklift trucks, as the director of its Northern Division. His contract of employment included a term that for a period of 12 months after the termination of the contract the defendant would not be engaged or concerned in any business which competed with the plaintiff or associated companies. The covenant was worldwide in scope except for those geographical areas where the business did not compete with the plaintiff or its associated companies. Other terms of the contract of employment required the defendant not to divulge trade secrets or confidential information about the company nor to solicit customers of the company. On the 26 June 1990 the defendant resigned from the plaintiff and by mutual agreement he left the company on 6 July. On 30 July he was appointed managing director of another company which manufactured forklift trucks in competition with the plaintiff. The plaintiff brought an action against the defendant seeking, *inter alia*, an interim injunction restraining the defendant from working for the other company or divulging trade secrets or confidential information about the company or soliciting customers of the company. On 4 September Knox J refused to grant the injunction, on the grounds that the trial of the action could not be arranged before March or April 1991, by which time the 12-month period of restraint would have almost certainly expired and since a worldwide covenant against competition would probably not be upheld at trial because it was too wide the balance of convenience came down against the plaintiffs. The plaintiffs appealed. Between the hearing at first instance and the hearing of the appeal the plaintiffs served further evidence to support the injunction application and a statement of claim. The statement of claim was materially different from the writ in that it alleged misrepresentation and fraud and on this basis particularly the plaintiff argued that the judge was wrong in his finding that the injunction hearing would effectively determine the proceedings between the parties. In particular it was said that there were further issues relating to the amount of damages which the parties would wish to have tried and the allegations on fraud and/or misrepresentation would have to be tried. The Court of Appeal dismissed these ambitions as unrealistic. The Court of Appeal upheld the approach of Knox J and his application of the approach in *Cayne v Global Natural Resources plc*, ie that the court was bound to consider the strength of the plaintiffs' chances of success at trial because by the date of trial substantially the whole period of the restraint would have expired.

In *Business Seating (Renovations) Ltd v Broad* [1989] 1CR 729, Millett J, in deciding to grant an injunction, applied *American Cyanamid* and in doing so said 'I really cannot avoid taking into account the likely prospects of success at the trial, particularly since they do not depend on any further investigation of the facts.'

In *Lock International Plc v Beswick* [1989] 1 WLR 1268 at 1274–5 when considering an application to discharge an executed Anton Piller order Hoffman J, in examining whether the order should ever have been made, decided not to apply *American Cyanamid*. He stressed the fact that this was not a case in which the plaintiff's case might be improved on discovery; because of the execution of the Anton Piller order he had had unrestricted access to every piece of relevant paper in the defendants' possession. Therefore the facts on which the plaintiff could rely were clear.

Conclusion

(1) In the vast majority of restraint of trade and breach of confidence cases the interlocutory injunction application will effectively dispose of the action. Therefore *American Cyanamid* will not apply. Most cases will be governed by the principles in *Cayne v Global Natural Resources plc* [1984] 1 All ER 225.

(2) Even if a trial may be envisaged or desired it is unlikely to occur before a period of restraint has expired. Therefore *American Cyanamid* does not apply. *Lawrence David v Ashton* was a very unusual case because a five day trial was to be heard in October, whereas the case had first come before the lower court at the end of May (the Court of Appeal considered the matter in July).

(3) A long period of restraint causes particular difficulties. Unless a trial date is available within a reasonable time then damages will invariably not compensate a defendant. In which case applying *American Cyanamid* may militate against granting an injunction (unless it is felt necessary to maintain the status quo).

(4) If the issues of fact and law are clear and it is therefore possible for the court to decide whether the clause is *prima facie* bad or good then it should make that decision (see also O'Connor LJ in *John Michael Design plc v Cooke* [1987] 2 All ER 332).

(5) It is still therefore advisable for the party seeking to enforce a restraint of trade or business secrets clause or duty to be armed so far as possible with affidavit evidence which proves that he has a strong case on the merits in addition to demonstrating that damages are not an adequate remedy for him and that the balance of convenience lies in favour of granting the injunction.

(6) NB: in an application for a mandatory injunction *American Cyanamid* does not apply; the onus on the applicant is very heavy: see *Locabail International Finance Ltd v Agroexport* [1986] 1 WLR 657 CA.

4 Special considerations in some restraint of trade cases

4.1 The general position

Specific performance is not usually granted of employment contracts. It has long been the view of the courts that to force an employee to work for an employer smacks of slavery. Until very recently (see 4.2 below) there was only one case in which a court had ordered reinstatement on common law grounds (*Hill v Parsons (CA) and Co Ltd* [1972] 1 Ch 305). The statutory powers regarding reinstatement/re-engagement of an employee under s 69 Employment Protection (Consolidation) Act 1978 are an entirely foreign concept to the common law.

Further, the courts will not grant an injunction if this will amount to indirect specific performance of an employment contract or if to do so will perpetuate a relationship based on mutual trust and confidence or if the applicant is seeking to enforce an unreasoanble restraint of trade. It is frequently said that the special considerations only apply to the employer/employee relationship however it is important to understand that the concept of mutual trust and confidence (see below) can encapsulate relationships much wider than those based on employment contracts (per eg agency).

The position, so far as employees are concerned, is now partly dealt with by s 16 of the Trade Union and Labour Relations Act 1974. This provides that no court shall, whether by way of an order for specific performance of an employment contract or an injunction restraining a breach or threatened breach of such a contract compel an employee to do any work or to attend at any place for the doing of any work.

However, it is still necessary to consider the common law rules and the cases. Regarding prohibiting interlocutory injunctions there are three important primary questions.

(1) Is there an unreasonable restraint of trade? If so, then quite clearly no interlocutory injunction will be granted. Such an answer must involve examining the strength of each party's case and it can thus be seen that the approach of Lord Denning MR in rejecting the broad *American Cyanamid* approach seems sensible.

(2) Would the interlocutory injunction, if granted, perpetuate a relationship based on mutual trust and confidence which has ceased to exist? This question will clearly be of importance in some cases which do not involve employers and employees such as some agency and management contracts.

(3) Would the award of an injunction amount to the indirect specific performance of a contract of personal services?

However, this area of law is very complex because it may be possible to argue when dealing with cases within (2) and (3) above that the courts should grant a negative injunction restraining the defendant from performing the type of services stipulated in the contract for anyone else but the plaintiff. Whether the court can, must or must not grant an injunction in these cases is a matter of debate for there are three distinct lines of authority.

The first view, which in our opinion is the correct one, is that the court simply has a discretion to grant an interlocutory injunction if that is just and convenient in the circumstances of the particular case. We see no reason why s 37 of the Supreme Court Act 1981 should not govern in this instance. However, this discretion is subject to a well-established principle laid down by the cases: this is that the court will not grant an injunction if the effect of it is to force the defendant either to perform his contract with the plaintiff or to remain idle. Authority for this principle is found in *Warner Brothers Ltd v Nelson, Ehrman v Bartholomew* [1898] 1 Ch 671 and in *Page One Records Ltd v Britton* [1968] 1 WLR 157. The question of idleness is one of fact: in the *Warner Brothers* case (rather surprisingly) it was found that the defendant, Bette Davis, would be able to find alternative employment even though it might not pay as well as if she had performed her contract with Warner Brothers. However, in *Page One Records*, it was found that the group in question, the Troggs, needed a manager and if the negative covenant had been enforced by injunction then they would either have had to accept the plaintiff as their manager or starve. In that case Stamp J held, in what appear to be entirely separate reasons for refusing the injunction, that a court will not grant an injunction to enforce a negative covenant either:

(a) if there is no mutuality (it was on this basis he distinguished *Lumley v Wagner* (1852) 1 De GM & G 604) and/or
(b) if the defendant's obligations are not only obligations of personal service but also involve trust and confidence and/or
(c) if the totality of the obligations between the parties approximates to a joint venture or partnership.

It used to be generally accepted that there was no mutuality in contracts of personal services (ie there is usually no possibility of the defendant enforcing the plaintiff's obligations to employ by way of specific performance or injunction). However, in the light of the cases discussed at 4.2 below, this will depend upon the facts in each case.

The second view states that the court will never grant the type of negative injunction referred to. This approach, founded on the doctrine of 'automatic determination', is supported by the Court of Appeal judgment in *Denmark Productions Ltd v Boscobell Productions* [1969] 1 QB 699. The court held that even though the defendant's repudiation had not been accepted and that the plaintiff thus purported to keep the contract alive, the contract, being one for personal services, had been brought to an end unilaterally. The plaintiff could therefore only sue for damages after the date of repudiation and could not claim for an account of the defendant's earnings after that date. Furthermore, the plaintiff was under a duty to mitigate his damage. Further support for this doctrine can be found in *Decro-Wall International SA v Practitioners in Marketing Ltd* [1971] 1 WLR 361. Also *Sanders v Neale (Ernest A) Ltd* [1974] ICR 565 per Sir John Donaldson '... repudiation of a contract of employment is an exception to the general rule. It terminates the contract without the necessity for acceptance by the injured party...'. There are dicta in other cases which also purport to follow the doctrine, see for example the dissenting judgment of Shaw LJ in *Gunton v Richmond-upon-Thames LBC* [1981] Ch 448. However, the doctrine has been doubted in *Marshall (Thomas) (Exports) Ltd v Guinle* [1979] Ch 227 and in the majority judgments in *Gunton*. In the former case, Megarry V-C said:

> If cases of master and servant are an exception from the rule that an unaccepted repudiation works no determination of the contract, and instead are subject to . . . the doctrine of automatic determination, the result would be that many a contract of employment would be determined forthwith upon the commission of a fundamental breach or a breach of a fundamental term, even though the commission of this breach was unknown to the innocent party, and even if had he known he would have elected to keep the contract in being.

He also went on to reject a narrower formulation of the rule which said that, in employment cases, a breach amounting to a repudiation did not forthwith determine the contract unless the party breaking the contract intended to bring it to an end. In conclusion one can say that there is some authority which supports a rule of automatic determination; however the trend in recent cases is against such a doctrine. The doubts about the rule, which we feel are well founded, concern the fact that it allows the defendant simply to say that the contract is at an end and to be free from the contractual restrictions which applied whilst employment or the relationship continued.

It would be anomalous if as a matter of law an employer was entitled to affirm the contract after repudiation by the employee (*Evening Standard v Henderson* [1987] ICR 588) but that the employee did not enjoy the same entitlement. The unilateralist view has been challenged by a number of recent authorities (and backed up by a growing number of cases where injunctions have been granted) which indicate that in principle an employee can affirm a contract. In *Rigby v Ferrodo* [1988] ICR 29 HL, the employer unilaterally imposed a reduction in wages on the workforce. This variation was never accepted by them but they carried on nevertheless. Mr Rigby commenced proceedings claiming damages for breach of his contract of employment, an order for payment of a weekly wage at the rate prevailing before the reduction and a declaration. Lord Oliver made it quite clear that a repudiatory breach in a contract of employment as a matter of law is no different from any other contract. At p 34 he said:

> whatever may be the position under a contract of service where the repudiation takes the form either of a walkout by the employee or a refusal by the employer any longer to regard the employee as his servant, I know of no principle of law that any breach which the innocent party is entitled to treat as repudiatory of the other party's obligations brings the contract to an end automatically.

The third view is that the court *must* always grant an injunction to prohibit a party to a contract breaching a valid express negative covenant and has no discretion to do otherwise. The theory supporting this approach is that the injunction reflects what the parties have agreed. Authority for this view is found in the dictum of Lord Cairns LC in *Doherty v Allman and Dowden* (1878) 3 App Cas 709. Although in *Warner Brothers Pictures Inc v Nelson (L)* [1937] 1 KB 209 and more recently in *Hampstead and Suburban Properties Ltd v Diomedous* [1969] 1 Ch 248 the judgments purported to follow and apply Lord Cairns' words it is submitted that they did not do so and that the dictim should be consigned to legal history. It would seem extraordinary if there were no discretion to grant a discretionary remedy.

The law is inconclusive and may well change further. For practical purposes the only advice we can give is that the parties should proceed on the basis that the court does have discretion to award an injunction to enforce a negative covenant except in those instances set out in the *Page One Records* case. Indeed the approach of Stamp J has recently been applied in the Court of Appeal in preference to that of Branson J in *Warner Brothers*.

In *Warren v Mendy* [1989] 1 WLR 853; [1989] IRLR 210 the Court of Appeal upheld Pill J's discharge of an injunction in a case between boxing promoters. The facts were that in January 1988 the plaintiff, a manager and promoter licensed by the British Boxing Board of Control, entered into a written agreement in the Board's standard form to manage the professional affairs of B, a talented young boxer, for three years. By clause 2 of the agreement the plaintiff agreed to supervise B's training programme and to use the best endeavours to arrange suitable professional activities and secure for him proper reward. By clause 4, B agreed to be managed exclusively by the plaintiff for the duration of the agreement. Thereafter the plaintiff acted both as B's manager and promoter in respect of a number of professional contests. By June 1988 B had lost confidence in the plaintiff, and, asserting that the agreement was unenforceable as an unreasonable restraint of trade, began an action against him for, *inter alia*, an account on the ground that he held undisclosed funds as constructive trustee. At about the same time B entered into an agreement with the defendant for the introduction of commercial opportunities. The plaintiff obtained *ex parte* injunctive relief against the defendant on commencing proceedings to restrain him from inducing B to act in breach of the agreement and from acting for B in relation to his professional career. On the defendant's application to discharge the injunctions the judge found that as a boxer B's professional career was relatively short-lived involving the continuing need to exercise a specialist skill, that the boxer-manager relationship gave rise to mutual trust which B no longer felt and that the plaintiff was likely to seek relief not only against the defendant but against any other person attempting to supplant him. He concluded that the effect of the relief sought against the defendant would be to compel B to perform his agreement with the plaintiff and discharged the injunctions. On B's application he joined him as a party to the proceedings.

The Court of Appeal held (a) that where a contract for the performance of personal services involved the continuing exercise of some special skill or talent and a high degree of mutual trust and confidence the court would not enforce negative stipulations under the contract if to do so would effectively compel performance of the positive obligations; (b) that compulsion, being a question of fact, might be inferred where relief was sought against a third party who might be the only alternative master, or where the current master was likely to seek relief against any other alternative master; and (c) that since the plaintiff's position as both manager and promoter gave rise to a potential conflict of duty and interest and since the evidence filed in B's action supported his assertion that the plaintiff held undisclosed funds as constructive trustee, it would be inappropriate to grant relief which tied B to any further contractual relationship with the plaintiff.

4.2 Recent developments

However, the general rule that a court will not order re-instatement of an employee (save where statute makes provision for this) has been abrogated recently in some cases. See *Irani v Southampton Health Authority* [1985] IRLR 203; *Powell v Brent LBC* (1987) IRLR 466; *Hughes v Southwark LBC* [1988] IRLR 55; *Wadcock v Brent LBC* [1990] IRLR 223 and *Robb v London Borough of Hammersmith & Fulham* [1991] IRLR 72. In *Wadcock v Brent LBC* the court granted an injunction restraining the council from acting on its purported determination of the employee's contract coupled with an order that he be paid his salary pending trial. The result of this case may turn on the special fact that the plaintiff apparently gave an undertaking to the court which went to the root of the litigation. However, it should be noted that in other recent cases the plaintiff has failed to bring his case within the limited exception to the usual rule: see for example *Alexander v STC Ltd* [1990] IRLR 55 and *Wishart v National Association of Citizens Advice Bureaux Ltd* [1990] 1RLR 393.

The general rule may also appear to have been disregarded in cases concerning what are called 'garden leave' clauses. The first case dealing with this topic is *Evening Standard Co Ltd v Henderson* [1987] 1RLR 64. Mr Henderson had been employed on the London *Evening Standard* for about 17 years. In 1979 he was appointed manager of the production room. His contract of employment provided for one year's notice on either side. It also contained a provision preventing him from working for anyone else during the currency of the contract.

During 1986 it became known that a rival publisher was planning to start another London evening newspaper that would compete with the *Evening Standard*. Mr Henderson agreed to join the staff of that proposed rival and in September he sent a letter to his employers saying that he wished to terminate his contract as from November 1986. He therefore failed to give the one year's notice that his contract required.

The company applied for an injunction to restrain Mr Henderson from working for a rival newspaper during the period of about ten months between the time the notice he had given expired and the contractual one year's notice. That application at first instance was refused notwithstanding that the company had given an undertaking that they would carry on paying Mr Henderson throughout the contractual notice period. In the course of proceedings before the Court of Appeal, the company offered to let Mr Henderson continue to perform his work if he so wished and undertook not to seek any damages against him for the period when he was not working for them. The Court of Appeal granted the injunction.

The second case was *Provident Financial Group plc v Hayward* [1989] 3 All ER 298. The defendant was employed by the plaintiffs as financial director of the estate agency business they operated from offices in various towns in the north of England and the Midlands. Under his contract of service the defendant was required to perform the duties assigned to him, although the plaintiffs were under no corresponding obligation to assign any duties to him or provide him with work. The contract further required him to devote the whole of his time to carrying out his duties under the contract and prohibited him from undertaking any other business or profession during the continuance of his employment. On 1 July 1988 the defendant tendered his resignation to the plaintiffs and it was mutually agreed that the period of notice should be six months instead of the 12 months specified in the contract provided the defendant undertook not to disclose any confidential information to any person, including future employers, for a period of two years from the date of the end of employment. The defendant continued to work for the plaintiffs until 5 September, when, at their request and for the purpose of preventing him from acquiring any further confidential information, he ceased to work on their premises and was sent home while continuing to receive full pay and other benefits. On 13 October the defendant notified the plaintiffs of his intention to start work for a supermarket chain as financial controller of their estate agency offices, which were situated in their stores throughout the country. The plaintiffs sought an injunction to restrain the defendant from working for anyone else until the period of his notice expired (on 31 December). The judge refused their application. The plaintiffs appealed. The Court of Appeal held that since the court would not specifically enforce a contract of personal service between an employer and his employee, it would not grant an injunction in very wide terms, reproducing a term in the contract, preventing the employee from working for anyone else during the continuance of his service agreement if the effect of granting such an injunction would be to compel the employee to return to work for his previous employer. However, an express negative covenant not to work for anyone else during the term of the service contract was not a mere corollory of the positive obligation to devote his whole time to the employer's business and, accordingly, was enforceable by the court as a matter of discretion. However the court would not enforce such a term where the other business for which the employee wished to work had nothing whatever to do with the employer's business, even if the employee was offered full pay, because an employee had a concern to work and exercise his skills. In the circumstances, an injunction would not be granted because the defendant did not have any relevant confidential information of the plaintiffs which would be of use to the rival company and there was no real prospect of serious or significant damage to the plaintiffs from the defendant working as financial controller for the rival company for the short period which remained of his contract. The appeal was dismissed.

This case was important because unlike in the *Evening Standard* case the plaintiffs were not even prepared to allow Hayward to spend the remainder of the notice period at work. They offered him no choice; they required him to stay at home.

From these two cases the following principles can be stated. In order to have a chance to obtain a 'garden leave' type injunction the court will have to be satisfied of the following:

(a) That the employer has not accepted the employee's repudiatory breach.

(b) That the employer has not agreed to provide the employee with any particular type of work. If there is such an agreement and the employee is required to be on 'garden leave' he can argue that the employer has repudiated the agreement.

(c) That the employee will receive the same salary and benefits whilst on garden leave as he did whilst at work.

(d) That the employer can demonstrate existing or likely detriment. In *Provident* it was said that fostering the profitability of a trade rival can constitute detriment: one obvious way in which that can exist is if the employee possesses confidential information which may be of use to his employer's competitor.

(e) That the period for which garden leave is sought is not excessive.

(f) That the employee is not engaged in an activity where to grant a garden leave injunction might deprive him of future work or if his skills might atrophy during the relevant period.

5 Business secrets cases

The special rules which apply to some restraint of trade cases do not apply to cases, or those parts of cases, in which business secrets are alleged to have been betrayed.

The defences on which the defendant will rely are either that the information was not in fact secret, that there has been no breach, or that the public interest militates against granting an injunction. In *Lion Laboratories Ltd v Evans* [1984] 2 All ER 417, the plaintiff failed to get an interlocutory injunction because of the public interest factor. That case concerned the Lion Intoximeter which is used to measure alcohol levels in the breath. The plaintiff company learnt that two of its ex-employees were trying to contact national newspapers with copies of some of the plaintiff's internal correspondence. These documents were all confidential and indicated doubts as to the reliability and accuracy of the instruments. The plaintiff issued a writ claiming an injunction restraining the defendant from using/disclosing the information and damages for breach of confidence and/or copyright. An *ex parte* injunction was granted in the terms of the writ. The following day a national newspaper published an article stating that the plaintiff's products were prone to serious error but did so without breaching the precise terms of the injunction. The defendants then applied to have the *ex parte* injunction discharged but the judge continued it. The defendants appealed to the Court of Appeal relying on the public interest point and succeeded.

Three further points are of special importance in business secrets cases. Firstly, an injunction to restrain a breach of secrecy will only be granted to a party who is the beneficiary of the duty of confidence: see *Fraser v Evans* [1969] 1 QB 349. Secondly, it is frequently sought to draw an analogy between confidential information cases and defamation actions in which there is a rule that if the defendant asserts in his affidavit that he will plead justification or qualified privilege or fair comment as a defence, then an interlocutory injunction will not be granted against him. There is no rule in confidential information cases concerning a plea of public interest. See *Lion Laboratories* per all members of the court who said that the defendant must specify the reasons in which the public interest in publication should defeat the public interest in maintaining confidence. See also *Francome v Mirror Group Newspapers Ltd* [1984] 1 All ER 408. Thirdly, even if an injunction is refused it may be possible in some cases to argue that the defendants undertake a duty to keep an account of royalties on each item produced which sums be put into a special joint escrow account and to supply monthly production figures to the plaintiff. See *Coco v Clark (A N) Engineers) Ltd* [1969] RPC 41.

Chapter 22

Anton Piller Orders and Miscellaneous Other Orders

1 Anton Piller orders

The Anton Piller order is, together with the interlocutory prohibitory injunction, probably the most useful form of interlocutory relief for a plaintiff in a business secrets case; indeed the case of *Piller (Anton) K G v Manufacturing Processes Ltd* [1976] Ch 55 was a business secrets/copyright case. Although it is unusual, it is also possible for a defendant to apply for such an order: see *International Electronics Ltd v Weigh Data Ltd* [1980] FSR 423. Power to grant an Anton Piller order arises from the inherent jurisdiction of the court and not from statute or rules of court for its existence came about because applications for orders for detention, custody, preservation and inspection under Ord 29, r 2 have to be made by summons or by notice: Ord 29 r 2(5). Because surprise is a vital element in the execution of such an order, applications are made *ex parte* usually in the Chancery Division and in camera. However, before any application is contemplated the words of Browne-Wilkinson J in *Thermax Ltd v Schott Industrial Glass Ltd* [1981] FSR 289 should be borne in mind.

> As time goes on and the granting of Anton Piller orders becomes more and more frequent, there is a tendency to forget how serious an intervention they are in the privacy and rights of defendants. One is inclined to forget the stringency of the requirements as laid down by the Court of Appeal

(ie in the *Anton Piller* case itself). Accordingly, the plaintiff must have a very strong case in order to obtain such an order.

Browne-Wilkinson J's concerns have been amplified recently by Hoffman J in *Lock International plc v Beswick* [1989] 1 WLR 1268. The facts were that in February 1989 the plaintiff, a manufacturer of metal detectors, obtained an *ex parte* Anton Piller order against eight of its former employees and a competing company with whom they had since commenced employment. Under the Anton Piller order, which was executed the next day, the plaintiff was allowed to search not only the competing company's premises but also the homes of three of the other defendants, and to remove not only documents containing specified confidential information but also the competing company's drawings, commercial documents, computer records and prototypes. The plaintiff undertook not to use the information except for prosecution of its action, and in support of a cross-undertaking in damages the plaintiff disclosed what was said to be its latest report and accounts for the 18 months ended on 31 December 1987, which showed net assets of about £800,000 and a pre-tax profit for the period of £1.76m. In fact, as appeared from accounts for the six months ended on 30 June 1988 which had been filed at the Companies Registry, the plaintiff had recently given financial assistance to H plc to enable it to purchase the plaintiff and associated companies. That assistance took the form of a guarantee of a £94m overdraft facility, supported by a charge over the plaintiff's assets. Since its purchase of the plaintiff, H plc had announced the closure and sale of another subsidiary.

The defendants applied to discharge the order on the ground of material non-disclosure (see below at p 221). Hoffman J granted the application and in his judgment made a number of general observations about the appropriate circumstances in which such an Anton Piller application should be allowed. He said that there must be proportionality between the perceived threat to the plaintiff's rights and the remedy granted. The fact that there is overwhelming evidence that the defendant has behaved wrongfully in his commercial relationships does not necessarily justify an Anton Piller order. People whose commercial morality allows them to take a list of the customers with whom they were in contact while employed will not necessarily disobey an order of the court requiring them to deliver it up. Not everyone who is misusing confidential information will destroy documents in the face of a court order requiring him to preserve them.

In many cases it will therefore be sufficient to make an order for delivery up of the plaintiff's documents to his solicitor or, in cases in which the documents belong to the defendant but may provide evidence against him, an order that he preserve the documents pending further order, or allow the plaintiff's solicitors to make copies. The more intrusive orders allowing searches of premises or vehicles require a careful balancing of, on the one hand, the plaintiff's right to recover his property or to preserve important evidence against, on the other hand, violation of the privacy of a defendant who has had no opportunity to put his side of the case. It is not merely that the defendant may be innocent. The making of an intrusive order *ex parte* even against a guilty defendant is contrary to normal principles of justice and can only be done when there is a paramount need to prevent a denial of justice to the plaintiff. The absolute extremity of the court's powers is to permit a search of a defendant's dwelling house, with the humiliation and family distress which that frequently involves. Having analysed the evidence, Hoffman J concluded that it came nowhere near disclosing an 'extremely strong *prima facie* case' or clear evidence that the defendants had in their possession incriminating documents or things or that there was a grave danger or real possibility that the defendants might destroy evidence. Moreover:

> the lack of specificity in the plaintiff's affidavit was such that I have some doubt whether it could be said to have raised a triable issue. Furthermore, these defendants were no fly-by-night video pirates. They were former long service employees with families and mortgages, who had openly said

that they were entering into competition and who the plaintiff knew to be financed by highly respectable institutions.

He also questioned why it was necessary to make an *ex parte* order which had the effect of allowing the plaintiff's employees to have immediate access to all of the confidential documents and prototypes owned by the company set up by the defendants. He went on:

> In the Anton Piller case, one of the conditions mentioned by Lord Denning MR for the grant of an order was that 'inspection would do no real harm to the defendant or his case' [[1976] Ch 55, 61]. Even if it was thought that the defendants were the kind of dishonest people who would conceal or destroy incriminating documents, it would surely have been sufficient at the *ex parte* stage to allow the plaintiff's solicitors to remove the documents and make copies for their own retention pending an application by the plaintiff *inter partes* for leave to inspect them. The defendant would then have had the opportunity to object or to ask for a restricted form of inspection, such as by independent expert only. I do not regard the right to apply to discharge the order as a sufficient protection for the defendants. The trauma of the execution of the Anton Piller order means that in practice it is often difficult to exercise until after substantial damage has been done.

1.1 The ambit of an Anton Piller order

A typical Anton Piller order will allow the following or a combination of the following:

(1) A fixed number of people authorised by the plaintiff and a fixed number of legally qualified members of staff of the plaintiff's solicitors to go to specified premises, usually the defendant's business premises, between certain hours and to enter them with the defendant's permission. If the defendant is not there they cannot enter, even by an open door or window. (See *AB v CDE* [1982] RPC 509 which indicates what the plaintiff should not do on the execution of an Anton Piller order.)

(2) The defendant must disclose the whereabouts of all relevant articles and documents.

(3) The plaintiff's representatives can seize and remove into the custody of the plaintiff's solicitors all incriminating documents or articles as specifically identified by the order or of a class identifed by the order.

(4) Further, they can inspect and photograph documents and articles specified in the order. This power is in addition to the normal powers of discovery.

(5) They can test specified articles.

(6) Moreover, the order will restrain the defendant until judgment or further order from doing certain acts in the same way as a typical interlocutory prohibitory injunction would.

(7) The court also has the power to order a defendant to disclose to those serving the order the names and addresses of suppliers of the infringing articles

or information and forthwith to place in the custody of those persons all relevant documents relating thereto: see *EMI v Sarwar and Haidar* [1977] FSR 146. Moreover, the defendant can be ordered to reveal the names and addresses of those to whom he has supplied infringing articles or information: see *Gates v Swift* [1982] RPC 339 and in either case he must necessarily be ordered not to warn his suppliers/customers of the existence of the order and of his compliance with it.

(8) A further extension of the ambit of an Anton Piller order occurred in *Yousif v Salama* [1980] 3 All ER 405. The plaintiff was a procuring agent in the Middle East. He entered into an agreement with the defendants in which he undertook to try to procure business for them and if successful he was to be paid commission. Having procured business for them he was not paid and so he visited their offices and was handed two files and a diary which showed the amount due to him. He then began an action to recover his commission. He also moved for an Anton Piller order regarding those documents. Order 29, r 2 did not apply as the documents themselves were not the subject matter of the action but were simply evidence in the action. Moreover, unlike the normal Anton Piller case, the documents were not in any way similar to infringing copies. The Court of Appeal however granted the order. Lord Denning MR did so because the documents were the best possible evidence and there was a genuine fear that the defendant might destroy them if given notice. Brightman LJ did so because there was *prima facie* evidence that essential documents were at risk. Donaldson LJ dissented as to the result but thought that such an order could only be made, as in all Anton Piller cases, if (a) there was a very clear *prima facie* case that the defendant would conceal or destroy essential evidence and (b) that to do so would deprive the plaintiff of any evidence on which to put forward his claim and so frustrate justice.

(9) There is the power to order not only disclosure of documents but for the defendant to answer interrogatories at the interlocutory stage. However in *Rank Film Distributors Ltd v Video Information Centre* [1982] AC 380 the House of Lords in a judgment which affirmed the decision of that Court of Appeal said that such a power was circumscribed by the principle against self-incrimination in those cases where criminal proceedings were contemplated against the defendant; (note, it was expressly stated that the primary parts of an Anton Piller order were not, however, subject to the privilege against self-incrimination). This case has now been effectively overruled by s 72 of the Supreme Court Act 1981 insofar as intellectual property rights are concerned. Section 72(1) says:

> In any proceedings to which this subsection applies a person shall not be excused, by reason that to do so would tend to expose that person, or his or her spouse, to proceedings for a related offence or for the recovery of a related penalty—
>
> (a) from answering any question put to that person in the first mentioned proceedings; or
> (b) from complying with any order made in those proceedings.

Subsection 2 goes on to say that subs 1 applies to proceedings in the High Court for infringement of rights pertaining to any intellectual property or passing off or proceedings brought to obtain disclosure of any information relating to any infringement of such rights or any passing off and proceedings brought to prevent any apprehended infringement of such rights or any apprehended passing off. Section 72(5) says that 'intellectual property' includes 'technical or commercial information'. It is submitted that this includes not only business secrets which are related to a design or process but also, for example, a list of customers. However, in those cases which do not involve intellectual property as defined, the privilege against self-incrimination still exists. Note that s 72(3) prevents the use of statements or admissions made by the defendant pursuant to an Anton Piller order in any criminal trial for a 'related offence'. See also *Charles of the Ritz Group Ltd v Jory* [1986] FSR 14 in which Scott J held that s 72 applies even when criminal proceedings have already begun. However the existence of pending criminal proceedings is a matter to be taken into account by a judge in deciding whether to exercise his discretion to order the discovery sought. The real issue is whether, if the order is made, there is a serious risk of injustice to the defendants at the criminal trial. However 'injustice' amounts to more than putting the defendant at a disadvantage. The safeguards provided to a defendant by s 72 (and by s 31 of the Theft Act 1968) may not apply in a large number of cases (eg where the likely criminal charge is a conspiracy of any type) which means that in many cases the defendant can assert the privilege. The inadequacy of the present law caused difficulties for the plaintiffs in *Sonangol v Lundqvist* [1990] 3 All ER 283 and *Tate Access Floors v Boswell* [1990] 3 All ER 303. There is much pressure for reform of the law in this area.

(10) Anton Piller orders nowadays frequently deal with breach of copyright and confidence in computer programmes. An order regarding an identified computer programme may include a further order that the defendant print-out material in computer readable form; this may even include computer readable material in his possession over and above the identifying material: see *Gates v Swift* [1982] RPC 339.

(11) Moreover in *Bayer (AG) v Winter* [1986] 1 WLR 497 it was held by the Court of Appeal that if necessary, to aid compliance with an Anton Piller order, a defendant could be ordered to surrender his passport and be prevented from leaving the jurisdiction. Once, however, compliance is demonstrated, such an order becomes unnecessary.

1.2 Criteria for the award of an Anton Piller order

The applicant must show:

(1) An extremely strong *prima facie* case. This requirement is mentioned in many cases: see the *Anton Piller* case itself. In *Universal City Studios v Hubbard* [1983] Ch 241 the evidence was that Hubbard was associated with running a factory making counterfeit films. He had been recognised entering the factory building, he had hired 14 video recorders and had purchased a machine capable of manufacturing video cassettes from 16mm film. It had cost £26,000. This was, on the face of it, compelling evidence against him at the interlocutory stage.

What is clear is that the plaintiff is not allowed to use an Anton Piller order as a fishing expedition (ie some form of pre-action discovery). (See the judgment of Lawton LJ in *Hytrac Conveyors Ltd v Conveyors Intl Ltd* [1983] 1 WLR 44, 'Those who make charges must state right at the beginning what they are and what facts they are based upon'.)

(2) The potential or actual damage is very serious to him (ie 'where it is essential that the plaintiff should have inspection so that justice can be done between the parties' per Denning MR in the *Anton Piller* case).

(3) Clear evidence that the defendant has in his possession incriminating documents or articles.

(4) That there is a 'real possibility' that the defendant might destroy, hide or take beyond the jurisdiction vital documents or articles before an *inter partes* application could be made. The plaintiff might be able to do this by simply showing the defendant has been dishonest. However this requirement may have been modified by the majority judgments in *Yousif v Salama* [1980] FSR 405. The only basis on which the plaintiff argued that the defendant might destroy vital evidence was an allegation of forgery of an endorsement on a cheque. As Donaldson LJ said, in a powerful dissenting judgment: 'This has nothing whatever to do with the destruction of documents which the plaintiff says he fears'.

However, if the defendant is operating openly or is a respectable company this may be a decisive factor in refusing an application. See *Systematica Ltd v London Computer Centre Ltd* [1983] FSR 313 and *Booker McConnell plc v Plascow* [1985] RPC 425 in which Kerr LJ strongly criticised the plaintiffs for having sought Anton Piller orders against the second and third defendants who were 'highly reputable public companies'. On the other hand, the order had been rightly sought against the first defendant, an individual who had been responsible for removing business secrets belonging to the plaintiffs. Dillon LJ said, in a judgment which sought to remind lawyers of the proper basis for an application for an Anton Piller order,

> ... the making of an Anton Piller order against a trading company may well be regarded as a serious stigma on that company's commercial reputation ... it follows that there is a responsibility in each case on the plaintiff's advisers to consider seriously whether it is justifiable to seek an Anton Piller order against the particular defendant or whether it would be enough to obtain negative injunctions with, if appropriate, an order to deliver up . . . .

(5) In the *Anton Piller* case, Lord Denning MR said that an order would only be made in circumstances in which inspection would do no real harm to the defendant or his case. He further said in the *Yousif* case that if the defendant was honest then he had nothing to fear from an order. It may well be that this part of the Anton Piller judgment, if it did constitute part of the ratio, has been neglected in some cases. However, in *Wardle Fabrics Ltd v Myrstis (G) Ltd* [1984] FSR 263, Goulding J discharged an Anton Piller order partly on the ground that as the defendant was honest it was unnecessary. Moreover, primary importance was attached to this requirement in the *Jeffrey Rogers* case.

(6) When the plaintiff makes his application for an Anton Piller order he

must make full disclosure. This means that he must put before the court all relevant matters including those which may militate against granting such an order. In *Thermax Ltd v Schott Industrial Glass Ltd* [1981] FSR 289 the importance of this requirement was brought home to the plaintiff when the court discharged an Anton Piller order without investigating the merits of the case when the plaintiff had omitted material matters from the affidavits supporting the *ex parte* application even though it seems such non-disclosure was innocent and was the result of an error of judgment rather than a conscious decision to mislead the court. The important points were that the plaintiff had omitted to mention that the defendant company was not simply a creature of the second to fifth defendants, all former directors of the plaintiff, but was a subsidiary of the Carl Zeiss Foundation, a reputable company which had extensive experience in manufacturing relevant goods. Secondly, that there were business secrets at the defendant's premises which belonged exclusively to them. Finally, and less importantly, that in a parallel action based on breach of confidence, the defendant's solicitors had already refused inspection of the premises in question. In *Wardle Fabrics Ltd v Mysistis (G) Ltd* [1984] FSR 263 the defendant said that the plaintiff had not informed the court of antecedent dealings between the parties to the extent that the defendants had co-operated with the plaintiffs in revealing names of suppliers, parallel importers and invoices. There had also been correspondence between the patent agents and solicitors acting for the parties. Goulding J said in granting an application to discharge the mandatory parts of an Anton Piller order that the test of full disclosure was not whether, if the judge had the fresh facts before him he would have come to the same conclusion, but whether the court had been informed of all relevant facts. He came to this conclusion even though, had all matters been revealed at the *ex parte* stage, he would still have awarded the Anton Piller order. In *Yardley and Company Ltd v Higson* [1984] FSR 304 the Court of Appeal held that even though there had been non-disclosure of a material fact in an initial application, this did not of itself prevent the grant of further relief at a subsequent hearing when that fact was fully before the court. However, that case concerned an application for an interlocutory prohibitory injunction and not for an Anton Piller order. It is submitted that, because an Anton Piller order combines mandatory parts as well as prohibitory elements, if the case had been concerned with such an order then the outcome should have been decided in the defendant's favour. The duty to make full disclosure also involves making full and proper enquiries before any action is taken. This was not done in *Systematica Ltd v London Computer Centre Ltd* [1983] FSR 313 nor in *Bank Mellatt v Nikpour* [1985] FSR 87 which was an application for a Mareva injunction. In *Jeffery Rogers Knitwear Productions Ltd v Vinola (Knitwear) Manufacturing Co* [1985] FSR 184 an Anton Piller order was set aside with costs on a common fund basis because insufficient enquiries had been made by the plaintiff.

The usual penalty for material non-disclosure, whether inadvertent or not, is the discharge of the *ex parte* order. However there is a discretion to maintain the order if the court is satisfied that no injustice has been caused to the defendants: see *Brink's Mat Ltd v Elcombe* [1988] 1 WLR 1350.

In *Lock International plc v Beswick* [1989] 1 WLR 1268 Hoffman J discharged an Anton Piller order because of a failure to disclose. The facts are set out at p 215 above.

See also *Manor Electronics Ltd v Dickson* [1988] RPC 618. The plaintiffs manufactured and sold electronic devices. The first four defendants were a former director and three former employees of the plaintiffs and the fifth defendant was a company for which they now worked. The plaintiffs believed the defendants had conspired to injure them by going into competition with them using their confidential information. There was also a claim for breach of copyright in relation to printed circuit boards and circuit diagrams. The plaintiffs obtained *ex parte* orders restraining disposal of certain assets, and for delivery up and discovery. They gave the usual cross-undertaking in damages but failed to disclose that their financial situation was 'parlous'; no evidence of their financial worth had been offered. They also undertook to issue and serve the writ forthwith, but there had been delay in serving it. On the basis of documents disclosed on the first order, they then sought and obtained an Anton Piller order, again failing to disclose their financial position. The order read in part 'It is ordered that . . . [the plaintiffs' solicitor accompanied by a director of the plaintiffs] shall be entitled to enter the dwelling house, workshop and garage of Mr Dickson . . .'. The plaintiffs' solicitor, who attended on the execution of the Anton Piller order, was the daughter of the plaintiffs' chief executive. On the return date, the plaintiffs sought an interlocutory injunction restraining use of confidential information. The defendants applied to discharge the *ex parte* orders.

Scott J discharged the *ex parte* orders and refused injunctive relief on the following bases:

(1) The form of the Anton Piller order, in providing that the plaintiffs' representatives 'be entitled to enter' the first defendants' premises, instead of requiring the first defendant to permit such entry, was defective.

(2) The plaintiffs' solicitor's failure to honour the plaintiffs' undertaking to serve the writ as soon as issued was regrettable (albeit an oversight) as it left the defendants in doubt as to the cause of action asserted against them.

(3) The requirement that a plaintiff's solicitor supervise the execution of an Anton Piller order is to ensure that there is some responsible person who can give reliable evidence of what has taken place. The evidence of a solicitor, as an officer of the court, is likely in the event of a dispute to be believed in preference to that of the defendant and it is desirable that the solicitor should have no personal connection with the plaintiff. Here, it had been unwise, though not a breach of the order, that the solicitor in attendance should have been closely related to the plaintiffs' chief executive.

(4) There had been material non-disclosure of the plaintiffs' financial difficulties, so that their cross-undertaking in damages was worthless. In the absence of reference in the evidence to a plaintiffs' financial substance, the *ex parte* judge will assume that it is adequate to support the cross-undertaking; he depends upon the plaintiff making full disclosure. If there has been such material non-disclosure, then the court's practice is to discharge the *ex parte* orders without going into the merits.

(5) The plaintiffs had been unable to identify the alleged confidential

information with sufficient particularity for the court to distinguish between protectable 'trade secrets' and the unprotectable technical expertise gained by the first four defendants which they were entitled to use.

In *Columbia Picture Industries Inc v Robinson* [1987] 1 Ch 38, the defendants, R and a company controlled by him, carried on business at Frederick Street selling pre-recorded video cassettes, blank tapes and video equipment. R was skilled at recording films onto video tapes and by 1981 a large proportion of the defendants' business was the recording of motion pictures onto tapes. Some of those films were recorded in breach of the plaintiffs' copyright in films they had made or distributed. At a shop in Mill Street, the defendants employed a manager mainly to run a video club hiring films to members but also to sell video cassettes. The stock at those premises contained a large quantity of pirate tapes. The chief investigation officer of the plaintiffs' trade organisation began to watch the defendants' premises. R recognised him and invited him to inspect the Frederick Street premises and permitted him to take away tapes so that they could be checked to see if they were in breach of the plaintiffs' copyright. Some were and some were not. The latter were returned to R. They had further meetings and R supplied the officer with information about video pirates.

The first 17 plaintiffs, having made a test purchase, became aware that a number of pirate tapes were being supplied from the Mill Street premises and they applied *ex parte* for an Anton Piller order and a Mareva injunction. Their solicitors' affidavit in support of the application did not refer to R's meetings with the investigation officer and did not indicate that there was a legitimate side to the defendants' business. The orders were granted and the Anton Piller order was executed in June 1982 at both the business premises and R's home. Documents and cassettes were taken that were not included in the order but R had agreed to their being removed. The solicitors retained the items seized, including items that formed no part of the claim in the action for, *inter alia*, breach of copyright brought by the 17 plaintiffs who had applied for the Anton Piller order and the other plaintiffs. A number of seized items were lost while in the custody of the plaintiffs' solicitors. The defendants, as the plaintiffs had hoped would result from the obtaining of the Anton Piller order and the Mareva injunction, ceased trading.

On the defendants' motion for, *inter alia*, the Anton Piller order to be set aside and for damages, Scott J held that:

(1) The purpose of an Anton Piller order was to preserve evidence that a defendant, warned of impending litigation, would be likely to conceal or destroy so that it would not be available as evidence supporting a plaintiff's cause of action; that it was an order obtained in secrecy requiring the defendant to permit his business premises and often him home as well to be entered and searched and, since it was frequently accompanied by a Mareva injunction, it could have the effect that the defendants' business would be destroyed without the defendant being in a position to apply to the court for the order to be set aside before it was executed; therefore, applicants for an order of such severity were under a strict duty to make to the court a full and frank disclosure of all

matters that could be relevant and, having obtained the order, neither to act oppressively nor abuse their power in executing the order.

(2) The plaintiffs' solicitors in their affidavit in support of the application had in a number of respects seriously failed in their duty to make a full and frank disclosure of all relevant matters of which they knew or ought to have known so that the impression was given that the defendants' business was secret and clandestine and so that the evidence was misleading in important respects.

(3) The plaintiffs and their solicitors had acted oppressively and in abuse of their powers in the execution of the order in that they had seized items not covered by the order and, in so doing, they were not protected by obtaining R's signature to a consent to remove those items; that, in addition, they had abused their position by retaining items not covered by the order and, in losing some of the seized items, they were in breach of their undertaking.

(4) The plaintiffs and their solicitors had also acted improperly in applying for and obtaining an Anton Piller order to achieve the closure of the defendants' business; but that it was for the court to keep the balance between the parties when considering making the order and the plaintiffs owed no duty to ensure that they did not obtain the order in unnecessarily wide and onerous terms.

(5) Although the plaintiffs' breach of duty in obtaining the Anton Piller order was a sufficient ground for the court to set aside the order, no purpose was served by doing so; but that the plaintiffs, including those plaintiffs joined as parties to the action after the obtaining and execution of the Anton Piller order, were liable in damages to the defendants; and that, in the circumstances, those damages would be assessed at £10,000 to include both compensatory damages for the defendants' loss of their legitimate business resulting from the obtaining and execution of the order and aggravated damages.

Scott J also pointed out:

(1) An Anton Piller order should be so drawn as to extend no further than the minimum extent necessary to achieve the preservation of documents or articles which might otherwise be destroyed. An order cannot be justified that allows the plaintiffs' solicitors to take and retain all relevant documentary material and correspondece. Once the plaintiffs' solicitors have satisfied themselves what material exists and have had an opportunity to take copies thereof, the material ought to be returned to its owner. It is essential that a detailed record of material taken should always be required to be made by the solicitors who execute the order before the material is removed and no material should be taken unless it is clearly covered by the order.

(2) It is inappropriate that seized material, the ownership of which is in dispute, should be retained by a plaintiff's solicitor pending trial. If the administration of justice requires that material taken under an Anton Piller order from defendants should, pending trial, be kept from them, then those responsible for the administration of justice might reasonably be expected to provide a neutral officer of the court charged with the custody of the material. In lieu of any such officer, the plaintiffs' solicitors ought to be required to deliver up the material to the defendants' solicitors on their undertaking for its safe custody.

In *Intercontex v Schmidt* [1988] FSR 575 Peter Gibson J refused to continue Anton Piller and Mareva orders in a passing off case because, *inter alia*,
- (a) the plaintiffs had failed to honour the undertaking given at the *ex parte* hearing forthwith to issue a notice of motion;
- (b) the plaintiffs had misrepresented that they were the proprietors of registered trade marks;
- (c) the plaintiffs were in breach of their statutory obligation to file accounts; and
- (d) the plaintiffs had failed to satisfy the court that their undertaking regarding damages would be fulfilled.

(7) The court will also require the plaintiff to give certain undertakings. The nature of these undertakings has been recently reviewed in *Booker McConnell plc v Plascow* [1985] RPC 425 at 442 per Dillon LJ.
- (a) An undertaking by the plaintiffs that the order will be served on the defendant by a solicitor and that the solicitor who serves the order would at the same time supply the defendants served with copies of all affidavits and other documents which are put before the judge on the *ex parte* application or, insofar as there were no such affidavits, with draft affidavits or at the least written statements setting out the substance of the matters of fact which were explained to the judge by counsel for the plaintiff on that application.
- (b) An undertaking by the plaintiffs that the solicitor who serves the order would explain its terms to the defendant served and will advise him to seek immediate advice. (A negligent failure to explain the order accurately can amount to a contempt of court: see *VDU Installations Ltd v Integrated Computer Systems and Cybernetics Ltd* [1989] FSR 378 per Knox J.)
- (c) Express liberty to each defendant to apply to the court on short notice to vary or discharge the order.
- (d) An undertaking in damages (see further *Fletcher Sutcliffe Wild Ltd v Burch* [1982] FSR 64).
- (e) An undertaking by the plaintiffs to issue a writ in substantially similar form to the draft writ if the *ex parte* application for the Anton Piller order is made before there has been time to issue the writ.

In addition, it is common for the plaintiffs to undertake:

- (f) That any articles or documents seized under the order shall be retained by the plaintiff's solicitor in safe custody;
- (g) Not to use any documents or information obtained as a result of execution of the order save for the purpose of civil proceedings in connection with the subject matter of the case without the leave of the court;
- (h) Within 48 hours to file affidavits (ie, the evidence on which the plaintiff relies as a basis for the award of the order).

(8) To what use can the plaintiff put the information he obtains pursuant to an Anton Piller order? If the information is obtained for the purposes of pursuing third parties, which may frequently happen in business secrets cases,

there seems no implied undertaking that the information will be used solely for the purpose of the existing action. See *Sony Corporation v Anand (RS)* [1981] FSR 398. If there is such a restriction, then it will be necessary to apply to the court to make such use. *Roberts v Jump Knitwear Ltd* [1981] FSR 527 illustrates problems which may arise in a copyright action against customers of an infringer. However, the general rule, recently affirmed in *General Nutrition Ltd v Pattni* [1984] FSR 403 is that documents can only be used in proceedings in which the order has been made. Warner J, on an application by the plaintiffs for leave to hand over documents seized and information gathered pursuant to an Anton Piller order, said that the mere fact that such documents might show that a criminal offence had been committed did not, in itself, justify a departure from the general rule. See also *Commissioners of Customs & Excise v Hamlin (AE)* [1984] 1 WLR 509. In *Piver v S & J Perfume Co Ltd* [1987] FSR 159, whilst executing an Anton Piller order on behalf of one client (P), a private investigator (L) came to the conclusion that the defendants were counterfeiting the goods of another client (R). He removed an empty box and later obtained a similar box through legitimate means. The court granted a second Anton Piller order, L having explained to the court how he had obtained the first box. The defendants sought an *ex parte* injunction to restrain the plaintiffs from dealing with any goods not related to the first Anton Piller order. Walton J refused the relief sought on the basis that it is irrelevant how evidence is obtained if it is not of a confidential nature and can be freely passed on. Provided there has been full disclosure to the court as to how the evidence was obtained, the court has a discretion whether to admit it. Rather confusingly Walton J went on to say that if L had actually seized a bottle of counterfeit scent (the subject matter of the action) then the court would never give leave for that to be used in another action. That statement by the judge must be wrong: it conflicts with the principle set out above and with common sense.

(9) What use can a plaintiff make of documents which have been obtained on the execution of an Anton Piller order which is subsequently discharged? *ITC Film Distributors Ltd v Video Exchange Ltd* [1982] 1 Ch 431 is authority for the proposition that the judge has a discretion to exclude evidence obtained as a result of such an order. Such a discretion was exercised in *Guess? Inc v Lee Seck Moa* [1987] FSR 159. The plaintiffs had obtained an Anton Piller order in an action for, *inter alia*, infringement of copyright. At the *inter partes* hearing of the summons the defendants applied to discharge this order. The judge found that there had been substantial and serious non-disclosure of relevant facts by the plaintiffs and that the evidence did not support the inference that there existed a real possibility that documents or things would be destroyed, and so he discharged the order. After an adjournment the plaintiffs applied for a fresh Anton Piller order and an interlocutory injunction. The judge rejected the application for the Anton Piller but granted the injunction. In doing so he took the 'yield' from the Anton Piller into account on the ground that it would be pedantic to exclude evidence which had been extensively referred to during the hearing.

On appeal the seventh defendant contended that the judge, having discharged the Anton Piller order, should not have taken the 'yield' into consideration when deciding whether to grant the injunction. The Court of

Appeal in Hong Kong held that even though the non-disclosure had been innocent, the court should not lightly allow a party to keep the benefit of it. Where the disclosure was serious and substantial, as here, the court should only allow use of the 'yield' for good and compelling reasons. The reasons relied upon by the judge fell far short of that standard, and so the 'yield' ought not to have been taken into consideration. In the absence of the 'yield' the evidence did not establish that there was a serious question to be tried.

(10) To what extent can a defendant refuse to comply with the mandatory parts of an Anton Piller order, ie the real essence of the order, and contend that he is not in contempt of court? There is no doubt that it is very dangerous for a defendant to refuse compliance with an Anton Piller order. If he does so and fails to obtain discharge of the order then he will clearly be in contempt of court and liable to a fine, sequestration and even imprisonment. Moreover, if the defendant uses the breathing space given by his application in order to breach the order, eg by destroying records, then the consequences for him will be very grave indeed. See *WEA Records Ltd v Visions Channel 4 Ltd* [1983] 1 WLR 721. The decision to refuse to comply with the terms of an Anton Piller order should only be taken in the clearest of circumstances where (i) the defendant has very strong grounds for saying either there were insufficient grounds to justify the grant of the order in the first place or (ii) that the attempted execution of the order was improper or (iii) that there was a material non-disclosure by the plaintiffs when applying for the order. However, even if the defendant successfully challenges the Anton Piller order can he still maintain that he is not in contempt of court? The answer is uncertain although it appears to be accepted that he will be in contempt unless the order was void *ab initio*. In all other circumstances the fact that he obtains a discharge goes to mitigation of penalty but does not provide a defence. This is certainly the orthodox view and the recent authority for it is the judgment of Goulding J in *Wardle Fabrics Ltd v Mysistis (G) Ltd* [1984] FSR 263. It was argued in that case by the defendant that a discharge of an order is a complete answer to any allegation of contempt of court for disobeying it. This was rejected by Goulding J who said unless the order is void *ab initio* it must be obeyed. However, he took into account the fact that the order was subsequently discharged and penalised the defendants by awarding the plaintiffs their costs of the contempt application on an indemnity basis. However, there are indications in other cases that the orthodox view is not necessarily held by everyone. In *Hallmark Cards Inc v Image Arts Ltd* [1977] FSR 150 Buckley LJ said that if an Anton Piller order was subsequently discharged then it could be argued that there had been no contempt at all by the defendant in refusing to comply with the order or alternatively that the contempt was merely a technical one which would not leave the defendant open to any penalties. Moreover, subsequently in the *WEA Records* case Sir John Donaldson MR said in a case in which there was an express undertaking given by the plaintiffs that the defendants be at liberty to move to vary or discharge the order upon giving 24 hours' notice of their intention to do so,

> They could, if they had wished, have refused immediate compliance and instead have made an urgent application to have the order discharged . . . . However, I must emphasise . . . that defendants who take this line do so

very much at their peril. If they succeed in getting the order discharged, all well and good. But if they fail, they will render themselves liable to penalties for contempt of court.

It is submitted that it is implicit in that passage that the Master of the Rolls thought that it was possible for the defendant to refuse compliance and yet not be in contempt of court if he succeeded in getting the order discharged. Moreover, see *Fields v Watts* (1985) 129 SJ 67 as quoted by Kerr LJ in the *Booker McConnell* case. The full transcript of the *Fields* case included a passage from the judgment of O'Connor LJ with which the other members of the court specifically agreed: 'If an order has been obtained on a wrong basis, I am satisfied that the proper order for this court to make . . . is to discharge the order'.

As the orthodox view stands, a defendant who refuses to comply with the mandatory parts of an Anton Piller order can only be exonerated if he can show that the order was a nullity. What amounts to a nullity is not mentioned in any of the cases. It seems however that if the basis on which the order is made is dishonest or fraudulent then that will be sufficient. However, should it be necessary for the defendant to go that far? In our submission, the judgment of Buckley LJ in the *Hallmark Cards* case is to be preferred to that of Goulding LJ in *Wardle Fabrics*. The reason for this is that the court should surely take a practical and strict approach to what is primarily an *ex parte* mandatory injunction. In these special circumstances it must be open to a defendant to choose to ignore the order at his peril but at the same time not be penalised if the order is subsequently discharged. By complying with the order he gives the plaintiff that which, as it subsequently turns out if the discharge is given, he should never have got. That should be sufficient to provide a defendant with the defence for a motion for contempt especially as that motion is brought by a party to the action, ie the plaintiff. As there is no public authority involved in prosecuting the motion or application for contempt then the whole matter should be viewed as a private one between the parties in which the court has assisted the plaintiff when it should not have done so. There is some support for this view in *Bhimji v Chatwani* [1991] 1 All ER 705. In that case an Anton Piller order was served at 8am on the defendants. By about 11am they were in contact with their solicitors and had received advice from them. Later in the morning instructions were sent to counsel on their behalf and that afternoon an application to set aside or vary the order was made to the judge who had granted it. He heard the application about 5pm and declined to set aside the order but made some variations to it. As soon as the hearing was concluded the defendants gave permission to the plaintiffs to enter their premises and the amended order was executed. The plaintiffs sought an order for the committal of the defendants for not obeying the original order. It was quite clear that the defendants had been advised by their solicitors that they should comply with the original order *or* apply immediately to have it discharged. However there were negotiations between the solicitors on both sides in order to obviate the need for an application to the court for a variation of the order so as to allow a search of the premises immediately to proceed. It was suggested by the defendants' solicitors that solicitors for both sides carry out a joint search of the premises and that the documents required by the plaintiffs' solicitors should be safeguarded by the defendants' solicitors for a short period to enable the defendants to make an application to the judge to have the order discharged or varied. That compromise was rejected by the plaintiffs' solicitors. Scott J concluded:

(1) The order on its true construction required entry at the latest after the defendants had received advice from their solicitors. Thereafter until they complied with the amended order the defendants were in breach of the order truly construed.

(2) The exact moment at which entry was to be allowed under the order was not clear from its terms, judging the matter by the standards of the ordinary layman.

(3) The defendants' failure to allow entry over the period 11am to 6pm was deliberate and, accordingly, the requisite *mens rea* for contempt of court was present.

(4) But in the circumstances the breach was not contumacious in the ordinary meaning of the word since:

    (a) it was accompanied by advice from solicitors that suggested that it was permissible for entry to be postponed until after the application to the court;

    (b) a reasonable offer to provide protection of the documents was made at an early stage, was not withdrawn, but was not accepted by the plaintiffs;

    (c) there was no evidence to suggest that the making of the application was merely a device to postpone the search;

    (d) there was no evidence of any impropriety in respect of the documents in any of the premises to be searched that took place over the period of the delay; and

    (e) where delay in allowing execution of an Anton Piller order is under review, the court should take into account the nature of the order and the *prima facie* injustice that has already been done to the defendant in being subjected to an inherently oppressive order of the court made after a hearing at which he was not able to be heard and sought to be enforced before he has had an opportunity to have it set aside or vaired.

The judge concluded that when a committal application is made something more than a mere technical breach of the obligation to allow entry forthwith was required.

(11) Once an order has been made it is unlikely that the court will suspend it on an *ex parte* application by the defendant which is made purely by way of counsel's address. Any such application should be supported by affidavit evidence. See *Hallmark Cards Inc v Image Arts Ltd* [1977] FSR 150. A party dissatisfied with an order made *ex parte* should apply to have it set aside under the terms of RSC Ord 32, r 6. However, there is no doubt that there is authority for the court to grant the retrospective discharge of a fully executed Anton Piller order. See the *WEA Records* case and the *Fields* case. This area has recently been reviewed by the Court of Appeal in *Booker McConnell plc v Plascow*

[1985] RPC 425. In that case, the first defendant had been poached by the second and third defendants just before a takeover bid by the second and third defendants of the plaintiffs was to be considered by the Monopolies and Mergers Commission. The first defendant had taken business secrets with him to the other defendants. An Anton Piller order was made and executed against all three defendants. The next day, the defendants sought to discharge the Anton Piller order and did not wait for the return date. The court said that if the order has been fully executed then the application to discharge is not usually one of overwhelming urgency and therefore any application should be made on the return date in the Chancery Division or a few days after the date of the order in the Queen's Bench Division. The court went on to say that there were a few occasions when an urgent application by a defendant could properly be made. In the instant case, it found that there were grounds for such an urgent application but in our submission failed to take into account that in a large number of cases it is a matter of overwhelming urgency for the defendant to make such an application. In circumstances where the plaintiff has been able in execution of the order to seize documents which also contain the defendant's business secrets, then in our view an urgent application on affidavit should always be permissible.

(12) A plaintiff who is dissatisfied with answers provided or disclosure made by a defendant on whom an *ex parte* order requiring such answers/disclosure, can take three courses of action: he can apply to cross-examine the defendant at the interlocutory stage as to his compliance with the court's order; apply for further specific disclosure; or he can apply for his committal for breach of the order. The power to order cross-examination is found in RSC Ord 39 r 1 and was recently considered in an Anton Piller order application: *CBS United Kingdom Ltd v Perry* [1985] FSR 421. There Falconer J laid down guidelines as to when cross-examination is appropriate:

(a) The object of the application must be to obtain further information which it is believed is in the possession of a person subject to an Anton Piller order but which was not discovered when he purported to comply with the order.
(b) The existence of that further information must be proved by the plaintiffs.
(c) The object of the application must not be to enable contempt proceedings to be brought so as to punish the person served with the order.
(d) The object must not be to obtain information which is to be used for the purposes of the trial of the action.

See also *House of Spring Gardens Ltd v Waite* [1985] FSR 173.

In *Bayer AG v Winter (No 2)* [1986] 1 WLR 540 Scott J distinguished *House of Spring Gardens*. The plaintiffs had obtained an Anton Piller order directing the defendants, *inter alia*, to disclose the whereabouts of all relevant correspondence and documents and also the full value of their assets within and without the jurisdiction. The defendants were also ordered to verify that information by affidavit within 14 days. The plaintiffs were disatisfied with the disclosure they obtained and they sought an order for cross-examination of the first defendants and that his liberty to depart the country be restricted until after such cross-examination had taken place. Scott J refused the applications. He did so despite assuming that a strong *prima facie* case had been made out to show that the first defendant was engaged in selling counterfeits of Baygon, the plaintiffs' product. He said:

> I do not think an order for the cross-examination of the first defendant would be a proper use of the power of the court. I do not consider the cross-examination of the first defendant would be a proper use of the power of the court. I do not consider the cross-examination of him in advance of any statement of claim, in advance of any proper opportunity for him to deal with the plaintiff's evidence put before the court on the *ex parte* application and, obviously, in advance of trial is appropriate. If it be the plaintiffs' view that he had made inadequate disclosure in compliance with the court order, then there are other courses that the plaintiffs can take. They can apply for his committal. They can apply for an order that further specific disclosure be made. Applications of that character would produce a liaison between the parties on which both could adduce evidence and on which the court would adjudicate. In the *House of Spring Gardens* case the defendant had consented to the order for his cross-examination. So the court did not have to decide whether, as a matter of discretion, the order was one which it would be right to make. For my part I find it very difficult to envisage any circumstances in which, as a matter of discretion, it would be right to make such an order as is sought in the present case and as was made by consent in the *House of Spring Gardens* case. The proper function of a judge in civil litigation is to decide issues between parties. It is not, in my opinion, to preside over an interrogation.
>
> The police, charged with the upholding of the public law, cannot subject a citizen to cross-examination before a judge in order to discover the truth about the citizen's misdeeds. How then, as a matter of discretion, can it be right in a civil case, in aid of rights which, however important, are merely private rights, to subject a citizen to such a cross-examination? *A fortiori* it cannot be right to do so in a case where the plaintiff seeking the cross-examination of the defendant is holding itself free to use the defendant's answers for the purpose of an application to commit him to prison for contempt.

It is now true to say that generally judges and masters are extremely reluctant to grant orders for cross-examination; it is difficult envisaging one being made. The plaintiff will therefore have to decide whether to pursue one of the other two options: an order for further specific disclosure or committal. The former is perhaps easier to achieve although formulating the grounds for the further disclosure is usually a very difficult exercise.

1.3 The foreign defendant and Anton Piller orders

In *Cook Industries Incorporated v Galliher* [1979] Ch 439 it was held that an English court had jurisdiction to order a foreign defendant to disclose the contents of a flat which was in his name, even though it was in Paris, and to permit the flat to be inspected by a French advocate who was also an English lawyer and an inventory made of its contents and that they be photographed. That case was however distinguished by Scott J in *Altertext Incorporated v Advanced Data Communications Ltd* [1985] 1 All ER 395 in which the plaintiff sued six defendants for breach of copyright, passing off, breach of confidence, procuring a breach of contract and misuse of confidential information. The first five defendants were all resident in the United Kingdom and Anton Piller orders were granted against them. However, the real difficulty concerned the sixth defendant which was a Belgian company with no place of business in the United Kingdom. The second and third defendants were directors of the sixth defendant and the first, second and third defendants were its principal shareholders. Although it is normal not to serve the writ until the Anton Piller order is served at the time of execution the question for the court was whether that could be done regarding a foreign defendant. Although the judge gave leave under RSC Ord 11 to serve the writ out of the jurisdiction he was concerned about granting an Anton Piller order intended to be executed against the sixth defendant's premises in Belgium before any service of process which founded jurisdiction had been effected on that defendant. Unless the defendant submits to the jurisdiction or can be served in person (as happened in *Cook Industries*) then until service under Ord 11 is effective the defendant is not subject to the jurisdiction of the court and if not so subject then it was arguable that no Anton Piller order should be made. Moreover, once service under Ord 11 is effected the defendant is always given the chance to challenge the jurisdiction of the court without actually submitting to it. If the Anton Piller order is executed before the application to set aside the writ under Ord 11, then damage will have been done to him even if the defendant eventually succeeds on the jurisdiction point. The judge decided that where an Anton Piller order against a foreign defendant has to be accompanied by leave under Ord 11 for service abroad then the Anton Piller order ought not to be executed until the foreign defendant has been given the opportunity to apply to set aside the Ord 11 leave. The judge did offer to grant an Anton Piller order against the sixth defendant but with the proviso that execution be suspended for a short period in order to enable that defendant to apply under Ord 11 to have the writ set aside. However this offer was declined by the plaintiff on the reasonable grounds that the element of surprise which is so crucial to the effectiveness of an Anton Piller order would be entirely lost. Scott J further decided that he would not issue an Anton Piller order regarding the sixth defendant's premises against the second and third defendants because he declined to do indirectly what he had already declined to do directly. It seems the only way out for the plaintiff would have been to issue concurrent proceedings in Belgium as well as in the United Kingdom and apply there for the equivalent of an Anton Piller order. By the end of his judgment Scott J had decided that his earlier pronouncement that he had no jurisdiction in this type of case was wrong. Instead he came to the conclusion that although he did have jurisdiction once leave was given under Ord 11 he declined to use it in this case. In our view, the judge was right to say that he did have a discretion. However, it is difficult to see why he did not rule in the plaintiff's favour. The plaintiff would in any event have been required to give an undertaking as to damages and if the defendant were successful in challenging the Ord 11 jurisdiction then the plaintiff's undertaking could have been called upon. See further *Protector Alarms Ltd v Maxim Alarms Ltd* [1978] FSR 442.

2 Miscellaneous orders

2.1 Detention, custody, preservation and inspection orders

In cases in which an Anton Piller application is inappropriate, where eg the defendant is a reputable company then Ord 29, rr 2 and 2A provide similar types of relief although applications based on these rules are usually made on notice.

RSC Ord 29, r 2 says:

(1) On the application of any party to a cause or matter the court may make an order for the detention, custody or preservation of any property which is the subject matter of the cause or matter, or as to which any question may arise therein, or for the inspection of any such property in the possession of a party to the cause or matter.

(2) For the purpose of enabling any order under para (1) to be carried out the court may by the order authorise any person to enter upon any land or building in the possession of any party to the cause or matter.

(3) Where the right of any party to a specific fund is in dispute in a cause or matter, the court may, on the application of the party to the cause or matter, order the fund to be paid into court or otherwise secured.

(4) An order under this rule may be made on such terms, if any, as the court thinks just.

(5) An application for an order under this rule must be made by summons or by notice under Ord 25, r 7.

(6) Unless the court otherwise directs, an application by a defendant for such an order may not be made before he acknowledges service of the writ or originating summons by which the cause or matter was begun.

The important points to note about the powers under Ord 29, r 2 are as follows:

(a) Any party can apply for such order, but if it is the defendant then compliance with Ord 29, r 2(6) must be demonstrated.

(b) It appears, following the words of Ord 29, r 2(5) that an order cannot be made on *ex parte* application. However in *EMI v Pandit* [1975] 1 WLR 302, Templeman J did not consider r 2(5) precluded an *ex parte* application.

(c) 'Property' includes money but not a manufacturing process. See *Tudor Accumulator Company Ltd v China Mutual Steam Navigation Company* [1930] WN 200 and note it must be property which is the subject matter of the action. That is why in *Yousif v Salama* [1980] 3 All ER 405, Ord 29, r 2 did not apply.

(d) The property in question must be in the possession of a party to the action or possibly he must have or claim to have property in the documents or articles, etc.

(e) There is a power to allow photographs to be taken under this provision.

(f) Inspection will, in certain cases, be permitted by an employee of the plaintiffs rather than by an independent expert: *Centri-Spray Corp v Cera International Ltd* [1979] FSR 175.

Note, in addition to the powers under Ord 29, r 2 the existence of Ord 24, r 10 which allows for inspection of any documents referred to in the pleadings or affidavits of any party.

2.2 Delivery up of goods under Order 29 Rule 2A

Order 29, r 2A provides:

(1) Without prejudice to r 2, the court may, on the application of any party to a cause or matter, make an order under s 4 of the Torts (Interference with Goods) Act 1977 for the delivery up of any goods which are the subject matter of the cause or matter or as to which any question may arise therein.

(2) Paragraphs (2) and (3) of r 1 shall have effect in relation to an application for such an order as they have effect in relation to an application for the grant of an injunction. (See Ord 29, r 1).

The scope of s 4 of the Torts (Interference with Goods) Act 1977 which is the enabling provision for Ord 29, r 2A is in fact wider than Ord 29, r 2A since the former extends to proceedings which have not yet been commenced as it states that it applies to 'any goods which . . . may become the subject matter of subsequent proceedings'. The most important limitation of Ord 29, r 2A is that it only applies to 'goods' which are the subject matter of proceedings for wrongful interference with goods. Section 1 of the Torts (Interference with Goods) Act 1977 defines 'wrongful interference with goods' as including conversion, trespass to goods, negligence insofar as it results in damage to goods or to an interest in goods and, most importantly, in the context of business secrets, any other tort apart from detinue so far as it results in damage to goods or to an interest in goods. In most business secrets cases a claim for breach of confidence will also inevitably involve an allegation of conversion. Moreover, a jurisdictional basis for a breach of confidence action is tort and it can sensibly be argued that the tort of breach of confidence results in damage to an interest in goods in some cases.

In *CBS (UK) Ltd v Lambert* [1983] Ch 37, a case in which the court made a combined Anton Piller and Mareva order, it was said that in addition to the basic requirements of Ord 29, r 2A the following guidelines should also be followed when making an interlocutory order for the delivery up of chattels:

(1) There must be clear evidence that the defendant is likely, unless restrained by order, to dispose of or otherwise deal with the goods in order to deprive the plaintiff of the fruits of any judgment.

(2) The court should be slow to order interim delivery up of the defendant's property unless there is some evidence or reasonable inference that the

property has been acquired by the defendant as a result of his alleged wrongdoing.

(3) No order should be made for delivery up of the defendant's clothing, bedding and furnishings, tools of his trade, or any materials or stock in trade which it is likely he uses in lawful business. However, it is clear that furnishings which were bought in order to frustrate creditors can be included within the order.

(4) All orders should specifically identify the goods or classes of goods which are to be delivered up and vagueness on the plaintiff's part will invariably militate against any order being made.

(5) The order should only authorise entry and seizure with the defendant's permission.

(6) The order should permit the delivery up only to the plaintiff's solicitor or to a court official.

(7) The court should follow the appropriate guidelines for the grant of an injunction laid down in *Z Ltd v AZ and AALL* [1982] QB 588, so far as applicable to goods in the possession, custody or control of third parties.

(8) Provision should always be made for liberty to apply to stay, vary or discharge the order.

Ultimately, the court has complete discretion which it appears is not limited to cases where there is a risk that the goods will be disposed of or lost or destroyed or otherwise be unaccounted for and therefore where goods are not readily available on the open market and damages would not compensate the plaintiff for the difficulty in continuing his business without them and the balance between the plaintiff's needs for the goods and the defendant's grounds for withholding them is strongly in favour of the plaintiff, the court will order the defendant to deliver up the goods to the plaintiff. See *Perry (Howard E) and Co Ltd v British Railways Board* [1980] 2 All ER 579.

Chapter 23

Practice and Procedure

1 The appropriate court

The first choice for the plaintiff lies between the county court and the High Court. The county court may only grant an injunction if it is ancillary to a substantive claim within the court's jurisdiction; in most restraint of trade and business secrets cases this will be a claim for damages (see *Hatt and Co (Bath) Ltd v Pearce* [1978] 1 WLR 885). However, the county court usually only has jurisdiction to grant up to £5,000 by way of damages in actions in tort or contract and therefore if damage claims are above or may be above this figure or if the relief sought does not involve a substantive claim the case should be started in the High Court. The final factor of importance is that applications for injunctions in the county court are made in open court unlike in the Queen's Bench Division of the High Court. In most cases, it is safe and appropriate to start proceedings in the High Court especially when a more 'exotic' form of interlocutory relief, for example an Anton Piller order or a Mareva injunction, is sought.

Assuming that the case is to be started in the High Court the only question is which division is appropriate. There are some cases over which the Chancery Division has exclusive jurisdiction: see Sched 1 to the Supreme Court Act 1981. These include 'copyright' cases. Many cases involving business secrets also involve questions of copyright; however it is not unusual though not common for copyright actions to be begun in the Queen's Bench Division. In most restraint of trade and business secrets cases the choice between the Chancery Division and the Queen's Bench Division will be determined by whether the plaintiff desires publicity of his claim or not. Hearings in the Chancery Division as in the county court are held in open court, hearings in the Queen's Bench Division take place in chambers. When publicity is positively not required then the Queen's Bench Division, which includes the Commercial Court, is the most appropriate forum. However, even in the Chancery Division it is possible for interlocutory hearings to be held in camera. Applications for Anton Piller orders are always heard in camera. The decision to conduct the hearing in camera is one of discretion for the judge. It is common for business secrets cases to be heard in camera if a public hearing would defeat the ends of justice (eg, if the particulars of a secret process have to be disclosed and discussed in detail). A further consideration may be that of court availability. In the general Queen's Bench list, summonses estimated to last more than 30 minutes require a special appointment; in the Chancery Division the motions judge will hear cases of up to two hours in length. The new procedure in QB cases is set out at [1989] 1 WLR 359.

2 Is an *ex parte* application necessary?

In some cases the answer to this question is very clearly in the affirmative: Anton Piller order and Mareva injunction applications must be made *ex parte* if they are to have practical value. In others, the answer is reached by considering whether there is such urgency or secrecy about the case that delay or disclosure would materially prejudice the plaintiff's position. The power to grant *ex parte* relief is found generally in RSC Ord 8, r 2(1):

> Except where an application by motion may properly be made *ex parte*, no motion shall be made without previous notice to the parties affected thereby, but the Court, if satisfied that the delay caused by proceeding in the ordinary way would or might entail irreparable or serious mischief may make an order *ex parte* on such terms as to costs or otherwise, and subject to such undertaking, if any, as it thinks just; and any party affected by such order may apply to the Court to set it aside.

In respect of injunctions the power is found in Ord 29, r 1(2):

> Where the applicant is the plaintiff and the case is one of urgency such application may be made *ex parte* on affidavit but, except as aforesaid, such application must be made by motion or summons.

Even though it may be necessary, for reasons of urgency, to proceed by way of an *ex parte* application, it may still be possible to avoid this by notifying the defendant or his solicitors that unless certain undertakings are given then such an application will immediately be made. In those cases which require an urgent *ex parte* application but in which surprise is not a relevant consideration, it may be tactically wise to notify the defendants of the time and place of the hearing so that they can attend. The hearing is then described as '*ex parte* on notice' and this procedure is especially relevant if the defendant is a reputable individual or company. In those cases which rely on the element of surprise such notification is inappropriate.

So far as the plaintiff is concerned he must be able, in the usual course of matters, to give an undertaking as to damages when he makes his application in case the defendant succeeds at trial or whenever the case is effectively concluded. Secondly, the plaintiff must show the utmost good faith when he makes his application. In practical terms this means he must put before the court in affidavit and exhibit form relevant facts known to him including ones which are not favourable to his case. If it can be shown that he has not done so then the *ex parte* order will be discharged.

3 *Ex parte* applications

In order to obtain *ex parte* relief the plaintiff must have:

    (a) a writ;
    (b) an affidavit;
    (c) draft order of the relief sought.

4 The writ

Where time permits the plaintiff should issue the writ before the *ex parte* hearing. However, in cases of extreme urgency this is not always possible and therefore a draft writ can be produced at the hearing. An undertaking will have to be given to issue it forthwith and failure to comply with this constitutes a contempt of court. See *Refson (PS) and Company Ltd v Saggers* [1984] 1 WLR 1025. It is usual though not essential to include in the writ a claim for an injunction.

If a writ is generally endorsed (ie, if it does not also contain the statement of claim) then the statement or points of claim must be served in accordance with terms RSC Ord 18, r 1 even if interlocutory relief is granted unless the defendant agrees to extend time for service. See *Hytrac Conveyors Ltd v Conveyors Intl Ltd* [1983] 1 WLR 44 in which failure to heed the normal rules resulted in the plaintiff's claim being struck out.

5 The affidavit

The affidavit produced by the plaintiff and the exhibits attached to it are vital as they constitute the only evidence at the *ex parte* hearing. RSC Ord 41 sets out the basic rules for the structure of affidavits and was supplemented by two practice directions in 1983. It is important to note that any defects can be cured with the court's leave, under the power contained in Ord 41, r 4. Normally, affidavits cannot contain statements of information or belief. However under Ord 41, r 5(2) such statements are specifically allowed in interlocutory proceedings only so long as the sources and grounds of the information or belief are also set out. This provision is especially useful in *ex parte* applications as it allows the plaintiff's solicitor to make the affidavit on information given to him by the plaintiff. It may not always be possible to swear the affidavit if the application is a matter of urgency or it is made outside working hours. In such cases, an undertaking will have to be given by counsel to have the affidavit sworn and filed after the application for interlocutory relief. If the writ has not yet been issued then the affidavit must be headed 'In the matter of an intended action'. The actual contents of the affidavit are very important because not only do they set out the facts upon which the judge will be asked to give the injunction or other interlocutory relief, but they are potentially dangerous if the case goes for trial. A deponent can be cross-examined on any discrepancies between his affidavit or any affidavit made on information provided by him and his oral evidence. There is also power under RSC Ord 39, r 1 for an order to be made that the deponent attend at the interlocutory stage for cross-examination. However, over-extensive use of this facility was severely criticised by the Court of Appeal in *Booker McConnell plc v Plascow* [1985] RPC 425. A major problem for a plaintiff in a business secrets case which involves a secret process or something similar is just how far he should go in his affidavit in revealing the substance of the information which is only partly known by the defendant. In *Under Water Welders and Repairers Ltd v Street and Longthorne* [1968] RPC 498 the plaintiff sought interlocutory injunctions against the defendants restraining them from using confidential information. The defendants claimed in their evidence that there was nothing confidential in the process, whereas the plaintiffs, although denying this, did not specify its confidential characteristics. Buckley J held, *inter alia*, that although the plaintiffs' evidence did not condescend to any details as to the secrecy of the process, it was clear that they regarded it as such, whereas the defendant's evidence did not sufficiently negative the possibility of confidentiality in order to refute the plaintiffs' *prima facie* claim for relief. He said that it is not to be expected that a plaintiff seeking to protect a secret would disclose it to the court particularly in interlocutory proceedings. This case may seem more liberal than in fact it was. There appears to have been other evidence before the court from which it could reasonably infer that the process was secret. (See also *Amber Size and Chemical Co Ltd v Menzel* [1913] 2 Ch 239.) However the plaintiff was not so fortunate in the case of *Zink (John) Co Ltd v Lloyds Bank Ltd* [1975] RPC 385 where a statement of claim was struck out under the provisions of RSC Ord 18, r 19 for not condescending to particulars. The court was convinced that the plaintiff's refusal to provide particulars was an indication that no confidentiality attached to the relevant information. See also *Diamond Stylus Co Ltd v Bauden Precision Diamonds Ltd* [1973] RPC 675. No details of a process were given by the plaintiff in his application for an interlocutory injunction. Graham J refused the application and said:

> ... each case must be judged in the light of its own particular facts and the governing principle in every case is that a plaintiff must make out a *prima facie* case.... It may be in some cases that a plaintiff is able to do that without disclosing much in the way of detail about his particular pro-cess. . . . On the other hand . . . depending on the surrounding circumstances and the state of knowledge generally in the art, he may have to go further and disclose at any rate the essential features of the process which he says have been taken.

It is submitted that this approach which pre-dates *American Cyanamid Co v Ethicon Ltd* [1975] AC 396 is just as valid now even if *American Cyanamid* does apply to business secrets cases. After all the plaintiff still has to show an arguable case and the balancing of convenience is very difficult if the details of a business secret are not to some extent revealed. Once the allegedly secret information is revealed to the other side there are ample powers to prevent its use or disclosure other than for the purposes of litigation. Firstly, there is the general implied duty not to use documents produced on discovery for a collateral or ulterior purpose (*Riddick v Thames Board Mills* [1977] 3 All ER

677). Secondly, the defendant may be required by the court to give an undertaking that only a certain number of people (usually himself, his lawyer and experts) be allowed access to the information disclosed by the plaintiff (*Warner-Lambert Co v Glaxo Laboratories* [1975] RPC 354).

The affidavit in a business secrets case is of crucial importance for it must distinguish what are truly the business secrets of the plaintiff. In *Lock International plc v Beswick* [1989] 1 WLR 1268 Hoffman J commented:

> In cases in which the plaintiff alleges misuse of trade secrets or confidential information concerning a manufacturing process, a lack of particularity about the precise nature of the trade secrets is usually a symptom of an attempt to prevent the employee from making legitimate use of the knowledge and skills gained in the plaintiff's service.

In *Lawrence David Ltd v Ashton* [1989] IRLR 22 Whitford J at first instance is reported to have refused an injunction in respect of a breach of confidence claim because the affidavits failed to identify 'with any real particularity any particular secret'. This part of his judgment was upheld in the Court of Appeal [1991] 1 All ER 385. Balcombe LJ said that it is a cardinal rule that any injunction must be capable of being framed with sufficient precision so as to enable a person injuncted to know what it is he is prevented from doing. The inability of the plaintiffs to define with any degree of precision what they sought to call confidential information or trade secrets militated against an injunction of this nature being granted.

6 General points

(1) Injunctions are not available as of right; whether they are granted is a matter of discretion.

(2) Parties: usually the plaintiff applies for an interlocutory injunction; the defendant is not able to do so unless:

    (a) he has filed a counterclaim; or
    (b) relief sought by him arises out of relief sought by the plaintiff; or
    (c) he has issued a writ in a cross action.

Frequently the plaintiff will claim not only against his former employee etc, but also against the new employer or another third party if there is any evidence that the latter knowingly induced the first defendant to breach his contract. In some cases, of which *Hivac*, is an example, the plaintiff chose to sue only the new employer.

(3) Security: in some cases the plaintiff may actually be required to lodge security with the court or pay money into court before being given interlocutory relief. This may happen if the plaintiff is outside the jurisdiction or if there are serious doubts as to his solvency. See *Harman Pictures NV v Osborne* [1967] 1 WLR 723.

(4) The period covered by an injunction: it is normal for the order which embodies an interlocutory injunction to last until the determination of these proceedings or further order in the Queen's Bench Division and until the return

date in the Chancery Division when it may be renewed following the *inter partes* hearing. (There is also liberty to apply to have the order discharged or varied.) The case of *Fisher Karpark Industries Ltd v Nichols* [1982] FSR 351 was an example of such a renewed injunction and concerned the 'springboard doctrine' in business secrets law. A period of five months intervened between the *ex parte* injunction being granted and the *inter partes* hearing and the defendant argued on the latter occasion that that was a sufficient period to negate any headstart that might have been improperly obtained. The judge continued the injunction but only for another six months in order to cancel any such advantage. See also *Bullivant (Roger) Ltd v Ellis* [1987] ICR 464 in which the Court of Appeal decided that in the case of the former injunctive protection should only last for a limited period. In this case as there was a year-long restraint of trade clause that period was accepted as being appropriate for the protection of the confidential information.

7 Order for a speedy trial

It is not uncommon for an application to be made during interlocutory proceedings for an order for a speedy trial in restraint of trade and business secrets cases. The power to make such an order is found in RSC Ord 29, r 5. An early trial was ordered in *Littlewoods Organisation Ltd v Harris* [1978] 1 All ER 1026 because of the urgency involved and in *Commercial Plastics Ltd v Vincent* [1965] 1 QB 623 an order was made for a speedy trial and that the affidavits sworn for the purposes of the interlocutory hearing should stand as the pleadings.

Part VIII

Final Remedies

Chapter 24

Damages

1 Introduction

The most common remedies sought at the conclusion of a trial by a successful plaintiff in restraint of trade and business secrets cases are an award of damages and a permanent injunction. In some cases a declaration is vital. Of secondary importance are an account of profits and an order for delivery up or destruction.

An award of damages is intended to compensate the plaintiff for loss and to attempt to put him in the position in which he would have been had the contract or duty not been breached. This approach is to be compared with that underlying an account of profits where it is the defendant's gain rather than the plaintiffs' loss which is relevant.

In both restraint of trade and business secrets cases damages can only provide a very approximate remedy as it is usually impossible to determine precisely what the plaintiff has lost and therefore what his compensation should be. However the court will not be deterred by this obstacle and will do its best to achieve justice between the parties (*Sanders v Parry* [1967] 1 WLR 53).

2 Damages for breach of a covenant in reasonable restraint of trade

If one takes the example of a former employee who has solicited a customer of his previous employer the court will assess the plaintiff's damages in the usual way for breach of contract. The plaintiff must show that the breach caused loss to him and that the particular type of loss was within the contemplation of the parties at the time of entry into the contract. Foreseeability is rarely a problem and even causation may be simple to prove. It is not open to the defendant to claim that the acts of a third party, such as a new employer who procures his breach of contract, have broken the chain of causation. The plaintiff is however, in these circumstances, wise to sue both his former employee and the new employer for it may only be the latter who can afford to pay any damages or even costs. The most common causation problem from the plaintiff's point of view is that clients who were actually solicited may well emerge at the trial as witnesses for the defence to say that they were open to solicitation by the defendant and that they were going to take their business away from the plaintiff in any event. In this case the plaintiff will have suffered nominal damage only and although he would usually be awarded costs the basis for such an award will frequently leave him paying a considerable amount of his own costs himself. Moreover, if the defendant unsuccessfully attempted to solicit a client of the plaintiffs although he will be in breach of contract the plaintiff will have suffered no loss and therefore once again will only be awarded nominal damages.

Therefore it is only in those cases where the defendant has successfully solicited the plaintiff's customers who, but for the approach by the defendant, were not intending to take their business elsewhere, that the plaintiff will be awarded more than nominal damages. The plaintiff will still have to persuade the court of the extent of his loss: typically he can provide evidence which shows the net worth of that client's custom. See, for example, *Sanders v Parry* [1967] 1 WLR 753. There, the defendant who was found to be in breach of the implied duty of fidelity to his employer, a solicitor, was ordered to pay damages to the plaintiff when he entered an agreement with an important client, T, of the plaintiff. Havers J awarded damages on the basis of a lost chance to do work for T and he accepted evidence of the net worth of that business over a period of 12 months. The reason he chose such a short time was because T had intended to change his solicitor anyway. See also *Robb v Green* [1895] 2 QB 1 per Hawkins J. These cases demonstrate how inadequate damages are as a remedy in most restraint of trade cases.

The relevant date for assessment of damages is usually the time of breach. However, this is not an invariable rule: if to choose that date would give rise to injustice then another time may be chosen (*Johnson v Agnew* [1979] 1 All ER 883).

3 Damages for breach of the duty of confidence

In nearly all cases the cause of action lies in contract. In some cases, however, there may be no contractual relationship between the parties (see eg *Saltman Engineering Co Ltd v Campbell Engineering Co Ltd* (1948) 65 RPC 203) or the court may choose to ignore the existence of the contract in which case the cause of action lies in the equitable doctrine of confidence. This is also especially useful when proceedings are against third parties who have induced the primary defendant to breach his contract. However, in the case of the equitable jurisdiction but for specific statutory provision it could be argued that the common law remedy of damages is usually inappropriate. However s 50 of the Supreme Court Act 1981 provides:

> Where the Court of Appeal or the High Court has jurisdiction to entertain an application for an injunction or specific performance, it may award damages in addition to, or in substitution for, an injunction or specific performance.

This section substantially re-enacts s 2 of the Chancery Amendment Act 1858 (Lord Cairns' Act). The jurisdiction contemplated in s 50 exists in all business secrets cases as there will always be the ability 'to entertain' such an application. It is submitted that these words mean that if injunctive relief is an option open to the plaintiff then the alternative remedy in damages may be available as well. Although *Saltman's* case and *Seager v Copydex* (No 2) [1969] 2 All ER 718 were decided prior to the enactment of s 50, they appear to support such a view.

Further, it should be noted that s 50 allows an award of damages in addition to an injunction not simply in substitution. In *Cranleigh Precision Engineering Ltd v Bryant* [1966] RPC 81 the court awarded both an injunction and damages.

In theory, there is an advantage to the plaintiff in an award of damages for breach of an equitable rather than a contractual duty. This arises from the fact that the contractual damages can only encompass past loss whereas equitable damages can take into account both past and future loss. In practice, however, the difficulty of successfully enquiring into future loss is very great and will rarely be fruitful.

Finally, the possibility of a claim for exemplary damages should not be forgotten in business secrets cases.

3.1 Quantum in business secrets cases

Typically in business secrets cases the secrets possess commercial value. The primary defendant may either have used the secret or allowed another to use it or he may have disclosed it to another or simply disclosed it by his use. Pure disclosure without use makes damages very difficult to quantify. If the defendant has disclosed secrets to another, the plaintiff should however recover more than nominal damages and even if an injunction is granted against any further use it may be difficult for, say, a trade competitor, to expunge from his memory a particular formula or client list which has been passed on to him. There may arise 'subconscious use' similar to the notion of 'subconscious copying' recognised in the law of copyright. See *Seager v Copydex* [1967] RPC 349. The plaintiff should be compensated for the real possibility of use by others as a result of unlawful disclosure to them. The plaintiff is only properly compensated however if he is awarded equitable rather than contractual damages as only then will the award take into account any future loss.

Where use is overt, then substantial damages will be awarded in line with the plaintiff's loss. Unlike restraint of trade cases, the Court of Appeal has laid down special rules for assessing quantum for use of business secrets. In *Seager v Copydex (No 2)* [1969] RPC 250 Lord Denning MR said that damages in a business secrets case were to be assessed on the basis of the value of the information which the defendant company took but then said that the value of the information depended on its nature. The nature or quality of information fell into three categories each with its own quantum, viz:

(1) If there was nothing very special about the information, ie if it involved no particular inventive step but was the sort of information which could be obtained by employing a competent consultant then the value was to be equivalent to the consultant's fee. The reason for this is that '. . . the defendant company, by taking the information, would only have saved themselves the time and trouble of employing a consultant'.

(2) However, if the information was 'something special', ie if it involved an inventive step or something so unusual that it could not be obtained by employing a consultant, then it has a higher value than information under (1). Quantum is to be assessed on the basis of the price which a willing buyer would pay for it and which a willing seller in the plaintiff's position would accept.

(3) If the confidential information is 'very special indeed' then it may be proper to calculate damages as a capitalised royalty.

In any event, whichever method is appropriate the court said that once the damages are paid then the property in the business secrets vests in the defendant in the same way in which it does in cases where damages are awarded for conversion.

These categories are novel and there seems little doubt that whichever is applied will be largely determined by the effect of expert evidence. It is submitted that the approach of the Court of Appeal in this case was most unfortunate. First, why should the compensation under category (1) be calculated in accordance with what the defendant company had saved rather than by what the plaintiff could reasonably have gained by the sale of the information? The court decided in *Seager v Copydex* that an account of profits would not be awarded—only damages—and yet the basis under (1) seems inconsistent with this. Regarding bases (2) and (3) the problem is that they assume that the plaintiff would willingly have sold and the defendant bought. However, in this case the negotiations as to sale between the parties had completely broken down. Moreover, why should the information vest in the defendants once the damages are paid? The logical result of such vesting is that he could in some cases obtain a patent, and then sue the plaintiff for infringement. Indeed *Copydex* had applied for a patent regarding the product to which the confidential information attached. Gurry suggests that the defendant should have obtained no more than a non-exclusive licence to use the information but it is submitted that even this compromise is unreasonably favourable to the defendant. We can see no reason why he should get any rights at all in the information. The analogy with conversion is fallacious because that rule is in itself an exception to the normal principles of compensation and the analogy fails to take account of the radical differences between a chattel and a piece of information. Once the former is transferred there is no residual aspect which can remain with the plaintiff. That is not so with information, especially business secrets which may have been crucial to a plaintiff's business. Is he to shut down his business because of the wrongful appropriation by another of his property? In our view this judgment amounts to a rogues' charter. It allows a defendant to buy the freedom to infringe the plaintiff's rights. Moreover what if *Seager*, having broken off negotiations with *Copydex*, had sold the information to another party and warranted that it was free from any encumbrances? If the judgment in *Seager v Copydex (No 2)* is applied then the other party would have grounds for a subsequent action against *Seager* for breach of warranty. Such a possibility produces a very unfair result.

Recently, in *Dowson and Mason Ltd v Potter* [1986] 1 WLR 1419, *Seager* has been distinguished. The plaintiffs developed a new type of landing leg for articulated lorries. In breach of his duty of confidence as the plaintiffs' employee, the first defendant disclosed to the second defendants information consisting of the names and addresses of the suppliers of the leg's component parts and the price which the plaintiffs had paid for them. The second defendants became the plaintiffs' competitors as manufacturers of landing legs and called a meeting of the suppliers and discussed the possibility of placing orders with them. The plaintiffs issued a write claiming against the defendants, *inter alia*, damages for the disclosure and use of the plaintiffs' confidential information. By a consent order an inquiry was ordered into the damages sustained by the plaintiffs. The defendants issued a summons seeking the court's determination of the proper basis for assessing the damages.

The district registrar held that the proper basis for the assessment was the plaintiffs' loss of profits resulting from the wrongful disclosure and use of the confidential information. The judge affirmed the district registrar's order.

The Court of Appeal held that since the purpose of damages was to put the plaintiffs in the position in which they would have been if the defendants had not wrongly obtained and used their confidential information to compete with them as manufacturers of landing legs, the proper basis for the assessment of the plaintiffs' damages was the loss of manufacturing profits. Sir Edward Eveleigh said that the particular position of the plaintiff in each case had to be considered. He gave examples. When dealing with someone who would have licensed the use of his confidential information, then almost invariably the measure of damages will be the price that he could have commanded for that information, and no question of loss of manufacturing profits will arise, as he was always ready to allow someone else to manufacture at a price. If the plaintiff was a manufacturer who would have licensed another to use his secret then he would, probably in all cases, be in the same position as the inventor who had sold it, because he would have exposed himself to competition and loss of profits for a price, the price for which he had sold the secret. If, on the other hand, he was a manufacturer who would not have licensed its use, then he would not have been exposed to competition at the time when he was exposed because of the defendant's wrongdoing.

He then went on to say that in *Seager* it was clear that S would have sold the information: he was an inventor who made his living from selling his inventions. He said the court in *Seager* was dealing with particular facts and was not laying down any principles. In this case the plaintiff was a manufacturer in a competing line of business. By using the plaintiff's confidential information the defendant was wrongly depriving the plaintiff by competition of manufacturing profits.

Chapter 25

Other Remedies

1 Permanent injunctions

At the end of a trial a plaintiff will frequently apply for a permanent injunction. Unlike a claim for an interlocutory injunction the request for a permanent injunction must be pleaded in the statement of claim. Unlike damages, which are available as of right, an injunction is an equitable remedy and is therefore discretionary. The power to grant a permanent injunction is nowadays found in s 37(1) Supreme Court Act 1981. However, despite the width of s 37(1) there are well established rules regarding what is 'just and convenient'.

1.1 Criteria for such an award

(a) Damages are not an adequate remedy: The primary consideration in all cases in which an injunction is awarded is whether damages or damages alone provide an adequate remedy. In most restraint of trade and business secrets cases damages will not be an adequate remedy because of the difficulty of quantification. Even if damages are not difficult to assess, if the plaintiff can show that there exists a real risk of future injury then he will be awarded a permanent injunction. A permanent injunction is unlikely to be sought in a restraint of trade case unless the covenant is not limited by time or if the period in question extends beyond the date of judgment: obviously if the covenant is struck down as being an unreasonable restraint of trade then no question of a permanent injunction arises. It is more common in business secrets cases for a permanent injunction to be awarded to a successful plaintiff, although in highly technological areas, where knowledge changes quickly, there may be little point in seeking such an award or the award may be limited as to time.

(b) Miscellaneous criteria: The court will also consider whether the plaintiff really deserves an interlocutory injunction. It will examine his conduct and especially whether he has clean hands or has delayed in bringing the action or has in some way acquiesced in what the defendant has done. The court will also examine the quality of the plaintiff's right and whether the breach is merely technical. However this is unlikely to be a consideration in most restraint of trade and business secrets cases. Further, the court will consider the defendant's behaviour. It is generally accepted that a defendant cannot buy the freedom to infringe the plaintiff's rights especially as in most business secrets

250

cases those are rights which the plaintiff has specifically refused to sell. The final criteria which are of especial importance are the public interest and the special rules concerning employees and those in positions of mutual trust and confidence; these topics have already been discussed at pp 207–11.

2 Account of profits

If the plaintiff has not suffered any or only minor loss or if he thinks that the defendant's gain is much greater than his loss, he may be tempted to sue for an account of profits Although it is usual in the pleadings to request both damages and an account of profits it is not possible for the plaintiff to be given both remedies as this would leave him with double compensation. The plaintiff must therefore elect at the end of the day and he will choose an account of profits if he wishes to have his recompense measured by the defendant's gain rather than, as in the case of damages, his loss. Technically, an account of profits is only available if the court is exercising its equitable jurisdiction. We, therefore, advise that if an account of profits may be requested then the statement of claim, even in the case of an express contractual term, should include an allegation of breach of both contract and the equitable duty of confidence.

In *My Kinda Town Ltd v Soll* [1983] RPC 15 Slade J made some general observations about an account of profits. He said 'the object of ordering an account in cases such as the present is to deprive the defendants of the profits which they have improperly made by wrongful acts committed in breach of the plaintiffs' rights and to transfer such profits to the plaintiffs'. He went on to say that in ordering an account of profits in a passing off or breach of confidence case the court will ordinarily direct that the account be in a form wide enough to include all profits made by the defendant from his acts in breach of evidence.

A good example of when such a claim is appropriate is found in *Industrial Development Consultants Ltd v Cooley* [1972] 2 All ER 162. The defendant was the managing director of the plaintiffs and on their behalf he entered into negotiations with the Eastern Gas Board to manage a large building project. However the Board made it quite clear that they disliked the plaintiffs' organisation and for that reason would not award them the contract. Subsequently, they approached the defendant and told him that if he were independent of the plaintiffs he would be chosen to do the work. The defendant procured a release from his employment contract on false grounds and eventually became the project manager. The plaintiffs sued him for acting in breach of his fiduciary duty as a director. They claimed:

- (a) a declaration that he was a trustee of the benefit of the contract for them;
- (b) an account of profits; and
- (c) alternatively damages.

They elected to pursue an account of profits. The advantage of doing so was that an award of damages would have, said Roskill J, been calculated as 10 per cent of the net value of the project to them as Eastern Gas Board would almost certainly not have awarded them the contract. The 10 per cent reflected the slight chance that they would have been chosen. Instead they received all the profits made by the defendant. However the dilemma of making each an award was recognised by the judge: '. . . if the plaintiffs succeed they will get a profit which they probably would not have got for themselves had the defendant fulfilled his duty. If the defendant is allowed to keep that profit he will have got something which he was able to get solely by reason of his breach of fiduciary duty to the plaintiffs . . .'. The problem was resolved on the basis that it was the defendant who had acted wrongly. An example where damages were chosen rather than an account of profits was *Saltman Engineering Co Ltd v Campbell Engineering Co Ltd* (1948) 65 RPC 203 in which the defendants had made a loss on sales of a product which had been manufactured using the plaintiff's business secrets. However, an account of profits appears to be rarely used:

(1) because of the difficulty of calculation and
(2) because of delay.

(1) The difficulty of calculation arises from the fact that the defendant is only liable to disgorge that element of the profit attributable to the wrongful use of the plaintiff's business secrets unless, of course, he is in a fiduciary position, in which case he disgorges all. There may be other factors which contribute: each has to be given value. There are however cases in which it can be said that apportionment is not an issue: these appear to be where the business secret is the final factor which creates the profit, ie it is the *sine qua non*: see *Peter Pan Manufacturing Corp v Corsets Silhouette Ltd* [1963] RPC 45 in which it was held that the account of profits was literally the difference between the amount expended by the defendants and the amount received. Pennycuick J rejected the argument that only that part of a profit attributable to the misuse of business secrets was relevant.

(2) Delay, so far as the plaintiff is concerned, arises from the fact that at the end of the trial, having waited a considerable period for judgment, the plaintiff will want to receive his compensation. Damages fulfil that need subject to the defendant's ability to pay. However, an account of profits can only be provided by the defendant. At the end of the trial, the defendant will be ordered to provide such an account. The defendant has little incentive, apart from the element of interest which may be awarded to the plaintiff, to get on with doing so. Once he has done so, there is often a dispute regarding the calculations made. There is frequently another trip to court and another trial, which is not always short, dealing with the profits disclosed. Judgment is then given and the plaintiff may find that at the end of the day he would have been much better off had he elected for damages. Once the election has been made however the plaintiff cannot change his mind.

It is submitted that only in the clearest cases where there is overwhelming evidence that there is a large and significant difference between an award of damages and an account of profits, that the plaintiff should be advised to choose the latter course.

However an account of profits is not an automatic remedy, like damages, but, like an injunction, it is a discretionary one. The court will therefore take into account factors similar to those already outlined when an application for a permanent injunction is made. Although Heydon claims that in practice an account of profits will not be awarded unless the defendant has acted dishonestly, we see no reason to adopt this as a general rule although it is true that in *Seager* there was a specific finding that *Copydex* had not been dishonest and damages only were awarded.

3 Delivery up/destruction

Apart from the powers of the court under RSC Ord 29, r 2A there is an equitable jurisdiction to make an order for delivery up/destruction. Such an order will only be made to perfect an injunction which has already been granted. The reasoning behind the equitable jurisdiction appears to be the removal of temptation from the defendant to break the terms of the injunction. It is usually the defendant who can choose between delivery up and destruction and if the latter course is chosen then the destruction must take place on oath. This means in practice that the defendant must swear an affidavit setting out the fact that destruction of certain articles has taken place. If the defendant has acted in a high handed or dishonest manner then the court may well decide, as it did in *Industrial Furnaces v Reaves* [1970] RPC 605, that the better course is to order delivery up. Other cases in which delivery up was ordered are *Measures Bros Ltd v Measures* [1910] 2 Ch 248; *Reid and Sigrist Ltd v Moss and Mechanism Ltd* (1932) 49 RPC 461 and *Ackroyds (London) Ltd v Islington Plastics Ltd* [1962] RPC 97. Delivery up means actual delivery to the plaintiff. The subject matter of an order for delivery up/destruction may encompass simply what the defendant has actually taken, for example, a customer list or a copy thereof but can go further and include what the defendant has made or has caused to be made using the business secrets.

4 Declarations

The power to grant a declaration is found in RSC Ord 15, r 1: No action or other proceeding shall be open to objection on the ground that a merely declaratory judgment or order is sought thereby, and the court may make binding declarations of right whether or not any consequential relief is or could be claimed.

The declaration can be a very useful form of 'remedy' in both restraint of trade and business secrets cases. It is particularly useful as a means of getting before a court in order to obtain judgment in those types of cases where either no contract as such exists, and/or if the party seeking relief is neither a member of a club whose rules are challenged etc nor is a party to a contract. A declaration was used in both *Eastham v Newcastle United Football Club Ltd* [1964] Ch 413 and in *Nagle v Feilden* [1966] 2 QB 633. Lord Denning MR in *Boulting v ACTAT* [1963] 2 QB 606 referred to 'the power of the court . . . to make a declaration of right whenever the interest of the plaintiff is sufficient to justify it'.

It is settled law that a declaration is not to be refused merely because the plaintiff cannot establish a legal cause of action apart from the rule, for its effect is to give a general power to make a declaration, whether there is a cause of action or not, since 'relief' in Ord 15, r 16 is not confined to relief in respect of a cause of action. See *Greig v Insole* [1978] 3 All ER 447 (in which the declaration was given to both the cricketers and WSC), *McInnes v Onslow-Fane* [1978] 1 WLR 1520 and *Dickson v Pharmaceutical Society* [1970] AC 403.

A further use was found in *White (Marion) Ltd v Francis* [1972] 1 WLR 1423 for the declaratory procedure. There the duration of the covenant had ended before the case could be heard in the Court of Appeal and therefore the dispute between the parties no longer effectively existed. However, the Court of Appeal allowed the applicants, the employers, to amend their grounds of appeal so as to include a claim for a declaration. This was done because the employers had an interest regarding their remaining employees who were employed under contracts containing a similar clause. Indeed, it is usual in all cases where the outcome of the instant case will inevitably be used as a basis for judging the validity of similar clauses, to claim a declaration.

A third, but rare, example of the use of a declaration occurred in *Greer v Sketchley Ltd* [1979] FSR 197. There the plaintiff wanted to join a rival company of the defendants; he had been employed by the latter for many years. On learning of this the defendants reminded him that in their view by working for the rival he would be in breach of a restraint of trade clause in his employment contract. Mr Greer, instead of joining the rival and waiting to see what might happen, issued a writ claiming a declaration that the clause was invalid. The defendants counterclaimed for an injunction. Lord Denning MR applauded the plaintiff for his sensible approach and in the event the clause was declared to be invalid. There can be no doubt that many covenantors would be wise to follow Mr Greer's example. Although the clause was clearly unreasonable and would have been judged so even if he had simply joined the rival company there may be situations in which the sympathy of the court may be a decisive factor. Mr Greer obviously had that sympathy.

Other examples of cases in which a declaration was sought are *Kores Manufacturing Co v Kolok Manufacturing Co* [1959] Ch 108 (because of a doubt whether there was an agreement at all); in *Esso Petroleum Co Ltd v Harper's Garage (Stourport) Ltd* [1968] AC 269 in which the defendants counterclaimed for a declaration; in *Industrial Development Consultants Ltd v Cooley* [1972] 2 All ER 192 in which a declaration was sought that Cooley was a trustee for the plaintiffs of all contracts with the Eastern Gas Board and was therefore liable; see also *Malone v Metropolitan Police Commissioner* [1979] Ch 344; *Schroeder v Macaulay* [1974] 1 WLR 1308, and *Commercial Plastics Ltd v Vincent* [1965] 1 QB 623 in which the plaintiffs claimed an injunction restraining the defendant from taking up employment with a specific competitor and a declaration that he was not entitled to work for any competitors in the PVC calendering field.

However, if an application for a declaration is contemplated the following points should be borne in mind:

(a) a declaration is not available as of right but is a discretionary remedy;

(b) a declaration will not be granted to answer an academic or hypothetical question. A declaration will not be granted where there is no breach and no threatened or intended breach of an agreement; see *Mellstrom v Garner* [1970] 1 WLR 603;

(c) the fact that declarations have been granted on the basis of the public interest does not mean, of course, that there is the type of public element sufficient to warrant an application for the judicial review variety of declaration under RSC Ord 53. See *Law v National Greyhound Racing Club Ltd* [1983] 3 All ER 300.

Appendices

Appendix 1

Ready Reckoner

Restraint of trade cases: quick reference guide to decisions in relation to employees

Case	Citation	Job	Time	Area	Valid
Bromley v Smith	[1909] 2 KB 235	Baker	3 years	10 miles	Yes (after severance)
Mason v Provident Clothing and Supply Co Ltd	[1913] AC 724	Canvasser	3 years	25 miles	No
Caribonum Co Ltd v Le Couch	(1913) 109 LT 385	Manufacturer	5 years	British Empire and Europe	Yes (but old-fashioned approach)
Continental Tyre and Rubber (GB) Co Ltd v Heath	(1913) 29 TLR 308	Salesman	1 year	UK, Germany, France	Yes (after severance)
Eastes v Russ	[1914] 1 Ch 468	Laboratory Technician	unlimited	10 miles	No
Hadsley v Dayer-Smith	[1914] AC 979	Estate Agent (partner)	10 years	1 mile	Yes
SV Nevanas and Co v Walker and Foreman	[1914] 1 Ch 413	Manager	1 year	UK	No

Case	Citation	Occupation	Period	Area	Enforceable
Herbert Morris Ltd v Saxelby	[1916] 1 AC 688	Engineer	7 years	UK and Ireland	No
Forster and Sons Ltd v Suggett	(1918) 35 TLR 87	Engineer	5 years	UK	Yes
The Great Western and Metropolitan Dairies Ltd v Gibbs	(1918) 34 TLR 344	Cashier	6, 12 and 18 months	20 miles	No
Whitmore v King	(1918) 87 LJ Ch 647	Salesman/Clerk	5 years	East Anglia	No
Ropeways Ltd v Hoyle	(1919) 88 LJ Ch 446	Draughtsman	5 years	Unlimited	No
Attwood v Lamont	[1920] 3 KB 571	Tailor	Unlimited	10 miles	No
Clarke, Sharp and Co Ltd v Solomon	(1920) 37 TLR 176	Salesman	5 years	5 miles	No
Hepworth Management Co Ltd v Ryott	[1920] 1 Ch 1	Actor	Unlimited	Worldwide	No
Bowler v Lovegrove	[1921] Ch 642	Estate Agent's Clerk	1 year	Portsmouth, Gosport	No
Fitch v Dewes	[1921] 2 AC 158	Solicitor's Clerk	Unlimited	7 miles	Yes
East Essex Farmers Ltd v Holder	[1926] WN 230	Manager	10 years	25 miles	No
Putsman v Taylor	[1927] 1 KB 741	Manager	5 years	Birmingham	Yes (after severance)
Express Dairy Co v Jackson	(1930) 99 LJKB 181	Milkman	2 years	customers	No
Vincents of Reading v Fogden	(1932) 48 TLR 613	Car Salesman	3 years	15 miles	No

Case	Citation	Job	Time	Area	Valid
Gilford Motor Co v Home	[1933] Ch 935	Managing Director	5 years	3 miles	Yes
Empire Meat Co Ltd v Patrick	[1939] 2 All ER 85	Butcher	5 years	5 miles	No
Chafer Ltd v Lilley	[1947] LJR 231	Salesman	5 years	Great Britain	No
Routh v Jones	[1947] 1 All ER 758	Doctor	5 years	10 miles	No
Jenkins v Reid	[1948] 1 All ER 471	Doctor	Unlimited	5 miles	No
Whitehill v Bradford	[1952] 1 All ER 115	Doctor (partner)	21 years	10 miles	Yes
Marchon Products Ltd v Thornes	(1954) 71 RPC 445	Chemist	1 year	UK	Yes
M and Drapers v Reynolds	[1956] 3 All ER 814	Salesman	5 years	customers	No
Vandervell Products Ltd v McLeod	[1957] RPC 185	Foreman	2 years	Any competitor	No
Kerchiss v Colora Printing Inks Ltd	[1960] RPC 235	Director	3 years	16 countries	Yes
Commercial Plastics Ltd v Vincent	[1964] 3 All ER 546	Researcher	1 year	Competitors, unlimited	No
Rayner v Pegler	(1964) 189 EG 967	Partner in Estate Agents	2 years	1 mile	No
GW Plowman and Sons Ltd v Ash	[1964] 2 All ER 10	Salesman	2 years	customers	Yes

				Districts worked	
Gledhow Autoparts Ltd v Delaney	[1965] 3 All ER 288	Salesman	3 years		No
SW Strange Ltd v Mann	[1965] 1 All ER 1069	Manager	3 years	12 miles	No
Scorer v Seymour Johns	[1966] 3 All ER 347	Estate Agent	3 years	5 miles	Yes
Technograph Printed Circuits Ltd v Chalwyn Ltd	[1967] FSR 307	Electronic Component Manufacturer	2 years	Unlimited	No
Under Water Welders and Repairers Ltd v Street and Longthorne	[1968] RPC 498	Diver	3 years	Unlimited	Yes
Lyne-Pirkis v Jones	[1969] 3 All ER 738	Doctor (partner)	5 years	10 miles	No
Home Counties Dairies Ltd v Skilton	[1970] 1 All ER 1227	Milkman	1 year	customers	Yes
Peyton v Mindham	[1971] 3 All ER 1215	Doctor (partner)	5 years	5 miles	No
Marion White Ltd v Francis	[1972] 3 All ER 857	Hairdresser	1 year	½ mile	Yes
T Lucas and Co Ltd v Mitchell	[1972] 2 All ER 1035	Salesman	1 year	Greater Manchester	No
Spafax (1965) Ltd v Dommett	(1972) 116 SJ 711	Salesman	2 years	customers	No
Financial Collection Agencies (UK) Ltd v Batey	(1973) 117 SJ 416	Debt Collectors/ Salesmen	6 months	4 cities	No

Case	Citation	Job	Time	Area/restricted activities	Valid
Stenhouse Australia Ltd v Phillips	[1974] AC 391	Insurance Broker	5 years	Walthamstow, Chingford	No
Calvert, Hunt and Barden v Elton	(1975) 233 EG 391	Branch Manager Estate Agents	3 years	3 miles	Yes
Standex International Ltd v CB Blades	[1976] FSR 114	Director	5 years	GB and Northern Ireland	Yes
Office Overload Ltd v Gunn	[1977] FSR 39	Employment Agency	1 year	6 miles	Yes
Luck v Davenport-Smith	[1977] EGD 73	Estate Agent	3 years	1 mile	No
Littlewoods Organisation Ltd v Harris	[1978] 1 All ER 1026	Director	1 year	Worldwide (but construed to be limited to UK)	Yes
Richards v Levy	(1978) 122 SJ 713	Solicitor's Clerk	3 years	London Borough of Ealing	Yes
Greer v Sketchley Ltd	[1979] FSR 197	Director	1 year	UK	No
Spafax Ltd v Taylor and Harrison	[1980] IRLR 442	Salesman	2 years	Customers	Yes
Marley Tile Co Ltd v Johnson	[1982] IRLR 75		1 year	Devon, Cornwall	No
Normalec Ltd v Britton	[1983] FSR 318	Agent	1 year	Yorkshire	Yes
Bridge v Deacons	[1984] AC 705	Solicitor (partner)	5 years	Hong Kong	Yes

Case	Citation	Position	Duration	Clause	Result
Rex Stewart, Jeffries Parker, Ginsberg Ltd v Parker	[1988] IRLR 483	MD Advertising Agency	18 months	Non-solicitation clause re any customer who 'is or has been' such of plaintiffs and associated companies	Yes but only after deleting 'is or' from definition of customer and reference to associated companies
Sadler v Imperial Life Assurance Co of Canada Ltd	[1988] IRLR 388	Insurance Agent	Unlimited	Payment of commission after termination reliant on agent abiding with clause which prevented him working in same type of business	No: clause un-reasonable (but severed: agent was paid)
Spencer v Marchington	[1988] IRLR 392	Manager Employment agency	2 years	25 miles Banbury/ 10 miles Leamington: not to work in similar business	No: 25 miles too far and adequate protection provided by a non-solicitation clause
Business Seating (Renovations) Ltd v Broad	[1989] ICR 729	Sales Rep	1 year	Soliciting customers of plaintiff or any associated company	Yes after severance of restriction for benefit of associated company

Case	Citation	Job	Time	Area/restricted activities	Valid
Dairy Crest Ltd v Pigott	[1989] ICR 92	Milkman	2 years	Non-solicitation	Yes
Hinton and Higgs (UK) Ltd v Murphy	[1989] IRLR 519	Unspecified	18 months	Not to work for any previous or present client of plaintiff group of companies	No: 'previous or present' too wide; extent too wide; application to other companies in group too wide
Briggs v Oates	[1991] 1 All ER 407	Employed Solicitor	5 years	5 miles: not practice nor solicit clients	No: partnership had dissolved prior to any breach
Lansing Linde Ltd v Kerr	[1991] 1 All ER 418	Divisional Director	12 months	Worldwide ban on working in similar business	No
Lawrence David Ltd v Ashton	[1991] 1 All ER 385	Sales Director	2 years	Not working in UK	Yes
Office Angels Ltd v Rainer-Thomas	(1991) The Times, 11 April, CA	Branch Manager	6 months	1,000 metres from branch in City of London	No

2 Business secrets cases: Quick reference guide

Case	Citation	Information	Relationship	Remedy
Prince Albert v Strange	(1849) 1 Mac & G 25	catalogue of etchings	third party	injunction
Morison v Moat	(1851) 9 Hare 492	secret formula	third party (partner's son)	injunction
Gartside v Outram	(1856) 2 LJ Ch 113	knowledge of fraud	employee	refused
Tuck and Sons v Priester	(1887) 19 QBD 629	drawings	contractor	injunction and damages
Gilbert v Star Newspapers Co Ltd	(1894) 11 TLR 4	plot of a play	third party (former employer)	injunction
Robb v Green	[1895] 2 QB 1	customer list	employee	damages and injunction
Exchange Telegraph Co Ltd v Central News Ltd	[1897] 2 Ch 48	newswire	subscriber and third party	injunction
Summers (William) and Co Ltd v Boyce and Kinmon and Co	(1907) 23 TLR 724	list of customers and business terms	employee and third party	injunction delivery up and damages
Rakusen v Ellis, Munday and Clarke	[1912] 1 Ch 831	solicitor's client	partner's knowledge	refused
Amber Size and Chemical Co v Menzel	(1913) 30 RPC 433	secret process	employee	injunction

Case	Citation	Information	Relationship	Remedy
Weld-Blundell v Stephens	[1920] AC 956	instructions to investigating accountants	accountant	damages
In re Keene	[1922] 2 Ch 475	formulae	trustee in bankruptcy	disclosure
Tournier v National Provincial and Union Bank of England	[1924] 1 KB 461	bank account	customer of bank	new trial ordered
Reid and Sigrist Ltd v Moss and Mechanism Ltd	(1932) 49 RPC 461	engineering	employee	injunction delivery up declaration
E Worsley and Co Ltd v Cooper	[1939] 1 All ER 290	prices and product types	employee	refused (as regards secrets) injunction
Hivac Ltd v Park Royal Scientific Instruments Ltd	[1946] Ch 169	manufacturing techniques	competitor	injunction
Saltman Engineering Co Ltd v Campbell Engineering Co Ltd	(1948) 65 RPC 203	engineering drawings	sub-contractor	delivery up and damages
Stevenson Jordan and Harrison Ltd v MacDonald and Evans	(1952) 69 RPC 10	business procedures	employee	refused
Bjorlow (GB) Ltd v Minter	(1954) 71 RPC 321	process	employee	refused
Nichrotherm Electrical Co Ltd v Percy	[1957] RPC 207	engineering drawings etc	disclosure for limited purpose	damages
Ackroyds (London) Ltd v Islington Plastics Ltd	[1962] RPC 97	tool design	sub-contractor	injunction and damages
Mustad v Allcock and Dosen	[1963] 3 All ER 416	engineering	employee	refused
Peter Pan Manufacturing Corp v Corsets Silhouette	[1963] 3 All ER 402	manufacturing	licensee	injunction and account of profits

Case	Citation	Subject	Relationship	Outcome
Paul (KS) Ltd v Southern Instruments Ltd	[1964] RPC 118	black box	lessee and third party	injunction
Printers and Finishers Ltd v Holloway	[1965] 1 WLR 1	printing process	employee and visitor	visitor injuncted but not employee
Cranleigh Precision Engineering Ltd v Bryant	[1965] 1 WLR 1293	engineering	director	injunction
Auto Securities Ltd v Standard Telephones & Cables Ltd	[1965] RPC 92	technical information	unclear	refused
Torrington Manufacturing Co v Smith and Son (England) Ltd	[1966] RPC 285	customer lists engineering	licensee	—
Terrapin Ltd v Builders' Supply Co (Hayes) Ltd	[1967] RPC 375	engineering	employee	injunction
Seager v Copydex Ltd	[1967] 1 WLR 923	engineering drawings and explanations	negotiations	inquiry as to damages
Franchi v Franchi	[1967] RPC 149	manufacturing process	employee	refused
Duchess of Argyll v Duke of Argyll	[1967] 1 Ch 302	marital confidence	spouse	injunction
Suhner and Co AG v Transradio Ltd	[1967] RPC 329	engineering drawings	distributor	refused
Under Water Welders and Repairers Ltd v Street and Longthorne	[1968] RPC 498	hull cleaning process	employees	injunction
Initial Services v Putterill	[1968] 1 QB 396	misconduct	employee	refused

Case	Citation	Information	Relationship	Remedy
Coco v AN Clark (Engineering) Ltd	[1969] RPC 41	engineering drawings etc	negotiations	refused
Fraser v Evans	[1969] 1 QB 349	report for government	consultant	refused
Industrial Furnaces Ltd v Reaves	[1970] RPC 605	engineering	employee	injunction damages delivery up
Baker v Gibbons	[1972] 1 WLR 693	agent's names	director	refused
Regina Glass Fibre v Werner Schuller	[1972] RPC 299	process	licensee	refused
Hubbard v Vosper	[1972] 1 All ER 1023	religious sect	sect member	refused
Church of Scientology v Kaufman	[1973] RPC 635	religious sect	student	refused
United Stirling Corp Ltd v Felton and Mannion	[1974] RPC 162	manufacturing process	employee	refused
Aveley/Cybervox Ltd v Boman and Sign Electronics Ltd	[1975] FSR 139	product design	employee	refused
Yates Circuit Foil Co v Electrofoils Ltd	[1976] FSR 345	chemical processes	employees	refused (undertakings given)
A-G v Jonathan Cape Ltd	[1976] QB 752	cabinet meetings	publisher of minister's diaries	refused
Potters-Ballotini Ltd v Weston-Baker	[1977] RPC 202	manufacturing process	employees	refused
Woodward v Hutchins	[1977] 1 WLR 760	private lives	press agent	refused

			appeal against use allowed
Riddick v Thames Board Mills Ltd	[1977] QB 881	evidence of defamation	discovery
Lennon v Mirror Group Newspapers Ltd	[1978] FSR 573	marital confidences	spouse/third party	refused
Dunford Elliott Ltd v Johnson and Firth Brown	[1978] FSR 143	report of company's finances	prospective underwriter	refused
Franklin v Giddings	[1978] Qd R 72	budwood	spouse and third party	delivery up
Thomas Marshall (Exports) Ltd v Guinle	[1979] 1 Ch 227	supplier and customer names	managing director	injunction
Malone v Metropolitan Police Commissioner	[1979] 1 Ch 346	telephone tapping		refused
Schering Chemicals Ltd v Falkman Ltd	[1981] 2 All ER 321	reaction to drug	public relations consultant	injunction
British Steel Corporation v Granada Television Ltd	[1981] 1 All ER 417	name of informant	third party	discovery
GD Searle and Co Ltd v Celltech Ltd	[1982] FSR 98	staff names etc	employee	refused
Sun Printers Ltd v Westminster Press Ltd	[1982] IRLR 292	company report	third party	refused
Home Office v Harman	[1982] 1 All ER 532	document disclosed in court	counsel	contempt
Fisher-Karpark Industries Ltd v Nichols	[1982] FSR 351	not clear from report	employee/director	injunction
Fraser v Thames Television Ltd	[1983] 2 All ER 101	concept for TV series	negotiations	damages
Trees Ltd v Cripps	(1983) 267 EG 596	value of bid	bidder	refused

269

Case	Citation	Information	Relationship	Remedy
Francome v Mirror Group Newspapers Ltd	[1984] 2 All ER 408	telephone tapping	third party	injunction
Lion Laboratories Ltd v Evans	[1984] 2 All ER 417	report on intoximeter	employee negotiations	refused injunction
Wheatley v Bell	[1984] FSR 17	advertising method	licensee	damages
House of Spring Gardens v Point Blank	[1985] FSR 327	design for armoured vest		
Speed Seal Ltd v Paddington	[1985] WLR 1327	engineering designs	employee	appeal allowed
Roger Bullivant Ltd v Ellis	[1987] ICR 464	customer index	employee	injunction
Faccenda Chicken v Fowler	[1986] 1 All ER 617	customers and prices	employee	refused
Dowson and Mason Ltd v Potter	[1986] 1 WLR 1419	Names and addresses of suppliers and prices paid to them	Employee	Claim admitted: case reported on quantum
Balston Ltd v Headline Filters Ltd	[1987] FSR 330	blends of microfibres, tests of identity of chemicals used in manufacturing process	Employee and director	Refused (partial undertakings given)
Johnson & Bloy Holdings Ltd v Wolstenholme Rink Plc	[1989] IRLR 499	knowledge of commercial use of the combination of 2 products	Employee	Injunction granted on appeal not to use/disclose/manufacture

Case	Citation	Information	Relationship	Result/Remedy
In Re a Company	[1989] 3 WLR 265	information about a company's tax & management	Employee	Injunction (subject to exceptions in the case of disclosure to FIMBRA and Inland Revenue)
W v Egdell	[1989] 2 WLR 689	psychiatrist's report	Doctor/Patient	Action dismissed on basis that disclosure to limited recipients in public interest
Ixora Trading Inc v Jones	[1990] 1 FSR 251	general technical knowledge of bureau de change business and of 2 manuals and a feasibility study	Employee	Claim struck out
Berkley Admin Inc v McCleland	[1990] FSR 505	details of a business plan	Employee	Claim dismissed
Systems Reliability Holdings plc v Smith	[1990] IRLR 377	ability to modify computers and information about customers of plaintiff and its subsidiaries	Employee and Shareholder	Injunction and enquiry as to damages
Lansing Linde Ltd v Kerr	[1991] 1 All ER 418	plans for development of new products	Divisional director	Undertakings

Appendix II

Restrictive Trade Practices Act 1976

1 Introduction

The Restrictive Trade Practices Act 1976 ('the Act') is, as its title suggests, concerned with the control of a limited range of trade practices. The Act regulates agreements and arrangements under which the parties either restrict their freedom to provide goods and services to others or supply each other with information on their terms and prices. The Act applies in two stages. Firstly, there is a formal test to determine whether any particular arrangement falls within the Act: if it does then it must be registered. Secondly, once it has been registered it must be brought before the Restrictive Practices Court where it must be shown not to be contrary to the public interest. As will be seen below, the Secretary of State can, on the advice of the Director General of Fair Trading, dispense with the need to go before the court in certain cases.

The expense of seeking to justify an agreement before the Restrictive Practices Court means that the only practical course which the parties to ordinary commercial agreements can take is to ensure either that their agreement is not registrable or that a direction from the Secretary of State dispensing with the need for a court hearing will be forthcoming. However trade associations and other groups may consider a hearing worthwhile.

2 Basic rule for registration

The Act applies to agreements. However the term agreement is widely defined in the Act and includes not only formal agreements which are intended to be legally binding but also informal arrangements which are intended not to be enforceable. In the remainder of this appendix the term agreement should be understood to include informal arrangements. In addition, the Act is concerned with the totality of the agreement between the parties and the fact that it may be divided into separate documents between the same or different persons will not prevent the whole arrangement from being looked at as one agreement.

The Act applies separately to restrictive provisions as to goods and restrictive provisions as to services. Whilst the rules for goods and services are similar it is necessary to examine any agreement twice, first considering any goods restrictions and secondly considering any services restrictions. Due to the similarity of the rules relating to goods and services the rules relating to goods are described and only the differences in the rules applying to services are mentioned.

The circumstances in which an agreement containing restrictions as to goods will be registrable are set out in s 6 of the Act which provides that the Act applies to agreements:

> between two or more persons carrying on business in the United Kingdom in the production or supply of goods, or in the application to goods of any process of manufacture, whether with or without other parties, being agreements under which restrictions are accepted by two or more parties in respect of [the specified matters].

Before dealing with the specified matters it is important to note the somewhat specialised meanings which have been given to the word 'persons' by the Act and case law.

Section 43(2) of the Act provides that, for most purposes, any two or more interconnected bodies corporate, or any two or more *individuals* carrying on business in partnership with each other, shall be treated as a single person. The term 'interconnected bodies corporate' is also defined in the Act and basically means members of a group of companies. Thus, in determining the number of persons carrying on business in the United Kingdom under the test in s 6 parent and subsidiary are treated as one person. However, the fact that a parent and subsidiary are counted as one person does not mean that restrictions accepted as between parent and subsidiary are to be disregarded. Thus where a subsidiary and an independent company both accept restrictions in favour of the parent company two parties will be treated as accepting restrictions (see *Registrar v Schweppes (No 2)* [1971] 2 All ER 1473). However where in an agreement between the same parties the parent and subsidiary each accept restrictions in favour of the independent company only one person will be treated as accepting a restriction.

In determining whether a person carries on business in the United Kingdom no account is taken of the activities of other members of that person's group. Therefore a company which does not carry on business in the United Kingdom will not be treated as doing so merely because its subsidiary does. It should be remembered, however, that in an agreement between multiple parties it is irrelevant that the parties who accept restrictions are different to the parties who carry on business in the United Kingdom. For an agreement to be subject to the Act all that is required is two of each.

3 Restrictions

The restrictions to which the Act applies are specified in s 6 for goods and s 11 for services. In summary these sections cover restrictions on the following matters:

> (a) prices to be charged, quoted for goods, services obtained or supplied

or the manufacture of goods or recommended in respect of resale of goods;
(b) terms of supply or acquisition of goods or services;
(c) quantities and descriptions of goods to be produced, supplied or acquired and the extent of any services to be supplied or obtained;
(d) the form or manner in which services are to be obtained or supplied;
(e) process of manufacture to be applied to goods;
(f) persons or areas to or from which goods are to be supplied or manufactured or services obtained or made available.

The word restriction is defined to include 'a negative obligation, whether express or implied and whether absolute or not' (s 43). In addition, ss 6 and 17 provide that provisions which confer a benefit or impose a detriment upon a party who complies with an obligation are treated as restrictions. Similarly, provisions which require payment at higher rates for excess production are treated as restrictions.

However, it is clear that the term restriction must be construed sensibly. In *Ravenseft Properties Application, Re* (1976) 120 SJ 834 it was held that covenants as to use of land accepted by a lessee in his lease were not 'restrictions' within the meaning of the Act for the lessee gave up no freedom which he otherwise would have had. It is interesting to note that in reaching its decision the court relied upon the principles enunciated in connection with the doctrine of restraint of trade by their Lordships in *Esso Petroleum Co Ltd v Harpers's Garage (Stourport) Ltd* [1968] AC 269. The precise limits of the *Ravenseft* decision are unclear. Further the Act provides that restrictions relating exclusively to the goods or services to be supplied pursuant to the Agreement are usually to be disregarded (ss 9 and 18).

4 Information agreements

The Act requires the registration of agreements for the mutual exchange of information in relation to matters which are broadly similar to the subject matter of the restrictions regulated by the Act (ss 8 and 12). However at the present time the provisions have only been applied to information agreements relating to goods (Restrictive Trade Practices (Information Agreements) Order 1969 No 1842). As this book is primarily concerned with the validity of restraints these provisions will not be considered further.

5 Exemptions

The exemptions thought most appropriate to the particular types of agreements are discussed in the main body of this book and are therefore only briefly mentioned here. Although the Act contains many detailed exemptions and exceptions the following are thought to be those of the most importance to the practitioner and cover many of the more commonly used types of agreement.

5.1 Schedule 3

Schedule 3 contains exemptions for exclusive dealing agreements, various types of licensing agreements, and for agreements with overseas operation. It should be noted that to claim the benefit of any exemption an agreement must fall wholly within its terms. It is thus not possible to obtain exemption where some of the restrictions in an agreement are covered by one exemption and the remainder by another.

5.2 Lending documents

The Restrictive Trade Practices Act 1977 exempted certain restrictions commonly found in lending and mortgage documents from the provisions of the Act.

5.3 Exempt services

Not all services are covered by the Act and accordingly restrictions relating to the provisions of such excluded services are not regulated (Sched 1). The excluded services include legal services, medical services and many other professional categories. In addition, certain categories of agreement including those relating to air and sea transport are given a degree of exemption by the Restrictive Trade Practices (Services) Order 1976.

5.4 Section 21(2)

Section 21(2) provides that if it appears to the Secretary of State, upon the Director's representation that the restrictions accepted are not of such significance as to call for investigation by the court, the Secretary of State may give directions discharging the Director from taking proceedings in the court. This provision is of great practical importance for there are many cases where it is not possible to structure an agreement so as to both avoid the need for registration and to meet the requirements of the parties. The Office of Fair Trading publishes a helpful guide to the provisions of the Act in which it gives an indication of the types of agreement which the Director is commonly able to represent to the Secretary of State without the need to go before the court. These include joint ventures, sales of businesses, codes of practice, standard terms and conditions promulgated by trade associations and agreements for group buying organisations. However, in the case of the last three types of agreement, it is advisable to consult with the Office of Fair Trading in advance of finalising the form of agreement.

It must be stressed that s 21(2) directions can only be given in respect of agreements which have been properly filed for registration.

5.5 Sale and purchase and share subscription agreements

The Restrictive Trade Practices (Sale and Purchase and Share Subscription Agreements) (Goods) Order 1989 (SI 1989 No 1081) and the corresponding Order for services (the Restrictive Trade Practices (Services) (Amendment) Order 1989 (SI 1989 No 1082)) provide a broad exemption for the restraints commonly imposed in share and business sale agreements and in share subscription agreements.

6 Special categories

6.1 Trade associations

Sections 8 and 16 contain special provisions relating to trade and services supply organisations. Where a trade or services supply association enters into an agreement containing restrictions accepted on the part of the association this is treated as an agreement entered into on behalf of the members. In addition where an association makes a recommendation to its members the Act has effect as if the agreement constituting the Association contained a provision binding the members to abide by the recommendation.

6.2 Co-operative wholesale societies

Section 32 contains provisions under which the Secretary of State may approve an industrial and provident society which satisfies certain specified conditions as to its business and membership; put simply it must be a wholesale co-operative society. If approved the society will not be treated as a trade association under the Act.

6.3 Coal and steel

Section 9(1) provides that no account is to be taken of goods restrictions relating to restrictions relating to coal or steel accepted by coal or steel undertakings where at least two such undertakings are party to the agreement.

6.4 Employment

No account is to be taken of restrictions relating to workers to be employed or to conditions of employment of such workers (ss 9(6) and 18(6)).

6.5 British Standards

Restrictions by which parties agree to meet standards of the British Standards Institution or other approved body are not to be taken into account in determining whether the Act applies (ss 9(5) and 18(5)).

6.6 Agriculture, forestry and fishing

Section 33 contains special exemptions for agricultural, forestry and fisheries associations (see also the Agricultural and Forestry Associations Order 1982 No 569).

6.7 The Stock Exchange

A special exemption has been granted to the Stock Exchange by the Restrictive Trade Practices (Stock Exchange) Act 1984.

7 Registration

The procedure for registration of agreements is set out in the Registration of Restrictive Trading Agreements Regulations 1984 No 392. Particulars of the whole agreement must be delivered and not just particulars of the restrictive provisions. Particulars must be delivered *before* the restrictions take effect and in any event within three months of the date of the agreement. It is now common practice to provide in agreements, which may be subject to registration, for the restrictions to take effect only upon delivery of particulars for registration in accordance with the Act. Variations and terminations of registered agreements must also be filed.

Agreements on the register are open to public inspection even if a direction is given under s 21(2) that court proceedings are not required. The Secretary of State may direct that confidential portions of agreements be placed upon a special confidential section of the register (s 23). However, the procedure is not automatic and parties would be well advised to seek guidance from the Office of Fair Trading before entering into a registrable agreement where confidentiality is of vital importance.

8 Gateways

If an agreement is registered and brought before the court, the restrictions will be held void unless they can be shown to be in the public interest in the terms of s 10 or s 19 for goods and services respectively.

9 Failure to register

Whilst no criminal proceedings lie in respect of a failure to register, an agreement which is not registered is void in respect of all restrictions accepted or information provisions included. It is also unlawful for any party to give effect to the restrictions (see s 35(1)(b)). Section 35(2) expressly provides that breach of s 35(1)(b) is actionable by third parties as a breach of statutory duty.

In addition, following a failure to register, the Director General of Fair Trading may apply to the court for an order prohibiting any party to the agreement from entering into any further registrable agreements which are not duly registered. Any further failure to register will be contempt of court.

Appendix III

EEC Provisions

We set out below in very brief form the essentials of the EEC provisions which may be relevant. Our purpose in doing so is to alert the reader to the relevance of EEC law which in our experience is frequently ignored by the parties to a contract or dispute and by their lawyers. A more detailed analysis of the EEC position is to be found in *Common Market Law of Competition*: Bellamy and Child and in *Competition Law* which is the most up-to-date treatment.

Articles 85 and 86 of the EEC Treaty form the starting point of any discussion.

Article 85
  (1) The following shall be prohibited as incompatible with the common market: all agreements between undertakings, decisions by associations of undertakings and concerted practices which may affect trade between Member States and which have as their object or effect the prevention, restriction or distortion of competition within the common market, and in particular those which:

   (a) directly or indirectly fix purchase or selling prices or any other trading conditions;
   (b) limit or control production, markets, technical development, or investment;
   (c) share markets or sources of supply;
   (d) apply dissimilar conditions to equivalent transactions with other trading parties, thereby placing them at a competitive disadvantage;
   (e) make the conclusion of contracts subject to acceptance by the other parties of supplementary obligations which, by their nature or according to commercial usage, have no connection with the subject of such contracts.

  (2) Any agreements or decisions prohibited pursuant to this Article shall be automatically void.

  (3) The provisions of paragraph (1) may, however, be declared inapplicable in the case of:

—any agreement or category of agreements between undertakings;
—any decision or category of decisions by associations of undertakings;
—any concerted practice or category of concerted practices;
which contributes to improving the production or distribution of goods or

to promoting technical or economic progress, while allowing consumers a fair share of the resulting benefit, and which does not:

   (a) impose on the undertakings concerned restrictions which are not indispensable to the attainment of these objectives;

   (b) afford such undertakings the possibility of eliminating competition in respect of a substantial part of the products in question.

Article 86

Any abuse by one or more undertakings of a dominant position within the common market or in a substantial part of it shall be prohibited as incompatible with the common market insofar as it may affect trade between Member States. Such abuse may, in particular, consist in:

   (a) directly or indirectly imposing unfair purchase or selling prices or other unfair trading conditions;

   (b) limiting production, markets or technical development to the prejudice of consumers;

   (c) applying dissimilar conditions to equivalent transactions with other trading parties, thereby placing them at a competitive disadvantage;

   (d) making the conclusion of contracts subject to acceptance by the other parties of supplementary obligations which, by their nature or according to commercial usage, have no connection with the subject of such contracts.

Article 85, which is likely to be the most relevant of the two, is not as simple as it might appear. The first question is whether there is an infringement of art 85(1). This divides into the following analysis:

(1) *Is there an agreement between undertakings?*
An undertaking is most obviously a company or firm, however individuals are also included: *Rai v Unitel* [1978] 3 CMLR 306. That case concerned opera singers who were freelance. There appears to be no authority to say that an employee *per se* is an undertaking; we do not think he is; and see *Sugar* (40/73) [1975] ECR 1663.

An agreement will usually be a contract but because of the phrase 'decisions . . . and concerted practices' the existence of a formal agreement is frequently irrelevant. No distinction is drawn between horizontal and vertical agreements.

(2) *Decisions*
Decisions are stated to be 'by association of undertakings' and this has been held to mean that a trade association may infringe art 85(1) by its very constitution (ASPA [1970] CMLR D 31).

In *Verband Der Sachversicherer* [1985] 3 CMLR 246 even a non-binding recommendation which was part of an official statement of an association's policy was held to infringe art 85(1).

(3) *Concerted practices*
The meaning of this phrase was established in two leading cases. In *ICI v Commission* (48, 49, 51–57/69) [1972] ECR 619, a concerted practice was defined as being 'a form of co-ordination between undertakings which, without having reached the stage where an agreement properly so-called has been concluded, knowingly substitutes practical co-operation between them for the

risks of competition'. This phrase may have led some to believe that a concerted practice was in some way a preliminary attempt at achieving an agreement which had not reached fruition. However in *Sugar* (40/73) [1975] ECR 1663, the European Court of Justice rejected the argument that a concerted practice always required the working out of an actual plan. It stressed that each undertaking must act independently towards market conditions including, where necessary, adapting to the conduct of competitors. However, what was clearly stigmatised as a concerted practice was direct or indirect contact between undertakings intending or resulting in influence over the conduct of an actual or potential competitor or the disclosure to such a competitor of the course of conduct which they themselves had decided to adopt or contemplated adopting on the market. The evidence which the Commission is able to produce of the existence of a concerted practice is often very similar to the natural reaction of firms in an oligopolistic market to a given set of circumstances and recently in *Cie Asturienne v Commission* [1985] 1 CMLR 688 the court allowed an appeal against a finding of a concerted practice because the appellants were able to show good economic reasons for their conduct.

(4) *The effect on trade between Member States*

The requirement is simply that there 'may' be such an effect; there is no need to show that there *has* been such an effect (*Technique Miniere* (56/65) [1966] ECR 235); nor that the effect is only prejudicial to such trade) *Grundig* (56 and 58/64) [1966] ECR 299). The most important consideration in the context of this book is whether the fact that all the parties to an agreement etc trade solely in the UK precludes the application of art 85. In the *Cement* case (8/72) [1972] ECR 977 an agreement relating solely to the Netherlands was still held to be caught by art 85(1).

It is necessary to examine the actual or potential effect of the agreement and if it does or is reasonably likely to affect inter State trade to a significant degree then art 85(1) will apply. See also *Carlsberg Beers, Re* [1985] 1 CMLR 735.

Given that an agreement etc is within art 85(1) it would seem logical to pass onto a consideration of the remainder of art 85. However, this may not be necessary in two situations. The first is when there is only a minimal actual or potential effect on competition. What amounts to such an effect is partially though not exhaustively defined by the Commission Notice on agreements, decisions and concerted practices of minor importance [1976] 3 CMLR 648. In the main these are those where the parties have less than 5 per cent of the relevant market between them and a combined annual turnover of less than 50 million ECU.

The second situation arises if a rule of reason approach is adopted towards art 85(1). This maintains that it is improper and commercially nonsensical to assume or accept that a certain agreement falls within art 85(1) and to concentrate on bringing it within the exemption provisions of art 85(3). The problem with the latter approach, which has been the traditional one, is that only the Commission and not national courts can grant individual exemptions under art 85(3). However, the Commission rarely has the resources to grant individual exemptions. The result is commercial uncertainty. No one knows whether the agreement is likely to be struck down. However, the rule of reason provides an answer to this difficulty. It says that even if an agreement may *prima facie* produce anti-competitive effects, closer examination may reveal that it does not do so or that the compensating factors result in a net consumer benefit. The Commission has consistently rejected such an approach although in some cases the court has accepted it (*see Nungesser v Commission 258/78* [1982] ECR 2015). However, this notion is still a relatively novel one. If there is doubt as to whether art 85(1) catches an agreement an application can be made for negative clearance under reg 17/62.

If, however, an agreement is caught by art 85(1), the next step is to consider art 85(3).

The most effective way of obtaining guidance as to the likelihood of an agreement falling within art 85(3) is to examine the block exemptions issued by the Commission in relation to certain classes of agreement. If the agreement falls squarely within a block exemption then it will be exempt from the rigours of art 85(2) and will be enforceable without the necessity of the parties notifying the agreement to the Commission under reg 17. The present block exemptions are:

(a) *Regulation 1983/83:*
categories of exclusive distribution agreements OJ [1983] L 173/1.
(b) *Regulation 1984/83:*
categories of exclusive purchasing agreements OJ [1983] L 173/5 (this includes special provisions regarding both beer supply and service station agreements).
    NB both 83/83 and 84/83 are the subject of a Commission Notice which provides guidelines as to their meaning and effect OJ [1984] C 101/2.
(c) *Regulation 2349/84:*
categories of patent licensing agreements OJ [1984] L 219/15 and OJ [1985] L 113/34.
(d) *Regulation 123/85:*
categories of motor vehicle distribution and servicing agreements OJ [1985] L 15/16.
    NB this regulation is the subject of an explanatory Commission Notice of 12 December 1984.
(e) *Regulation 417/85:*
categories of specialisation agreements OJ [1985] L 53/1.
(f) *Regulation 418/85:*
categories of research and development agreements OJ [1985] L 53/5.
    These should be examined in detail.
(g) *Regulation 2671/88:*
categories of joint planning, co-ordination of capacity, sharing of revenue and consultations on tariffs on schedule air services and slot allocation at airports.
(h) *Regulation 2672/88:*
categories of agreements for computer reservation systems for air transport services.

(i) *Regulation 2673/88:*
categories of ground handling services agreements.
(j) *Regulation 4087/88:*
categories of franchise agreements.
(k) *Regulation 556/89:*
categories of know-how licensing agreements.

Opposition procedures
Article 4 of reg 2349/84 (patent licensing), art 4 of reg 417/85 (specialisation agreements) and art 7 of reg 418/85 (research and development) are the only ones which provide for an opposition procedure. These allow for an agreement to be exempted in certain circumstances so long as the Commission does not oppose exemption within six months of notification of the agreement.

Individual exemptions
If an agreement is caught by art 85(1), but does not benefit from a block exemption, then an individual exemption must be sought. This involves notification of the agreement to the Commission. Notification of an agreement entered into after 1 January 1973 does not enjoy provisional validity and therefore until a decision is made by the Commission it is open to scrutiny before national courts. Frequently no decision is given or if it is, it is of an informal nature in say, a 'comfort letter'. These are not binding on the courts though they may provide guidance. In deciding whether art 85(3) applies so as to exempt an agreement it is necessary to examine the agreement in the light of the goals set therein. However, even if an exemption is granted it can take a long while to arrive; in *Carlsberg Beers, Re* it took four years from notification to exemption.

Article 85(2)
Should an agreement not be exempted then it is void. A similar result occurs if an agreement which should have been notified is not. A void agreement can attract fines until the time of any notification. In the recent case against 15 producers of polypropylene the fines announced by the Commission amounted to ECU 57.85 million. An Italian company was itself fined ECU 11 million. Notification acts as a barrier to fines regarding the agreement after that date in most cases. In the context of domestic courts, an agreement void under art 85(2) will be illegal and unenforceable. Moreover, so far as English law is concerned art 85 and 86 can be used as swords as well as shields so as to permit the recovery of damages and/or an injunction. See *Garden Cottage Foods Ltd v Milk Marketing Board* [1984] AC 130; *An Bord Bainne Co-operative Ltd v Milk Marketing Board* [1984] 2 CMLR 584; *Bourgoin SA v MAFF* [1985] 1 CMLR 528; *Cutsforth v Mansfield Inns Ltd* [1986] 1 WLR 558.

Article 86
Many of the points made about art 85 also apply to art 86 though it takes a different approach to anti-competitive practices: it is concerned with the abuse of full or partial monopoly power. There are two fundamental issues involved in its application. The first is whether the relevant undertaking has a dominant

position. The existence of dominance is tested by considering the economic strength enjoyed by an undertaking in a particular product market and geographical area which enables it to prevent effective competition being maintained therein by affording it the power to behave to an appreciable extent independently of its competitors, customers and ultimately of its consumers. This test makes it clear that the size of the undertaking is not always relevant: the important point is its economic power in a particular market (see *Argyll Group plc v Distillers Co plc* [1986] 1 CMLR 764).

The second question is whether there has been any abuse. Examples of what constitutes abuse are given in art 86. Of particular importance in the restraint of trade context is example (a). What amounts to an unfair trading condition is a question of fact. However, in *GEMA, Re* [1971] CMLR D 35 the Commission ruled that certain rules of a performing rights society amounted to unfair trading conditions; and in *Michelin v Commission* (322/81) [1985] 1 CMLR 282 it was decided that although a quantity discount to customers was not an abuse, a loyalty rebate was, as it tended to prevent a customer purchasing elsewhere. Finally, example (d) singles out requirements contracts. The consequences of the existence of an abuse of a dominant position are that any relevant contractual provision is void. A third party can use art 86 as a cause of action in national courts and sue for damages/an injunction: see *Argyll v Distillers* in which art 86 was used in an attempt at merger control by an unsuccessful suitor in a takeover battle.

Index